Kant after Derrida

Kant after Derrida

Editor
Philip Rothfield

Copyright © Clinamen Press 2003
Selection of essays © Philip Rothfield
Individual essays © contributors

First edition published Manchester 2003

Published by Clinamen Press
Clinamen Press Limited
Unit B,
Aldow Enterprise Park,
Blackett Street,
Manchester M12 6AE

www.clinamen.co.uk

Geoffrey Bennington, 'The End is Here' first appeared in the journal
Tekhnema: Journal of Philosophy and Technology,
issue 6, 2000, ISBN   2950994407,
reproduced here by kind permission of the editor.

   3 5 7 9 8 6 4 2

April 2004 reprint with corrections

All rights reserved. No part of this edition may be reproduced, stored in or introduced into a retrieval system, or transmitted, in any form or by any means (electronic, mechanical, photocopying, recording or otherwise) without the written permission of the publishers.

A catalogue record for this book is available from the British Library

ISBN 1 903083 25 7

Typeset in Times New Roman with ITC Officina display
Printed and bound by CPI Bath

dedicated to
Elayne Louise Rothfield
1942-2002

Contents

Notes on Contributors	ix
1 Introduction Kant *Par Excellence*: Introducing Kant after Derrida *Joanna Hodge*	1
2 Aporias of the *As If*: Derrida's Kant and the Question of Experience *Hager Weslaty*	18
3 The End is Here *Geoffrey Bennington*	50
4 Apocalyptic Imagination *Gary Banham*	66
5 After *parerga*: Kant, Derrida and the Temporality of Judgement *Jonathan Lahey Dronsfield*	80
6 Reflecting the Form of Understanding: The Philosophical Significance of Art *Andrea Kern*	106
7 System of (Kantian) Pleasure (With a Freudian Postscript) *Jean-Luc Nancy*	127
8 Kingdoms of God *Kevin Hart*	142
9 Kant after Derrida: Inventing Oneself Out of an Impossible Choice *Olivia Custer*	171
Select Bibliography	205
Index	213

Notes on Contributors

Gary Banham is Research Fellow in Transcendental Philosophy at Manchester Metropolitan University. He is author of *Kant and the Ends of Aesthetics* (2000) and co-editor of *Evil Spirits: Nihilism and the fate of Modernity* (2000). He has edited special issues of *Tekhnema: Journal of Philosophy and technology* on teleology and *Angelaki: Journal of the Theoretical Humanities* on aesthetics and the ends of art. He has recently completed a study of Kant's practical philosophy and is Series Editor of *Renewing Philosophy* for Palgrave.

Geoffrey Bennington taught for almost twenty years at the University of Sussex, where he directed the Centre for Modern French Thought, before moving to Emory University in 2001. His two most recent books are *Interrupting Derrida* (Routledge, 2000) and *La frontière kantienne* (Galilée, 2000).

Olivia Custer teaches philosophy at L'Ecole des Hautes Etudes en Sciences Sociales, Paris

Jonathan Dronsfield is a Lecturer in Philosophy & History of Art at the University of Southampton, where he is Director of the Centre for Contemporary Art Research.
This paper was begun with the aid of a Leverhulme Special Research Fellowship at the Centre for Research in Modern European Philosophy, Middlesex University.

Kevin Hart is the author of *The Trespass of the Sign* (Cambridge, UP, 1989; exp. ed. Fordham UP, 2000), *A. D. Hope* (Oxford UP, 1992) and *Samuel Johnson and the Culture of Property* (Cambridge UP, 1999). He is the editor of *The Oxford Book of Australian Religious Poetry* (1994). His most recent collection of poetry is *Flame Tree: Selected Poems* (Bloodaxe Books, 2002). He is Professor of English at the University of Notre Dame, Indiana.

Joanna Hodge is Professor of Philosophy at Manchester Metropolitan University, coordinating a research programme on time, teleology and phenomenology. She published *Heidegger and Ethics* (Routledge, London) in 1995 and has published articles on phenomenology, aesthetics and feminist critique. Her current main line of enquiry concerns the reconfiguration of conceptions of time in the writings of Jacques Derrida.

Andrea Kern is an assistant professor of philosophy (wissenschaftliche Assistentin) at the University of Potsdam. Her publications include: *Schöne Lust. Eine Theorie der ästhetischen Erfahrung nach Kant*, Suhrkamp Verlag, Frankfurt am Main 2000; *Falsche Gegensätze. Zeitgenössische Positionen zur philosophischen Ästhetik*, (co-edited with Ruth Sonderegger), Suhrkamp Verlag, Frankfurt am Main 2002.

Jean-Luc Nancy is Professor at the University Marc Bloch, Strasbourg, France. He has contributed at the highest level to contemporary debates on ethics, philosophy and literature, and has published numerous books and articles including *An Inoperative Community*, *The Birth to Presence* and *Hegel: The Restlessness of the Negative*.

Philip Rothfield was until recently a post-graduate research student in the Centre for Research in Modern European Philosophy at Middlesex University, London. His research interests include Kant, Heidegger, Derrida and specifically metaethics and ontology.

Hager Weslaty received her doctorate from the University of Lancaster in 1998. She is currently assistant professor at the faculty of letters, Manouba, Tunisia, mainly teaching contemporary American literature, art history, critical theory and media studies. Her research interests include German philosophy and continental philosophy/ critical theory.

1
Kant *Par Excellence*: Introducing Kant after Derrida

Joanna Hodge

There will be many volumes published to mark the bicentenary of Kant's death in 1804. None will be more apposite to the implied disjunction of time and history, to be marked in various ways, and here by the phrase *Kant after Derrida*. This series of essays traces a proximity and estrangement between Derrida's texts, his engagements and disengagements, with those of Kant, in response to the question: how to read Kant today? Derrida's readings have, over the past forty years, been open to a series of questions posed by Kant, to which Derrida's readers have responded by, in turn, reading and re-reading, re-reading and reading Kant. As a consequence, Kant's critical philosophy emerges as no less apposite than it did, when first presented to a doubting public in the last decades of the eighteenth century. In no particular order, Derrida has written of radical evil, hospitality, cosmopolitical intent, the history of the lie, secrets and exemplarity, the kingdom of ends, the apocalyptic tone of philosophy, the schematisation of space and time, the idea 'in the Kantian sense' and above all the question of experience, its possibility and its impossibility. Hence it might be thought that such a volume as this has been long overdue, and Philip Rothfield, its editor, deserves all due credit for bringing his contributors to this point of engagement.

1

Examples are the baby walkers of the
 power of judgment: and those who lack
 this natural talent cannot do without them.

Kant 3:173-4, 4: 134

The task of this introduction is to provide a chart of the encounters with Kant's writings to be found in those of Derrida.[1] This will also provide occasion to intimate how some of his readers have responded to those encounters; and how he, in his turn, has responded to those readings of Kant, which have contributed to the emergence of some of the philosophical innovations distinctive of the twentieth century: by Bergson, Benjamin, Freud, Lacan, Husserl, Heidegger, Levi Strauss, Levinas, to name a few. Kant's innovations, to which these various readers have variously responded, are the separation of an analysis of human reasoning from ontological and theological commitments, turning the question of knowledge into an analysis of the faculties and capacities for knowing; and, no less contested, the systematic exploration of the implications of this reversal, called by him the Copernican Revolution in philosophy, in the writing of his three Critiques, of pure reason, of practical reason and of judgment.[2] Derrida's responses to these responses to Kant have in the main taken up and returned to Kant, in the mode of restitution, Kant's own designated task for pure reason, *die Aufgabe der Vernunft*, a task which Derrida thinks in the mode of the futural: as that which remains to be undertaken. This futurity is linked to the performance of promising, the activity which Nietzsche notes is reserved for humanity, among living beings, but which is also the gesture distinctive of Abraham's God, who promises that Abraham's people shall be the chosen people.[3]

While Nietzsche's responses to Kant reaffirm the ontological cut whereby human destinies are cut free from theological moorings, Derrida's readings of Kant turn out from the beginning to have been inflected by an interest in the fate of religion, once thus set free from theology.[4] This religion released from theology is the focus for attention in his increasingly widely received 'Faith and Knowledge: The two sources of "Religion" at the limits of reason alone' (1994).[5] The potlatch effect of Derrida's readings, where a reading of one text runs over into another is conveniently performed by this title, which starts by quoting Hegel's text, *Faith and Reason or Reflexive philosophy of subjectivity in the completion of its forms in Kant, Jacobi and Fichte* (1802); continues into the title of Henri Bergson's text *The Two Sources of Morality and Religion* (1932); and only in the third place cites the title of Kant's text: *Religion within the Bounds of Mere Reason* (1794).[6] This text more clearly than any amount of refutation demonstrates why the attribution of a negative theologising to Derrida's texts was misleading at best, for negative theology presupposes the possibility of a rationalist theology: both concerned with the same field of phenomena, just in disagreement about how to set up descriptions of them. For Derrida, and indeed for Kant, by contrast, there is no such single field of phenomena to be disputed between proponents of positive and negative theologies, and for Derrida, there is more than one religion to be thought about.

The mode of restitution is analysed by Derrida at length in the discussion of Heidegger's essay 'The Origin of the Artwork', in the third part of his *The Truth in Painting* (1978).[7] It supplies a mark of difference between Derrida's response to Kant, and the manner in which, at the beginning of the last century, Benjamin proposed in 'On the Program for the Coming Philosophy' (1918) to rewrite Kant's *Prolegomena for any Future Metaphysics* (1783). Their intent however is not so very different, for each explores how: 'With a new concept of knowledge, therefore, not only the concept of experience but also that of freedom will undergo a decisive revision'.[8] In contrast to the separate spheres of neo-Kantianism, contrasting science and logic on one side and the historical and the moral sciences on the other, the task as taken up by Benjamin and Derrida is to explore the interdependencies of the moral and metaphysical sciences. For Derrida, there are also the interdependencies generated by juxtaposition: if Husserl is perforce or by chance read after Kant and before Heidegger, then the reading of Husserl is inflected by that of Kant, and the reading of Heidegger by that of Husserl. Derrida's reading of Husserl is also inflected by a response to Heidegger, and that of Kant, by a response to Husserl. Thus Kant after Derrida is also Kant after Heidegger and after Husserl, Derrida's Heidegger and Derrida's Husserl, that is.

Derrida's Heidegger is one whose emphatic reading of Kant remains in evidence. In *Kant and the Problem of Metaphysics* (1929) Heidegger argues for the constitutive role of imagination as the root joining together the other two faculties of sensibility and understanding, within which juncture the schematisation of a finite temporality takes place.[9] This then leaves wide open the terrain of the typology of pure practical reason, as a site for the articulation of non-finite temporalities, one which Derrida has explored with increasing confidence and enthusiasm in the course of the eighties and nineties, perhaps under the encouragement of Levinas' response to Kant, in *Totality and Infinity: an essay on exteriority* (1961). In *Otherwise than Being or beyond essence* (1974), Levinas develops his challenge to Heidegger, but he may also be responding to a Kant and to a Heidegger after Derrida. He writes: 'The fact that immortality and theology could not determine the categorical imperative signifies the novelty of the Copernican revolution: a sense that is not measured by being or not being; but being is on the contrary determined on the basis of sense'.[10] This marks a separation, in the Kantian sense, between moral imperatives and ontological commitments. Between these two texts, Levinas contributed to the journal *L'Arc* (1973) an essay on Derrida entitled 'Wholly Otherwise'. This begins with the following questions:

> May not Derrida's work cut into the development of Western thinking, with a line of demarcation similar to that of Kantianism, which separated dogmatic philosophy from critical philosophy? Are we again at the end of a naivete, of an unsuspected dogmatism, which slumbered at the base of that which we took for critical spirit? We may well ask ourselves. The Idea, as the completion of a series which begins in intuition without being able to end there; the Idea said to be 'in the Kantian sense of the term' would operate within intuition itself; a transcendental semblance itself generating metaphysics would create an illusion within presence itself, a presence that would ceaselessly be found to be wanting.[11]

Here Levinas makes a remarkably strong claim on behalf of the impact of Derrida's writings, one which is germane to the project of reading Kant after Derrida, and one which perhaps illuminates Levinas' attention in that later text to an unsaying in play in any signifying relation.

Heidegger's stabilisation of the faculties in an account of a finite time of schematism cannot hold for Kant's analyses in the *Critique of Practical Reason* (1788) and there opens out the domain explored by both Levinas and Derrida, of the excess of the moral claim over any empirical capacity to perform; and an excess of temporalities over any metaphysics of presence. Interruption and interval, *différance* and destinerrance, the time of weariness and the time of undecidability spring the contours of Heidegger's carefully constructed containment of a finite, self-temporalising auto-affection, on the site of imagination. This stabilisation of consciousness in terms of auto-affection is definitively displaced by Levinas' insistence on the hetero-affection of subjectivity already in evidence in *From Existence to Existents* (1947).[12] This is the unhinging of time, for which Derrida finds an anticipation in Kant's *Critique of Aesthetic Judgement* (1791*)*, as analysed in *The Truth in Painting*, from which the citation at the head of this section is taken.[13] Derrida centres his decentring reading of Kant, on truth and painting, on a series of remarks on the frame or ornament, the *parergon*, which Kant introduces in section 14: 'Elucidation by Examples'[14], hence Derrida's retrieval there of the notion of 'examples' from the *First Critique* in the given citation.[15] Derrida has returned to the thematisation of examples in Kant's writings on a number of occasions, to be adduced in what follows here. Kant's clarification of their status from a passage in the final pages of the *Critique of Aesthetic Judgment* runs as follows: 'Establishing that our concepts have reality always requires intuitions. If the concepts are empirical the intuitions are called examples. If they are pure concepts of the understanding, the intuitions are called schemata'.[16] The upshot of Derridean reading here is to destabilise the distinctions.[17]

Derrida's Heidegger is also one for whom a reception of the themes of classical phenomenology: the *a priori*, intuition, intention, constitution, time, remain close to the surface.[18] Derrida's restitution remarks Heidegger's reception of Husserl's constitution, and in so doing reveals the trace and iteration in Heidegger's text of the problematics of Husserlian phenomenology. In his analysis of his own theoretical development, given in 'The Time of the Thesis: Punctuations' (1980),[19] Derrida remarks the on-going impact on his work of his reading of Husserl:

> Naturally, all of the problems worked on in the Introduction to *The Origin of Geometry* have continued to organize the work I have subsequently attempted in connection with philosophical, literary, and even non-discursive corpora, most notably that of pictorial works; I am thinking for example of the historicity of ideal objects, of tradition, of inheritance, of filiation or of wills and testaments, of archives, libraries, books, of writing and living speech, of the relationships between semiotics and linguistics, of the question of truth and of undecidability, of the irreducible otherness that divides the self-identity of the living present, of the necessity for new analyses concerning non-mathematical idealities.[20]

In the course of the following discussion, he mentions his preoccupation with 'the modern concept of the university'[21], to be investigated in relation to Kant's *The Conflict of the Faculties* (1798). Part of this analysis is now available in both French and English, in French as *Du droit a la philosophie* (1990), and, in part, in English as *Who's Afraid of Philosophy? Right to Philosophy 1* (2002).[22] The first essay, 'Privileges', dated 1990, introduces the French volume, and is dedicated and not by chance to Jean Luc Nancy. There, Derrida rehearses Kant's response at the beginning of the *Metaphysics of Morals* (1797) to Christian Garve's requirement that philosophy be capable of being made popular.

> I gladly admit this with the exception only of the systematic critique of the faculty of reason itself along with all that can be established only by means of it; for this has to do with the distinction of the sensible in our cognition from that which is supersensible but yet belongs to reason. This can never become popular - no formal metaphysics can - although its results can be made quite illuminating for the healthy reason (of an unwitting

metaphysician.).[23]

Derrida writes:

Whether we adopt or critique it, the Kantian model exercises its authority over all the philosophical, that is European mechanisms of teaching across the most diverse (Hegelian-Marxist or Husserlian-Heideggerian) relays. This is no doubt unique, but we can take it up from at least three angles. The question of its singularity, that is, its absolute privilege, will only be the more pointed. Kantian critique and metaphysics are inseparable from modern teaching. They 'are' this teaching, that is to say that they 'are' teaching forms untried until now (p.50-51).

To which pair of ugly conjuncts we might add 'Wittgensteinian-Habermasian'.

Derrida then resumes two of these three angles: that Kantian critique and metaphysics propose a pedagogy; and that they lay claim to "a power of judgement, evaluation, and sanction, that is, the power of a jurisdiction, of an instance pronouncing the law, accompanying its declarations with an objective constraint (this is the very definition of right according to Kant)" (p.51). More provocatively, Derrida states as the third angle the discovery by Kant of the problematics of possibility and potentiation: 'Through numerous relays of potentialization, it participates in the most structuring, the most productive and the most destructive operations in the history to come of discourses, works, and European institutions. It informs European 'culture', which is also to say European 'colonization', wherever it operates' (p.53). This is a neo-Kantianism in which the inseparability of the moral and metaphysical sciences leave no hiding place for philosophy from the challenges of globalatinisation, as the ugly neologism has it. Derrida's readings of Kant in relation to a moment of violence in the institution of legal order and on a connection between a right to hospitality and asylum seeking suggest a reinvention of Kant's cosmopolitical intent for the twenty first century. [24]

2

In making this choice, I also hoped to go to meet those who, in one of the seminars of these ten days, have precisely organized their work by privileging the reference to a certain Kantian *caesura* in the time of philosophy.

Derrida

The Kantian moment in Derrida's thought erupts emphatically on to the surface of his texts in this remark from 'Of an Apocalyptic Tone Recently Adopted in Philosophy' (1980), the title of which replays the title of one of Kant's own essays, published in 1796, in the Berlin *Monatschrift*.[25] The *caesura* is the broken line distinctive of Hoelderlin's verse, analysed by Lacoue-Labarthe in 'The *Caesura* of the Speculative' (1978),[26] and Derrida's paper is thus advertised as advancing towards the thought that Kant's writings mark a decisive rupture and inception for philosophy. Derrida's paper was delivered to the 1980 Cerisy conference 'The Ends of Man: starting with the work of Jacques Derrida'.[27] Derrida traces out Kant's preoccupation with the feint whereby mystification takes the place of philosophy proper:

> [...] to be sure Kant is more closely interested in some recent examples of this mystagogic and psychagogic imposture, but he supposes at the outset that the usurpation is recurrent and obeys a law. There has been and will always be philosophical mystification, speculation of the end and ends of philosophy. This depends on an event that Kant himself does not date and that he seems to situate right against the origin, namely, that the name philosophy can circulate without its original reference, in other words without its *Bedeutung* and without guarantee of its value. While still remaining in the Kantian axiomatic as it were, we can already infer from this that no harm would have happened, no mystagogic speculation would have been credible or efficient, nothing or no-one would have detoned philosophy without this errance of the name far from the thing, and if the relation of the name philosophy to its originary sense had been insured against every accident.[28]

This errance is diagnosed by Heidegger as the destiny of being, to fall into oblivion, but the loss of originary sense is diagnosed by Husserl, in the work *Origin of Geometry*, in relation to the failure of transmission of understanding of the truths of scientific enquiry. Thus this Kant is read through both Husserlian and Heideggerian terminology. The lesson drawn by Derrida is that there can be no such insurance securing philosophy from contamination: the workings of language and the transmission of texts inextricably intertwines philosophical necessity and the accidents of chance; philosophy and mystification; critique and dogmatism. The work of separating them out again has always to be begun again, in a labour worthy of Penelope. The paper was first published in the conference proceedings, edited by Philippe Lacoue-Labarthe and Jean Luc Nancy, who went on to work together for several years on the research program, *Rethinking the Political*, and then in the *Collège Internationale de Philosophie*, founded in 1983.[29] The text itself refers back to Derrida's work in the seventies; among other texts cited are *The Post Card from Plato to Freud and Beyond* (1980), *The Truth in Painting* (1978), and *Glas; What Remains of Absolute Knowledge* (1974).

The text also refers forward to a body of work performed by Derrida in the famous seminar series, summed up in the opening pages of *Politics of Friendship* (1994):

> I count on preparing for future publication a series of seminar studies within which this one actually finds its place, well beyond the single opening session, which thus presupposes its premises and its horizon. Those that immediately preceded it, then, if it is anything but useless to recall the logical development at this point, were centred on: *Nationality and Philosophical Nationalism* (1: *Nation, Nationality, Nationalism* (1983-84); 2: *Nomos, Logos, Topos* (1984-85); 3: *The Theological-political* (1985-86); 4. *Kant, the Jew, the German* (1986-87)); and *Eating the Other (Rhetorics of cannibalism)* (1987-88). Subsequent seminars concerned *Questions of Responsibility* through the experience of the *secret* and of *witnessing* (1989-1993). [30]

These seminars find some resonance in the analyses undertaken in *The Other Heading: Reflections on Today's Europe* (1991).[31] For while the transcendental teleology explicitly invoked is that of Husserl in the *Crisis of the European Sciences* (1936),[32] the language of duty is both Kantian, and Levinasian, or, in the terms of this introduction, Kantian after Derrida: "The same duty dictates cultivating the virtue of such critique, of the critical idea, the critical tradition, but also submitting, beyond critique and questioning, to a deconstructive genealogy that thinks and exceeds it without yet compromising it".[33] The analysis of responsibility, while ostensibly Levinasian, is also proferred in Kantian terms: "The condition of possibility of this thing called responsibility is a certain experience and experiment of the possibility of the impossible: the testing of the aporia from which one may invent the only possible invention, the impossible invention".[34] To this Derrida adds a footnote invoking the papers collected together in the volume *Psyche: Inventions de l'autre* (1986).[35] This impossible invention marks a reconfiguration of Kant's analysis of genius from section 46 of the *Critique of Aesthetic Judgment* [36], as nature giving the rule for art. It opens up the challenge, emergent in the interaction between Derrida's writings and those of Levinas, of taking up Heidegger's rethinking of the Kantian modalities of impossibility, possibility, and necessity, the categories of the *First Critique*, as both subjective capacities, *Vermoegen der Vernunft*, faculties of reason, and objective potentialities, and as slippages arising from the conjunctions and disjunctions of the two.

3

> What is more we cannot do morality a worse service than by seeking to derive it from examples. Every example of it presented to me must first be judged by moral principles in order to decide if it is fit to serve as an original example - that is, as a model: it can in no way supply the prime source for the concept of morality. Even the Holy One of the Gospel must first be compared with our ideal of moral perfection before we can recognise him to be such.
>
> (Kant 4: 408)

This citation is taken in the first instance from Kant's *Groundwork for a Metaphysics of Morals* (1785),[37] that is, published after the first edition of the *First Critique*, the *Critique of Pure Reason* (1781,1787), and before its second edition, and before the *Second Critique*, the *Critique of Practical Reason* (1788). In the *Groundwork,* Kant prepares the terrain for the *Second Critique* by setting out the three layers of nesting between ordinary moral intuitions, a metaphysics of morals, and the critique of pure practical reason required in order to make sense of those moral intuitions. These words also appear in a footnote on exemplarity and secrets, in a footnote to Derrida's essay 'Passions: "An Oblique Offering"' (1993, 1992), which as the conjoined dates suggest, appeared first in English, as the first essay of eleven in *Derrida: A Critical Reader*, and then only subsequently in French.[38] In the same long footnote, Derrida goes on to cite from some pages later in the *Groundwork:* 'only we must never forget here that it is impossible to settle by example and so empirically whether there is any imperative of this kind at all: we must rather suspect that all imperatives which seem to be categorical may none the less be covertly hypothetical'.[39] Empirical evidence for there being categorical imperatives and obedience to them thus is in principle lacking, and therefore so far as Kant is concerned, there must be *a priori* reasoning, if moral requirements are to be made sense of. In response to this, still in footnote ten, Derrida adduces:

> This is a most radical claim: no experience can assure us of the 'there is' at this point. God himself cannot therefore serve as an example, and the concept of God as sovereign Good is an idea of reason. It remains that the

discourse and the action (the passion) of Christ demonstrates in an exemplary way, singularly, par excellence, the inadequacy of the example, the secret of divine invisibility and the sovereignty of reason; and the encouragement, the stimulation, the exhortation, the instruction is indispensable for all finite, that is to say, sensory beings, and for all intuitive singularity. The example is the only visibility of the invisible.[40]

For Kant, in this case, what is impossible by example is possible by *a priori* reasoning, but this is not so for Derrida, and conditions of possibility are for him equally conditions of impossibility. This is an emphatic rewriting of this Kantian modality, which has become familiar by repetition, but both the rewriting and indeed the implications of Kant's own phrase as a modalisation remain to be thought through.

In their prefatory note to the Cerisy volume, *Les Fins de l'Homme*, Lacoue-Labarthe and Nancy refer the reader back to the concluding words of the paper delivered by Derrida in New York in October 1968, under that title: 'The Ends of Man': 'La veille, la vigilance. En 1968, tel etait le dernier mot du texte intitule: "Les fins de l'homme"'[41], 'The Eve, Vigilance. In 1968, this was the Last Phrase of the Text Entitled "The Ends of Man."'[42] This paper installs the double gesture of proposing to read texts in two contravening modes: "to attempt an exit and a deconstruction without changing terrain, by repeating what is implicit in the founding concepts and the original problematic"[43]; and 'to decide to change terrain, in a discontinuous and irruptive fashion, by brutally placing oneself outside, and by affirming an absolute break and difference'. These apparently opposed strategies discover strangeness on the site of repetition and a familiar violence in the gesture of supposed immunisation from association with the old order. Derrida thus marks his departure from the model of antinomy set up by Kant in the *First Critique*[44]. Whereas for Kant the first two antinomies, concerning the nature of the universe, its beginning and constitution, pose two equally false arguments, and the second two antinomies, on freedom and the nature of the divine, propose two equally valid arguments, for Derrida there is a problem in principle of separating out two distinct lines of argument.

In 'The Ends of Man', Derrida treats of the transmission of a certain anthropologism and humanism in phenomenology, and its critique, in the texts of Hegel, Husserl and Heidegger. However, to mark a disrupted contemporaneity, he places its argument between citations on the first page, of Kant, of Sartre and of Foucault and, on the last, an invocation of Nietzsche's active forgetting. The first epigraph of the text is the following remark from Kant's

Groundwork for a Metaphysics of Morals (1785):

> Now I say that man, and in general every rational being, exists as an end in himself, not merely as a means for arbitrary use by this or that will: he must in all his actions, whether they are directed to himself or to other rational beings, always be viewed at the same time as an end.[45]

There is a long footnote on this ambiguity, where Derrida remarks: 'In Kant, the figure of finitude organizes the capacity to know from the very emergence of the anthropological limit'.[46] He diagnoses how even for Kant, human being is the only example, the only case of a rational being, even while Kant must hold open the thought that human being is only one instance of the more general case. The footnote has the form of the by now classic Derridean antinomic declaration: on the one hand, on the other hand, leaving both elements suspended in unresolved apposition. 'On the one hand, it is precisely when Kant wishes to think something like an end, the pure, the end in itself, that he must criticize anthropologism, in the *Metaphysics of Morals*' [47], Derrida announces. 'But, *on the other hand,* and inversely, man's specificity, man's essence as a rational being, as the rational being (*zoon logon ekhon*) announces itself to itself only on the basis of thinking the end in itself...' The second section continues: '[...]it is through the offices of this fact that anthropology regains all its contested authority. This is the point at which the philosopher says 'we', and at which in Kant's discourse 'rational being' and 'humanity' are always associated by the conjunction 'and' or *vel*'.[48] This 'and' or the inclusive 'or' permits a certain slide between interpretations of the bearer of reason of the *First Critique* as finite and human and the bearer of reason in the *Second Critique* as non-finite and human, as the bearer of an immortal soul, susceptible variously to eternal bliss and damnation.

Derrida, like Kant, scrupulously leaves open this question of status, although for rather different reasons. In the text, he diagnoses a further ambiguity between the notion of end, as limit, and the notion of end, as destiny, in the retrieval of Kant's philosophy in Husserl's transcendental turn:

> Transcendental phenomenology is in this sense the ultimate achievement of the teleology of reason that traverses humanity. Thus, under the jurisdiction of the founding concepts of metaphysics, which Husserl revives and restores (if necessary affecting them with phenomenological brackets or indices), the critique of empirical anthropologism is only the affirmation of a transcendental humanism. And, among these metaphysical concepts, which form the essential resource of Husserl's discourse, the concept of

end, or of *telos,* plays a decisive role. It could be shown that at each stage of phenomenology, and notably each time that a recourse to the 'Idea in the Kantian sense' is necessary, the infinity of the *telos*, the infinity of the end regulates phenomenology's capability. The end of man (as a factual anthropological limit) is announced to thought from the vantage of the end of man (as a determined opening or the infinity of a *telos*).[49]

The connection between his studies of Husserl and his interrogation of Kant could not be made more plain. The invocation of Kant in the texts on Husserl thus marked by Derrida is much remarked but perhaps never to incisively as in a short essay by Rudolf Bernet, on Derrida reading Husserl.[50] Having set up the distinctions "between real (factual) objects and ideal (essential) objects, as well as the separation between external (empirical) history and internal (*a priori*) historicity" (p.141), Bernet turns to a further refinement; remarked by Derrida,

> between ideal objects in the sense of essences and in the sense of "Ideas in the Kantian sense". These distinctions then permit Derrida to investigate in an exemplary phenomenological manner the peculiar linguistic nature of ideal objects as well as the intentional-teleological transmission of their original truth-content. In turn, this determination of the way in which an ideal truth is linguistically fixed and transmitted gives rise to a new understanding of the infinite idea, which guides scientific progress.[51]

These moves sketch out the argument for the impossibility of a purely phenomenological understanding of phenomenology and of the constitutive role in Husserl's arguments of a borrowing and interpretation of certain key Kantian terms: the *a priori*, transcendentalism, critical analysis, the forms of intuition as giving the *a priori* structure of temporality and, of course, the idea in the Kantian sense.[52]

Derrida thus performs a series of returns to Kant, under the various rubrics already remarked. His readings of Hegel, of Husserl, of Heidegger, of Levinas, indeed of Nietzsche and of Freud are mediated by a responsiveness to the impact of Kant on their writings, and the impact of Kant more generally on the shape of philosophy in the twentieth century. In the account of subjectivity as hypostasis, Levinas incisively complicates Kant's analysis of the Amphiboly of Concepts of Reflection, from the Transcendental Analytic of the *First Critique*[53]*;* and his analysis of substitution further disrupts Kant's analysis in the paralogisms of pure reason, of the dialectical implications of the 'I think', if falsely taken as a concept of the understanding, when, according to Kant, it is rather to be thought as a postulate of practical reasoning. Derrida can be read as decisively intervening in the articulation of the antinomies of pure reason, the second phase of Kant's analysis in the Transcendental Dialectic. He also traces the 'radical trembling' to which the distinction between an analysis of pure reason and an analysis of judgment can be subjected, when it is interrogated for the inside/outside of its framing ornamentation, Kant's remarks on the *parergon* and on examples. The essays, which follow, interleave themselves in this trajectory of intertextuality, rehearsing and confirming the thought that experience without *a priorism* is blind, while deconstruction without critique is empty.

Notes:

1 Kant's writings will be given in English, cited in the endnotes according to Akademie Ausgabe volume and page numbers, cited Ak., for ease of reference, while a reference to an English translation will be given in the appended note.

2 In one of the most astonishing outbursts of concentrated philosophical energy of all time, Kant published the *First Critique*, the *Critique of Pure Reason*, in 1781, publishing a second extensively rewritten version in 1787; the *Second Critique*, the *Critique of Practical Reason* followed in 1788 and the *Critique of Judgment* in 1790, by which time Kant was sixty seven.

3 For Nietzsche on promising, see the second essay of *Genealogy of Morals*, Colli and Montinari, eds (KSA 5, Berlin: de Gruyter, 1967): 'Indeed that is the long story of the development of responsibility. The task, to breed an animal which can promise, contains within itself, as we have just set out, as condition and preparation, the previous task to make human beings first up to a certain degree subject to necessity, uniform, similar according to a notion of equality, orderly and therefore subject to assessment.' (p.293).

4 There has been much writing on this strand of Derrida's thinking. Two among many significant contributions are Kevin Hart, *The Trespass of the Sign: Deconstruction, Theology and Philosophy* (Cambridge: Cambridge University Press, 1989), and John D Caputo, *The Prayers and Tears of Jacques Derrida: Religion without Religion* (Bloomington: Indiana University Press, 1997). See also Hart infra. For a collection staging the encounter between Jacques Derrida and Jean Luc Marion on the impossible donation, see John D Caputo and Michael J Scanlon, eds, *God, the Gift and Postmodernism* (Bloomington: Indiana University Press, 1999).

5 See Jacques Derrida, Gil Anidjar (ed.), *Acts of Religion*, (London: Routledge, 2002), pp.40-102. See also Hent de Vries, *Philosophy and the Turn to Religion* (Baltimore: John Hopkins University Press, 1999) and *Religion and Violence; Philosophical perspectives from Kant to Derrida* (Baltimore: Johns Hopkins University Press, 2002).

6 It scarcely needs to be reiterated, perhaps, but for the displacement of the relation between Kant and Hegel as a consequence of rigorously reading Derrida, see Paul de Man, Andrzej Warminski, ed. and intro, *Aesthetic Ideology* (Minneapolis: University of Minnesota Press, 1996) and Rodolphe Gasché, *The Tain of the Mirror: Derrida and the Philosophy of Reflection* (Cambridge MA: Harvard UP, 1986), and his collection of essays, *Inventions of Difference: On Jacques Derrida* (Cambridge MA: Harvard UP, 1994).

7 Jacques Derrida, *The Truth in Painting* (1978), trans. Geoff Bennington and Ian McLeod (Chicago: Chicago UP, 1987). For Bennington's own discussions of Derrida and Kant, see infra. and also Bennington and Derrida, *Jacques Derrida* (1991), trans. Geoffrey Bennington (Chicago: University of Chicago Press, 1993) and see Geoffrey Bennington, *Interrupting Derrida* (London: Routledge, 2000).

8 *Walter Benjamin: Selected Writings Volume 1, 1913-1926*, Marcus Bullock and Michael W. Jennings, eds (US: Belknap Press of the Harvard University Press, 1996), p.105. For a reading of Kant positioned mid-way between a reception of Benjamin and one of Derrida see Diane Morgan, *Kant Trouble: The Obscurities of the Enlightened* (London: Routledge, 2000).

9 Martin Heidegger, *Kant and the Problem of Metaphysics* (1929), fifth enlarged edition, trans. Richard Tart (Bloomington: Indiana UP, 1997).

10 See Emmanuel Levinas, *Otherwise than Being or Beyond Essence* (1974), trans. Alphonso Lingis (Pittsburgh: Duquesne University Press, 1981), p.129. See also Paul Davies' essay, 'Sincerity and Theodicy: Three Remarks on Levinas and Kant', in Simon Critchley and Robet Bernasconi, eds, *Levinas: the Cambridge Companion* (Cambridge: Cambridge UP, 2002), pp.161-187, an earlier version of which appeared in *Research in Phenomenology 28* (1998) pp.126-151.

11 Emmanuel Levinas, 'Wholly Otherwise' (1973), trans. Simon Critchley, in Robert Bernasconi and Simon Critchley, eds, *Re reading Levinas* (London: Athlone, 1991), pp.3-10. First published in the journal *L'Arc* as 'Tout Autrement', volume 54, 1973. For Simon Critchley's own discussion of the relation between Derrida, Levinas and Kant see his *Ethics of Deconstruction: Derrida and Levinas* (Oxford: Polity Press, 1991).

12 See Emmanuel Levinas, *Existence and Existents* (1947), trans. Alphonso Lingis (Nijhoff: Kluwer Academic Publishers, 1978).

13 This remark is cited by Derrida in the second part of the analysis of Kant's *Third Critique*, in *The Truth in Painting,* part One Section two: 'Parergon', p. 79. It is of course a citation from Kant's *Critique of Pure Reason*, the cogency of which Derrida seeks to unhinge, by bending back the instabilities of the *Third Critique* onto the certainties of distinctions set up in the *First*. The success of this manoeuvre is disputed. Kemp Smith has 'Examples are thus the go-cart of judgement; and those who are lacking the natural talent can never dispense with them.' (A 134, B 173-4.)

14 (Ak. 5:226)

15 For an excellent discussion of Derrida on Kant and Hegel, see Simon Malpas, 'Framing Infinities: Kant's Aesthetics After Derrida', in Andrea Rehberg and Rachel Jones, eds, *The Matter of Critique: Readings in Kant's Philosophy* (Manchester: Clinamen, 2000), pp.147-162. For Hegel after Derrida, see Werner Hamacher, *Pleroma - Reading Hegel* (1978), trans. Nicholas Walker and Simon Jarvis (London: Athlone, 1998) and Stuart Barnett, ed, *Hegel after Derrida* (London: Routledge, 1998).

16 (AR5: 351) Immanuel Kant, *Critique of Judgment*, trans. Werner S. Pluhar, with a forward by Mary Gregor (Indianapolis: Hackett, 1987), p.225.

17 For the apposition to Adorno's notion of models, see Jean Francois Lyotard: *The Differend: Phrases in Dispute* (1983), trans. Georges van den Abbeele (Manchester: Manchester University Press, 1988), paragraph 152, and *L'enthousiasme: la critique kantienne de l'histoire* (Paris: Editions Galilée, 1986).

18 These are the Husserlian themes listed by Heidegger in his lectures *History of the Concept of Time* (1925) GA 20, trans. Theodore Kisiel (Bloomington: Indiana UP, 1999).

19 See Jacques Derrida, 'The Time of the Thesis: Punctuations', trans. Kathleen McLaughlin, in Alan Montefiore, ed, *Philosophy in France Today* (Cambridge: Cambridge University Press, 1983), pp.34-50. Refered to here as TTP.

20 (TTP p.39) For the analysis of Husserl by Derrida, see Jacques Derrida, *Edmund Husserl's Origin of Geometry: An Introduction,* trans. and preface John P. Leavey (Brighton: Harvester, 1978). For an extended critique of the reception of Derrida's analyses of Husserl, see Len Lawlor, *Derrida and Husserl: The Basic Problem of Phenomenology* (Bloomington: Indiana UP, 2002).

21 (TTP p.43)

22 Jacques Derrida, *Who's Afraid of Philosophy? Right to Philosophy 1,* trans. Jan Plug (Stanford: Stanford University Press, 2002): *Who's Afraid of Philosophy: Right to Philosophy1* was originally published in French in 1990 as pp.9-279 of a book entitled *Du droit à la philosophie* (Paris: Editions Gallilée, 1990).

23 (Kant 6: 206) The translation is taken from Kant, *The Metaphysics of Morals*, Cambridge Texts in the History of Philosophy, Mary Gregor, ed. (Cambridge: Cambridge UP, 1996), p.4. To this Derrida appends a note which reads in part: 'I take this... as a pretext to refer, as I should in every sentence, to two great books by Jean-Luc Nancy that clear the way for so many discussions: *Le discours de la syncope: 1. Logodaedalus,* (Paris: Flammarion, 1976) and *L'imperatif categorique* (Paris: Flammarion, 1983). In the latter work, the fundamental article entitled '*Lapsus judicii*' must receive here a privilege to which I will return again later. On the passages from Kant that I cite or evoke at this moment, see in particular the chapter 'L'ambiguite du populaire et la science sans miel', in *Le discours de la syncope,* pp. 56 ff.' (pp.198-199).

24 For the beginnings of this analysis see Richard Beardsworth, *Derrida and the Political* (London: Routledge, 1996). See also Jacques Derrida, *On Cosmopolitanism and Forgiveness* (1997), trans. Mark Dooley and Michael Hughes (London: Routledge, 2001) and Jacques Derrida and Anne Dufourmantelle, *Of Hospitality* (1997), trans. Rachel Bowlby (Stanford: Stanford UP, 2000) and Jacques Derrida, 'Of hostipitality' (1997), in *Acts of Religion*, pp.356-420.

25 The edition of Peter Fenves, *Raising the Tone of Philosophy: Late Essays by Immanuel Kant, Transformative Critique by Jacques Derrida* (Baltimore: Johns Hopkins University Press, 1993) conveniently contains translations of both Kant's text, from volume eight of the Akadamie Ausgabe, and of Derrida's text. The more usual source for Derrida's text is Harold Coward and Toby Foshay, eds, *Derrida and Negative Theology* (Albany: State University of New York Press, 1992), cited here as DNT. Peter Fenves has a number of essays on the conjunction between Kant and Derrida. His acclaimed book, on the repeated return in transcendental philosophy to

the singular instance is Peter Fenves, *A Peculiar Fate: Metaphysics and World-History in Kant* (Ithaca and London: Cornell University Press, 1991).
26 Translated in Lacoue-Labarthe: *Typographies, Mimesis, Philosophy, Politics* (Cambridge MA: Harvard University Press, 1989).
27 The texts presented at the conference are printed in *Les fins de l'Homme: a partir du travail de Jacques Derrida,* Colloque de Cerisy, 23 Juillet à 2 aout, 1980, sous le direction de Phillippe Lacoue- Labarthe et Jean Luc Nancy (Paris: Editions Galilée, 1981), cited as CFH.
28 (DNT p.32)
29 Both projects have been controversial. Some of the circumstances surrounding the former are reconstructed for English readers in Simon Sparks, ed, *Retreating the Political: Philippe Lacoue- Labarthe and Jean Luc Nancy* (London: Routledge, 1997), in which Lacoue-Labarthe's and Nancy's contributions to the Cerisy Conference are to be found in translation: see Philippe Lacoue-Labarthe, 'In the name of....', pp.55-86 and Jean Luc Nancy, 'The Free Voice of Man', pp.32-55.
30 (PF p.vii) See Jacques Derrida, *Politics of Friendship* (1994), trans. George Collins (London: Verso, 1997).
31 See Jacques Derrida, *The Other Heading: Reflections on Today's Europe,* trans. Pascale Anne Brault and Michael B Naas (Bloomington: Indiana UP, 1991), cited as OH.
32 See Edmund Husserl, *The Crisis of the European Sciences and Transcendental Philosophy: An Introduction to Phenomenological Philosophy* (1936), trans. David Carr (Evanston: Northwestern University Press, 1970).
33 (OH p.77)
34 (OH p.41)
35 See Jacques Derrida, *Psyche: inventions de l'autre* (Paris: Editions Galilée, 1987).
36 (Ak. 5: 307)
37 (Kant 4:408)The translation is taken from H.J. Paton, ed., *The Moral Law: Kant's Groundwork for a Metaphysics of Morals* (London: Hutchinson, 1966), p. 73, cited as KML and with AK numbers.
38 See David Wood, ed., *Derrida; A Critical Reader* (Oxford: Blackwell, 1992), pp. 5-35, and the three texts published separately in French in 1993, gathered together under one cover in English, Jacques Derrida, Thomas Dutoit, ed., *On the Name* (Stanford: Stanford UP, 1995), cited as DCR. For David Wood's own discussion of these and other topics see his *Deconstruction and Time* (New Jersey: Humanities, 1986).
39 (Kant 4:419)
40 *Derrida: A Critical Reader* p.32
41 (CFH p.15)
42 See Jacques Derrida, *Margins of Philosophy* (1972), trans. Alan Bass (Brighton: Harvester Press, 1982), cited as MP.
43 (MP p.135)
44 (A 406-567, B 433-595)
45 (Kant 4: 428)
46 (MP p.121)
47 (MP p.121)

48 (MP p.122)
49 (MP p.123)
50 See Rudolf Bernet in Hugh Silverman, ed., *Derrida and Deconstruction: Continental Philosophy II* (London: Routledge, 1989), pp.139-153, cited as DD.
51 (DD p.142)
52 See Edmund Husserl, *Formal and Transcendental Logic* (1929), trans. Dorion Cairns (The Hague: Nijhoff, 1969), Appendix Two, for an especially clear enumeration of these borrowings and interpretations.
53 (A 261-292, B 316-349)

2
Aporias of the *As If*: Derrida's Kant and the Question of Experience

Hager Weslaty

> As if always lays down the law.
> Jacques Derrida (*Of Hospitality*)

Kant's system of knowledge seeks to answer three main questions on the possibility of knowing, action and hope.¹ The Possible, in the philosophy of Kant, comes with and through pure rational anticipation that thinks the logical and discursive 'conditions' of all that is *in itself* 'unconditional'. For that matter, the philosophy of Kant is, in the final analysis, a philosophy of form(s). It provides the receptacle that receives experience or anticipates its advent. Having dismissed the philosophical accuracy of the dialectic and speculative methods, the question of transition had been Kant's major concern from the *Critique of Pure Reason* to the *Opus Postumum*.² The Kantian notion of experience knows nothing of the Hegelian moment of the 'for itself'. It does not tremble or doubt, it is never subject to violence or estrangement, having various schemata that come to supplement its unifying principle with Understanding. Further, Kantian experience does not lack being (as in existentialist philosophy), and neither does it lack sense (as in Derrida's deconstruction). At least this is Kant's *Idea* of experience that is radically contested in Derrida's various encounters with the Kantian critical project where experience seems to be composed and untroubled. It has apparently achieved this peace of mind thanks to the *as if* that constantly comes to bridge the gap between the given and the impossible. Is it possible to talk about experience in the mode of the *as if*? In what follows, I explain why there are only forms of experience in Kant's philosophy, but no experience 'as such'. In his various encounters with Kant, Derrida preserves the idea of 'form' in experience. However, he defines its absent subject in terms of an irreducible 'singularity'. An 'infinite experience' staged between irreducible singularities re-opens the field of the questions that were put aside by the Kantian *as if*, but even here experience takes place only through anticipation, it constantly runs the risk of not taking place at all. This is best understood in the direct link this essay will try to establish between experience and the irreducible questions of alterity and temporality.

Experience and the philosophy of the *as if*: aporias of the 'as such'

Both Derrida and Kant contend that there is no such thing as a 'whole experience', an experience that is *in* and *for itself*, an experience that is both rational and real. For Kant, totality and extension are rational properties but they are not real as such. They belong to the critical instrument that thinks experience, institutes its moral imperatives and defines its aesthetic conditions. Totality and extension do not belong to the faculty of understanding or to that of intuition, hence they are not related to experience itself, as it takes place, but rather to its rational conditions that lie outside itself. Experience is also, by definition, phenomenal, it's that which *appears to be* from the point of view of reason in its speculative and practical uses. Kantian experience is: 1) fragmented since it is conceptual and sensuous (*a priori / a posteriori*); 2) never immediate. It is mediated by schemata and contained within concepts; and 3) it is never complete since, for instance, it strives towards the fulfilment of the postulates of the moral imperative: the immortal soul and the necessary God. Knowledge is also possible without experience (in the form of empty concepts) because what is *a priori* is knowable even if it does not '*come within* our experience.' This is the case particularly in the sphere of practical reason where the 'practical' has an objective, pure, universal and necessary unconditional condition.

Nowhere, in Kant's work, is it possible to see the entire picture of experience. Seen through the keyhole of the critical door, experience appears as a tantalising[3] perspective onto the abject elements that cannot be accommodated within the system. Within the Kantian architectonic, everything must fit into the right place. This (anal) obsession with order presupposes a static structure (as defined through the categories, time, space, the *a priori* ...). It is only because the existence of the structure can be proved and maintained that the work of 'arrangement' can take place. The critical act of putting into order can proceed also thanks to the methodological device of the *as if* that systematically brushes under the carpet (to continue with this metaphor of cleaning and tidying up) any question that might come to undermine the legitimacy of the whole structure (which is nothing other than the house of reason). For instance, the Kantian antinomies of pure reason, of practical reason as well as the antinomies of judgment, do not threaten the existence of one particular element in the Kantian system. They question the whole critical project, they are directed at the very rationality of reason.

Now, if on the other hand questions are maintained, this would render the progress towards the critical task (of arrangement, of putting into order, of tidying up) impossible because the very structure that would make this work possible is never complete. Each time a question comes up, a question takes place in place of something else, the whole critical project is brought to a halt. Derrida describes such an open structure or 'opening of the structure' in his conversation with the phenomenology of Husserl, his aim being to discover 'a concrete, but non empirical, intentionality, a "transcendental experience" which would be "constitutive," that is, like all intentionality, simultaneously productive and revelatory, active and passive.'[4] Derrida does not work with a static structure where experiences come to dwell in a particular prescribed or inscribed place. Questions are not put aside as if they were never raised in the first place. On the contrary, each time a question comes about the whole structure is dismantled and taken to pieces. If the Kantian experience can be seen only through the keyhole of the critical door, the Derridean experience cannot be seen at all because it takes place in an eternal construction site where everything is provisional. The very concept of experience is based on what Derrida describes, in his attempt to write a biography of his own work in *Aporias*, as 'the interminable list of all the so-called undecidable quasi-concepts that are so many aporetic places or dislocations.'[5] Experience is in this respect essentially non-phenomenal. It comes very close to the 'Idea in the Kantian sense [that constantly comes to] overflow the phenomenological system of self evidences or factual determinations.'[6]

Despite this 'infinite opening of what is experienced,'[7] Derridean experience does not lack form. This is, to my mind, the first insurmountable difficulty that we are faced with in our discussion of Derrida's understanding of experience. We are talking about experience that is non-phenomenal, that does not take place where the voyeuristic gaze of the Kantian subject is directed. We are not even sure whether anything takes place or *is* taking place at all. However, this experience has an unconditional *a priori* condition. The Derridean category of the *arché* is, I think, a structural *always already* that determines what I propose to call 'preliminary consent' that is implied in the positive reception of any utterance however hostile and negative. The main distinction between the Kantian critical project and Derrida's deconstructive discourse lays in an irreducible 'affirmation' that is formulated (with and) against the unconditional reply of the Kantian subject to the imperatives of the moral law. 'Affirmation that motivates deconstruction is unconditional, imperative, and immediate - in a sense that is not necessarily or only Kantian, even if this affirmation, because it is double [...] is ceaselessly threatened. This is why it leaves no respite, no rest. It can always upset, at least, the instituted rhythm of every pause.'[8] The affirmation of preliminary consent and the risk/y (responsibility) that it entails makes Derrida think of many 'troubled Saturdays, Sundays, and Fridays' *ahead of* oneself.[9] However, affirmation is not an absolute moment in the Derridean discourse on experience. For every 'yes, yes' there has to be an irreducible 'no' or a non-response, a secret that does not speak, an event that refuses to take place, a photograph that does not show anything,[10] basically a non-passage or an irreducible signature, a 'proper name' that guarantees the absolute singularity of the other. This is Derrida's experience of the *aporia*. The easy and rational transitions provided by the Kantian schemata are here formulated as an impossible 'passage' that is always conditioned by a possible 'advent', an unconditional 'perhaps', and a messianic justice and democracy 'yet-to-come'. Hence the imperative return to the primacy of 'experience' as in Derrida's writings about the gift, hospitality, friendship, forgiveness, envois, mourning, death, writing ... all such experiences taking place within the house of deconstruction reopen the questions of time and the other *qua* the (non-)concept of singularity.

In Kant's philosophy everything is preparing for, or anticipating experience. 'The principles of the pure understanding, whether constitutive *a priori* [...] or merely regulative [...] contain nothing but the pure schema, as it were, of possible experience.'[11] While experience is strictly defined through these 'forms of thought,' the categories have no use unless they are applied within the limits of experience. Their very existence requires experience. But in the sphere of experience the categories are not really 'put to the test' and as such their relevance or accuracy is not verified. They are rather employed, or used, as the defining containers of experience. However, it is in the field of practical reason that the categories become problematic in their relation to experience because where there is *duty* and *obligation* there is no experience as such. In the *Critique of Practical Reason*, Kant works with the main 'speculative' thesis of the first critique that 'the thinking subject is only an appearance to itself in inner intuition.'[12] Now even though Kant explains in his preface to the second *Critique* that this thesis has not been proved in the *Critique of Pure Reason*, he finds himself 'compelled' to accept this formulation *as if* it had already been proved. In practical reason, it is perfectly acceptable to apply the categories to *noumena*. The mediation between a theory of the subject (a being *in itself* in relation to natural law) and a theory of (moral) action performed by a phenomenal empirical reason rather than a pure consciousness is absolutely imperative otherwise 'the self-contradiction of reason is unavoidable.'[13]

Since the will acts outside the law of causality (i.e., it does not take into consideration the achievement of a 'desired effect'), it is radically dissociated from the 'sensuous world' or again the sphere of experience. What *can* be done is only that which *ought to* be done following the dictates of the moral law. 'The practical rule is therefore unconditional and thus is thought of *a priori* as a categorically practical proposition. [...] The will is thought of as independent of empirical conditions and consequently as pure will, determined by the mere *form*[14] of the law.' The unconditional does not 'borrow' anything from experience, as Kant says. The 'practical' in the Kantian ethics is not related to experience. It is pure reason that is practical *of itself* and *by itself* and as such it defines the unconditioned imperative of the moral law. The autonomy of the subject of this moral law (which is by implication a universal subject) does not depend on the empirical or sensuous incentive to act since such incentives belong to maxims and maxims are purely subjective.

While the first *Critique* establishes the absolute dependence of concepts on intuition and intuition on concepts (hence the importance of the objects of experience[15]), the second *Critique* revisits the sphere of *noumena*. Now it is possible to practically know something of the noumenal sphere, and this something is the moral law. This law 'provides a fact absolutely inexplicable from any data of the world of sense or from the whole compass of the theoretical use of reason, and this fact points to a pure intelligible world.'[16] The categories of practical reason are not empty (even though they lack intuition) because their objective condition is 'the concept of the highest good'. At this point it is possible to understand why the Kantian *as if* does not have the same function in the totality of Kant's system of knowledge. I think that, where Kant talks about experience defined through 'forms of thought', the 'as if', which ignores (but does not resolve) the antinomies of pure reason, achieves a necessary transition towards the sensuous world or objective reality. Without this necessary transition the concepts would remain empty and intuition would be blind and misguided. However, in the sphere of practical reason where, as I said earlier, I think that it is entirely impossible to talk about experience at all in terms of duty or obligation, the 'as if' has a completely different function. Instead of providing the transition from concepts to the field of 'possible experience', the 'as if' of practical reason turns away from experience altogether and points to the necessary existence of a 'supersensuous nature' where concepts need neither time nor intuition. In Alexandre Kojève's reading of Kant[17], it is the second 'as if' that marks the point at which the whole Kantian system of knowledge fails. The concept is no longer equated with phenomenal time (as in the first *Critique*)[18] but it now depends on something that is non-phenomenal (that is eternal time), something outside itself. The Kantian system of knowledge has already transgressed the limits of the phenomenal condition.

Kant divides his philosophy into that which is possible to know and that which is impossible to know. The highest principle of the possible and the impossible is the idea of an object that exists regardless of whether it is being or nothingness. Kant deduces that only the categories can be applied to objects in this fashion. The categories are superior to *noumena*. The noumenal as a 'content' is *in itself*. 'The categories are not in themselves knowledge, but mere *forms of thought* for the construction of knowledge from given intuitions.'[19] So whatever cannot be thought by or within the categories is deemed an 'unknown something'. It is at this point that Kant leaves an 'empty space'[20] in his system of knowledge for some undefined 'third something' where intuitions are without concepts and concepts without intuitions. The Kantian (impossible) moral and aesthetic experiences are located in place of this *chiasmus*, this X that (un)marks a (non-)place occupied by some 'third something'. This is why there are *ideas* that we can't understand that are yet practical and beautiful. Where there is no answer to a question there is silence (or the Kantian rational faith), even though it is possible to carry on talking about the impossibility of finding an answer. Silence is understood, in this respect, as the absence of any discursive progress. This is why I think that Kant's *Critique of Practical Reason* as well as his *Critique of Judgment* are silent books.[21] Kojève explains in his *Kant* that 'the thing-in-itself is a point that has no discursive extension in the Kantian system, but it cannot be excluded from this system because its exclusion would interrupt the development of discourse. The *as if* affects only one of the elements of the system which is no longer a homogenous system.'[22] But instead of stopping at the ineffable, like Parmenides, it is possible to carry on with the discursive development of the system 'as if' unresolved questions were not an object of questioning in the first place.

To sum up, we can say that in the Kantian system of knowledge, the *as if* is no more than: 1) a pacifying device that neutralises the unresolved problems of pure reason. Kant rejected the habit of thought which consists in 'making the mind revolt against itself, provide it with destructive weapons on both sides then step back and watch the conflict with calmness and sarcasm.' Besides being a pacifying device, 2) the *as if* keeps reason and understanding apart, assigning for each faculty its own independent sphere of knowing. Finally 3) the *as if* is a restrictive paradigm in the Kantian system. The *as if* marks the boundaries of knowledge and prevents it from expanding endlessly in new grounds. 'Knowledge does not extend its application to all that the understanding thinks. But, after all, the possibility of such *noumena* is quite incomprehensible, and beyond the sphere of appearances, all is for us a mere void.'[23] The Kantian *as if* is then essentially related to restriction for pure reason in its speculative use only. In its practical use, however, reason has an absolute 'right to extension' through the *as if*. The extension of reason signals the end of experience.

The *as if* marks, however, a third moment in the Kantian system of knowledge in the *Critique of Judgment*, where aesthetic experience is meant to bring together the sensuous nature that is essential in the first *Critique* and the 'supersensuous nature' that is necessary in the second *Critique*. The judgment of taste, Kant thought, should be as disinterested as the moral imperative even though it lacks its purposiveness. Experience is, at this point, independent of both desire and knowledge. Kant dissociates enjoyment from the aesthetic experience that is purely contemplative. The aesthetic object that brings together the faculties of Imagination and Understanding must be contemplated *as if* it had a purpose. Derrida revisits the third *Critique* at the very moment when it poses its antinomies of judgment on whether the production of material things depends on mechanical laws or not. The mechanism of nature is replaced by the principle of 'final causes'. Kant concludes that the concept of causality through a purpose cannot be derived from experience since 'taste is our ability to judge a priori the communicability of the feelings that (without a mediation by a concept) are connected with a given presentation.'[24] The faculty of taste in the *Critique of Judgment* has the same magnitude and scope as the 'moral feeling' in practical reason. In both examples, the concepts are not needed to provide experience with form. The aesthetic experience, for instance, is already rendered through aesthetic forms (of the Beautiful or the Sublime), it is an experience of that which is always already *trans*-formed in and by a supersensuous, non-phenomenal nature. 'We have a merely aesthetic power of judgment, an ability to judge forms without using concepts and to feel in the mere judging of these forms a liking that we also make a rule for everyone, though our judgment is not based on an interest and also gives rise to none.'[25] The aesthetic experience would require, in Derrida's words, an 'arid pleasure without concept and without enjoyment.'[26] The subject of the Kantian aesthetic experience is called on to act *as if* the presence or existence of the 'beautiful object' was totally indifferent to this subject. The beautiful object must be contemplated in a totally disinterested and detached way and no pleasure must be sought in such pure contemplation of that whose existence does not concern the subject because it cannot be determined by Understanding or Intuition. Here again, Kantian experience exceeds its phenomenal condition, because such experience, Derrida says, 'no longer depends on any phenomenal empiricity, of any determined *existence*, whether that of the object or that of the subject.'[27] At this point, Reason finds itself incapable of satisfying its moral needs as well as its aesthetic desire for the beautiful non-existence. The *as if* enters the work, the discourse on the beautiful (such as the third *Critique* that Derrida reserves the absolute right to *contemplate* as this very beautiful object), in the form of a *parergon*, the experience of the frame, or the act of framing that displaces a discourse outside its own pre-scribed or in-scribed limits or concepts. This *quasi concept* 'designates a formal and general predicative structure, which one can transport *intact* or deformed and reformed *according to certain rules*, into other fields, to submit new contents to it.'[28] Derrida's reading of Kant's critique of pure judgment of taste[29] defines the political economy of the Kantian discourse on art and on the beautiful. Derrida first finds a major difficulty in defining 'economy' that is formulated in terms of an irreducible *aporetic* antinomy. It is neither restricted nor general economy, and there is no relationship of identity or opposition between these two economic structures. There is instead a relation of non-relation through the act of haunting. Restricted economy of circulation and profit must come to haunt a pure economy of expenditure. A general economy that is essentially irreducible to the dictates and rules of restricted economy must come to haunt the restrictions of the restricted economy and its very rationale of circularity and exchange. Nothing should be pure *in* and *for* itself. Contamination is an irreducible experience in the Derridean discourse on experience. Kant evacuates the subjective condition from *mimesis* in so far as he equates *physis* with *mimesis* which is nature's relation to itself and not the subject's imitation of nature. Kant's 'apparently irreducible oppositions' are once again going to be 'dissolved' as 'they always do.'[30] The systematic dissolution of opposition in the Kantian system depends, according to Derrida, on the necessary 'production, propagation and multiplication' of the Kantian apparatuses of critical distinctions. Through these distinctions, Derrida uncovers the humanist project of Kant, in the field of the aesthetic, whose concept of art aims to 'erect a man-god [...] to mark an incontrovertible limit of anthropological domesticity.'[31] Kant thought that art should remain outside the economy of circulation. But because of the hierarchy created by different distinctions between good art and bad art, free art and mercenary art ...etc., it becomes legitimate for 'an-economy to render useful the economy of work.'[32] Hence Kantian oppositions are in Derrida's words 'false oppositions'. What is always already part of a restricted economy is in other instances presented in the form of play.[33] 'Liberal art relates to mercenary art as the mind does to the body, and it cannot produce itself, in its freedom, without the very thing that it subordinates to itself, without the force of mechanical structure which in every sense of the word it *supposes* - the mechanical agency, mercenary, laborious, deprived of pleasure.'[34] Contamination has already taken place.

In the terminology 'fine art' or 'beautiful art' that is never questioned by Kant, Derrida finds an implicit link that is never explicitly established and recognised between the product and a 'productive subjectivity.' The beautiful knows nothing of the subject who is lost in the contemplation of the beautiful. However, Derrida finds in this seemingly disinterested and detached act, that he also associates with the experience of mourning, a signature 'which remains marked at the limit of the work, neither in nor out, out and in, in the parergonal thickness of the frame.'[35] The beautiful does not belong to either the product or the producing act, but it is the property of the very producing subjectivity also called a 'parergonal effect' that signs the work or puts it in a frame. It is this very signature, this framing (subjectivity) that Kant sought to erase from mimesis that he identifies, as Derrida says with 'the free unfolding-refolding of the *physis*.'[36] It is at this point, that Derrida thinks that the 'as if' becomes essential, since 'a certain *quasi*, a certain *als ob* re-establishes analogical *mimesis* at the point where it appears detached.'[37] Subjective productivity is presented *as if* it were a pure product of nature. Derrida questions the 'scope' of this 'as if' which points to a 'pre-critical time, anterior to all the dissociations, oppositions, and delimitations of critical discourse, "older" even than the time of the transcendental aesthetic.'[38] In the third *Critique*, the *as if* opens up the Kantian system of knowledge on endless 'analogies' that reveal no purpose. This, according to Derrida, 'leads us back inside ourselves,'[39] to indulge once more in that silent conversation with the infinitude of the 'invisible self' in the moral law and the infinitude of the starry heavens of pure reason. The Kantian subject always stumbles against an insurmountable obstacle of the purpose-less. Here is where experience becomes essential from the point of view of Derrida. While the Kantian discourse about everything and anything proceeds without running the risk of contradicting itself, something comes about to betray the discursive limits of this very discourse. The *as if* plays with the conjunctions and disjunctions of the given and the impossible, it connects and disconnects, ties and unties the totality of the Kantian discursive edifice. In *The Truth in Painting*, Derrida compares philosophy to the art of architecture. Philosophy must 'represent itself, it *detaches itself*, detaches from itself a proxy, a part of itself besides itself in order to think the whole, to saturate or heal over the whole that suffers from detachment.'[40] In a crucial passage of Derrida's 'Economimesis' the working of the *as if* in its relation to discourse is staged in the confrontation between the orator and the poet in the third *Critique*. (Beautiful) discourse becomes an irreducible condition whereby there is no possible *hors-texte* for experience. However, silence, or the secret, is essential to this apparently irreducible and absolute discursive condition.

> The orator and the poet meet one another and exchange their masks, masks of an *as if*. Both pretend, but the as if of one is more and better than the as if of the other. In the service of truth, of loyalty, of sincerity, of productive freedom is the as if of the poet, who therefore expresses more and better. The orator's as if deceives and machinates. It is precisely a machine or rather a 'deceitful art' which manipulates

men 'like machines'. The orator announces serious business and treats it as if it were a simple play of ideas. The poet merely proposes an entertaining play of the imagination and proceeds as if it were handling the business of the understanding. [...] the orator promises understanding and gives imagination; the poet promises to play with the imagination while he nurtures the understanding and gives life to concepts.[41]

It seems that the Kantian system is perfectly capable of admitting negativity within its boundaries without running the risk of contradiction (because negativity can be accommodated within the antinomies and neutralised by the mask of the *as if*). It is rather something else that cannot be 'digested, or represented, or stated - does not allow itself to be transformed into auto-affection by exemplorality. [...] Vomiting lends its form to this whole system.'[42] What is vomited by the Kantian third *Critique* is something 'unrepresentable' and most of all it is something 'singular' and 'unnameable in its singularity.'[43] This thing renders economy impossible, it is something insensible and at the same time unintelligible; it is 'the absolute other of the system.'[44] Vomiting makes enjoyment possible because it interrupts the passage from consumption to idealisation. Disgust is linked according to Derrida to the experience of mourning. Vomiting, like mourning, interrupts discourse, it causes this discourse to tremble when it interrupts its economy of circulation as in the stream of promises flowing from the mouth of the orator to the ear of the poet and from the mouth of the poet to the ear of the orator.

The elements of the Kantian *as if*, such as the existence of God, the freedom of the will, the immortality of the soul, or the possible existence of a commonwealth of self-governing citizens, are essentially non-phenomenological. Hence what is foreclosed from the sphere of understanding reappears in the sphere of reason and causes the return of the repressed metaphysical tension in the seemingly perfectly composed and untroubled philosophy of Kant. Derrida reminds us of the distinction Kant makes between the critique or the empiricism of the critical project and the system of pure philosophy, also called metaphysics.[45] The impossible *Concept* is a possible *Idea*. The *as if* introduces within critical philosophy an area of silence that, paradoxically, allows metaphysics to be heard. Where there is the ineffable there is violence, according to the thesis of French philosopher Eric Weil.[46] Critical philosophy constructs a system with lacks and that is why philosophy remains for Kant an 'infinite task'. At the end of the *Critique of Pure Reason*, Kant explains that 'the *critical* path alone is still open.'[47] Discourse becomes the absolute condition of the Kantian system of knowledge. Kant speaks on top of his philosophical discourse while Hegel hoists the white flag as soon as the Absolute Spirit appears. At that point, there is nothing left for the philosopher to say after everything that could be said had been put into words. (Kojève's reading of Hegel that reaches the moment of absolute knowing presupposes the end of history thesis and the absolute closure of discourse/the book). According to Derrida, the infinite 'play' of substitutions, deferral and rearrangement of signification occurs only when the transcendental signified ('extimate' to the structure, i.e., both within and outside the structure) is re-inscribed within a system of difference. The Kantian *as if* allows this very play of infinite (in)signification to take place.

It seems that phenomenology remains an unresolved problem in the philosophy of Kant. The point of view of the *as if* achieves a double movement in the direction of, and away from, phenomenology. In Kant, the return to phenomenology via the *as if* and the setting aside of 'the question' is in reality a denial of phenomenology altogether. This presumed return suspends both reason and understanding in what Kant calls the *'metaphysics of experience'*, for Kantian ethics are not about revelations. Just as in Derrida, the ethics of Kant are essentially 'non-phenomenal'. The point of view of the *as if* does not lead (back) to phenomenology but only to 'deceptive appearances'. This *pseudo-phenomenology* is, according to Derrida, a form of violence. It seems that one cannot pretend to philosophise in perpetual peace. Appearance is recommendable in the context of Kantian morality. Deceptive appearance is not as bad as all that, is not always inadvisable, Kant concedes. Nature was wise enough to implant in mankind a felicitous aptitude for being deceived. Certainly illusion does not save virtue, but in saving appearance, illusion renders virtue attractive.'[48] Illusions are in that sense beneficial, hence the happy complicity between the orator and the poet. Derrida explains in *Aporias* that 'this formulation of the paradox and of the impossible, calls upon a figure that resembles a structure of temporality, an instantaneous dissociation from the present, a *difference* in being-with-itself of the present.'[49] Derrida thinks that in the context of Kant's system of knowledge, *aporia* is more accurate a term than 'antinomy'; 'the antinomy here better deserves the name of *aporia* insofar as it is neither an "opponent nor illusory" antinomy [...] nor even a "transcendental illusion in a dialectic of the Kantian type," but instead an interminable experience.'[50] The Kantian *as if* is in the context of Derrida's work of the same nature as the 'perhaps'; it is the identification of an unsurpassable boundary (a point at which no *relève* in the Hegelian fashion is possible) and yet this same boundary is also an opening onto the categorical or *pure* other. The Aporetic is an act of transgression, it is at the same time 'the non passage, which can in fact be something else, the event of a coming or of a future advent.'[51] By overcoming the antinomies through the 'as if' the Kantian system of knowledge seems to have overcome the problem of *alterity* altogether. But with Derrida, we say that the other is set aside, dismissed or repudiated (since the staging of a dialectical confrontation which reduces the other to same does not take place). And yet, the spectre of the other remains there within the system looming behind the *as if*.

Kant's three *Critiques* define the limits of knowledge and the knowable and as such, his philosophy defines an area of *différance*, a space where it is possible to locate the spectre of the other, the margin, the accursed share of philosophy that causes the sacrifice of philosophy. But it seems to me that this is not quite true of the philosophical system of Kant. If the Hegelian '*relève*' as Derrida says, is supposed to lead to absolute knowing, self-consciousness, the moment of this achievement is the very beginning of absolute expenditure. However, by multiplying the partitions and 'breachings' of the *as ifs* in his system and at the same time endowing the critical enterprise with an open project for pure and practical reason, as well as aesthetic judgment, Kant never brings about this moment of *différance*. The event of the 'other' never happens in the philosophy of Kant. The 'notion of the subject,' Kant thinks, lacks permanence. There are no absolute conditions which guarantee its absolute existence, or presence at all times. Kant contends in the section titled 'Transcendental Doctrine of Judgment', Chapter 3 in the first *Critique*, 'I can make nothing out of the notion, and draw no inference from it, because no object to which to apply the concept is determined, and we consequently do not know whether it has any meaning at all.'[52] The subject is also besieged in the sphere of practical reason since the subjective condition is deemed 'contingent' and as such it never leads to the 'objective condition' which is valid for the will of every 'rational being.' Kant assumes that 'for reason to be legislative, it is required that reason need presuppose only itself.'[53] The subject's desire or its 'susceptibility to pleasure or displeasure' cannot be known *a priori* and therefore it can never be raised to the status of an objective necessity. The subject of practical reason (if there is such thing at all) is defined in its absolute dependence on the law. 'A law would not be needed if we already know of ourselves what we ought to do and moreover were conscious of liking to do it.'[54]

Derrida's (missed) encounter with Kant is staged in a field 'extimate' to the transcendental, it is both within and without the sphere of what can be known, always anticipating the questions of what can be done and what can be hoped. Derrida explains that 'a theory of the subject is incapable of accounting for any decision. But this must be said *a fortiori* of the event, and of the event with regard to the decision. For nothing ever happens to a subject, nothing deserving the name "event".'[55] For Derrida, subjectivity is related to permanence, it is a continual Hegelian striving to do away with the fear of nothingness, the fear of the infinite, fear of that which refuses to overcome its other. The figure of otherness is associated with the event's occurrence, and always acts in a manner alien to the subject. The event, according to Derrida, 'must surprise both the freedom and the will of every subject, surprise the very subjectivity of the subject ... the passive decision, condition of the event, is always in me, structurally, another event, a rending decision as the decision of the other. Of the absolute other in me, the other as the absolute that decides on me in me.'[56] Unlike Kant, Derrida does not seek to re-establish in the empty field of experience a subjectivity that is identical to itself, subject to the irreducible categories of time and space. He rather posits a singularity that is capable of 'dislocating and dividing itself' in *the time and space of différance* which presupposes the irreducible singularity of the other.

Experience and the yet-to-come: *aporias* of the event

The Kantian event is defined at the end of the *Critique of Pure Reason* with much certainty. If something can be known at all, then *something is*, i.e., something does exist even though it is at times absolutely non-existent (as the beautiful object). This event is not purely intellectual since it also depends on the ethical question. What 'takes place' depends on 'something that *ought to* take place.' Kant associates practical pure reason with the 'principle of the possibility of experience.'[57] For Kant whatever is moral 'must be possible.' Here the Kantian system of knowledge leads us to the conclusion that is so reminiscent of the L'Oréal commercial where the piercing gaze of beautiful female models declares with such coldness and cruelty: 'because I'm worth it!' For Kant, acting in accordance with the moral law means that one should strive towards being 'worthy of happiness.' 'Do that which will render thee worthy of happiness.'[58] How is it possible to use knowledge of what can be known to understand what happens, what takes place, if by such expressions we mean *the event* itself? Let us ask with Derrida 'can one speak [...] of *an experience of the aporia*?'[59] For both Derrida and Kant there is no such thing as an experience in the present tense. Experience is expressed in the 'future anterior' (future of that which is necessary) or in the conditional future (future of that which would perhaps come about). The future also comes back, it returns even before it happens (it's the anticipated return of the Nietzschean eternal return). This future (event/tense) is the very basis of the entire (a)political and (an)economic theory of Derrida. The event as a concept, lacks time, it is never equated with time, and it never *lives up* to any promise, be it the promise of a poet or that of an orator.

The non-phenomenal Kantian 'as if' is, then, perverted in Derrida's thought of the trace. For Derrida, it is imperative that at the heart of every ethical law there is a 'question' 'that is always foreclosed, it never appears immediately *as such*'. The Kantian *as if* is a return to presence and identity as developed in the questions of Leibniz: on why there is something rather than nothing, and why things are such as they are and not otherwise. Kant recommends an imperative return towards a (virtual) centre that would reorganise and hold together the pieces of his entire critical project for 'the universe must sink in the abyss of nothingness, unless we admit that, besides this infinite chain of contingencies, there exists something that is primal and self-subsisting - something which, as the cause of this phenomenal world, secures its continuance and preservation.'[60] Derrida achieves a return towards a Kantian metaphysics of experience that is yet not inspired by the violence of 'light'. Derrida's metaphysics of ethical, political, philosophical or juridical experiences seek the guidance of a pacifying light before the enlightenment, and a critical path that is essentially pre-critical, i.e., non-conceptual, unwilling and undecided. The ethical relationship is, for that matter, 'a non-violent relationship' to the irreducible otherness of the other. And the infinitely other is most of all 'invisible', he/she is never seen, but simply pre-supposed in a non-phenomenal field. One must act as if the other is infinitely other. The *as if* is, however, on the side of illusion, light and violence because such experience would always require the metaphysical time, the future. 'The encounter of the unforeseeable itself is the only possible opening of time, the only pure future, the only pure expenditure *beyond* history as economy. But this future, this beyond, is not another time, a day after history. It is *present* at the heart of experience. Present not as a total presence but as a *trace.*'[61] Derrida was hoping that the other would present himself as absence, and appear as non-phenomenal. The event is written (off) with and in *aporias* of the event, an event that is preceded and anticipated by the *perhaps* rather than by any concept or any faith.

The Kantian ethical position, on the other hand, requires the introduction of the finite time of the phenomenal sphere, as Gilles Deleuze explains in *Difference and Repetition*, 'my undetermined existence can be determined only within time as the existence of a phenomenon, of a passive, receptive phenomenal subject appearing within time.'[62] For Derrida, 'ethics is metaphysics' and this would have to depend on the discreteness of the other who would remain confined within its/his/her 'secret interior'. Derrida's philosophy of the future is one of the main questions of the whole project of deconstruction. It determines its definition (the discovery within the text of that which always already undoes itself as trace, supplemented in and through writing) and its method (the thought of *différance*, the deferred, absence, and the yet to come). The work of deconstruction is ongoing and it has no dialectical resolution. It is in that sense an 'infinite task'. So if we talk about Derrida's philosophy of the future we will have to talk about the whole idea of, and behind, deconstruction rather than about one of its components or aspects. It is this sort of (metaphysical) questioning that 'reveals' deconstruction as the experience of the 'impossible', 'excess', 'transgression', and 'play', so many terms that bring to mind Batalllean general economy essentially based on the concept of sacrifice. Deconstruction requires an 'infinite patience' and a sustained 'passion' for *secrets* but also the work of mourning, and entombment. Derrida talks of unborn victims and a justice that is infinite and always to come. *It never arrives* because each actual manifestation is necessarily flawed and inherently unjust. Each instance of the law involves a violence. This lofty messianic justice-to-come floats on ahead of us, like Benjamin's angel of history, in an endless ascension towards the sublime beauty of the starry skies above the subject of the moral law. Kant had an enlightened faith that subjectivity could adhere to rational and universal ethical positions. The Kantian faith conceded, it is true, a lot to the subject's 'power of self determination', a freedom beyond understanding and beyond appearances, a noumenal freedom that remains the transcendental condition of the moral imperative. A condition that is not 'with' the subject but always transcendent to subjectivity, transcendent to the split Ego of reason and understanding. In contrast to Kant's metaphysics of experience, Derrida attempts to neutralise and at the same time rekindle the violence of general economy and the gift, friendship, hospitality, forgiveness ... He attempts to evacuate the 'subject' from such experiences to locate it way beyond the grasp, apprehension or credit of the subject, even the subject of the unconscious. In *Politics of Friendship*, for example, there has to be no love or hate, no debt, no potlatch, no humiliation, no mutual ruination and no *hainamoration*. Derrida seems to talk about an experience that isn't one, an experience that is, like the gift, nothing - a gift of nothing, an experience of nothing (in particular if by such a thing one can understand a predetermined, determined and conceptual experience).

The experience of friendship and the category of preliminary consent

In *Politics of Friendship*, Derrida strives to deconstruct the 'schematic of filiation' that has historically governed the way in which political subjects, communities, nations and races have organised themselves in relation to and in a certain continuity with, monarchical and imperial models. Throughout history, political groupings have always idealised, justified, and exercised authority and consolidated power through the rhetoric of 'fraternity' or a 'society of brothers'. Derrida's method to deconstruct the restricted economy of 'friendship' is based on a process of 'countersignatures'. For instance he reads the Aristotelian apostrophe, 'Oh my friends there is no friend,' with the Nietzschean apostrophe, 'Oh my enemies, there is no enemy.' The concept of friendship is not estranged in its other, its point of *unworking* being in this case the concept of enmity. In the Hegelian fashion, this process of estrangement which would have posited the possibility of overcoming, or *relève*, preserves the limits of discursive knowledge that Derrida describes as the 'anxiety of the infinite'.[63] This (anti-)Kantian anxiety can be enhanced through the antinomy or *aporia* of the friend/enemy, an antinomy at which reason, in its speculative as well as in its practical uses comes to stumble and ultimately loses its balance. Derrida's 'play' is based on the Kantian principle of the sudden 'irruption of the infinite into consciousness.'[64] In this case there is an endless anticipation, deferral and distancing that is radically different from the Hegelian dialectic that neutralises the infinite, and does away with the Kantian 'Idea'.

The reconciliation of the concepts of enmity and friendship is symptomatic of the persistence of the society of brothers. Derrida uncovers this project articulated in the name of the political in various canonical texts dealing with the concept of friendship. He is, however, much concerned with the recent discussions of the political after the waning of the communist threat. Western democracies, according to Karl Schmitt, for instance, need the concept of enmity in order for the political to survive. Via the 'seismic event signed Nietzsche', Derrida opens the end of friendship onto the end of enmity instead of reducing friendship to enmity. Countersignature is based on unresolved contradiction or what Derrida calls 'teleopoesis' a combination of the idea of distance (*tele*) and end (*telos*). The *teleopoetic* is by implication a rhetorical effect of distancing, deferral, or refraction of meaning by bringing together the performative and the reportive within one single statement. The apostrophes pronounced respectively by the Aristotelian 'dying sage' and the Nietzschean 'living fool' on the end of friendship and the end of enmity would be examples of synthetic *a priori* statements in so far as they presuppose connection without identity. If the apostrophes were analytic, presupposing the identity of friendship and enmity, this would make the recourse to experience irrelevant and unnecessary. However, the Kantian synthetic *a priori* can be the object of an infinite experience, one that is built on *différance*. Experience, in this context is not used in the empirical sense of the transcendental aesthetic as the act of 'receiving representations through sensibility.' It is experience that becomes possible when knowledge is denied to make room for faith. In the synthetic *a priori* there is this double effect of the Derridean *teleopoetic* which 'qualifies in a great number of contexts and semantic orders, that which renders absolute, perfect, completed, accomplished, finished, that which brings to an end. But permits us to play too with the other tele, the one that speaks to distance and the far removed.'[65] Derrida is concerned with the 'teleopoesis' of the event promised in the structure of the 'X without X' that is perhaps more simply conveyed in the uncertain promise of the word 'perhaps'. He takes up the contemporary political implications of Karl Schmitt's contention that political existence, even politics itself, depends on the relative *stability* of the friend/enemy distinction. Derrida follows Schmitt, in order to diverge from him, when he writes that 'losing the enemy would not necessarily be progress, reconciliation, or the opening of an era of peace and human fraternity. It would be worse: an unheard of violence, the evil of a malice knowing neither measure nor ground.'[66] Derrida questions and addresses the possibility of a political model 'beyond the principle of fraternity,' an 'arché-friendship' that would consist in both the necessity and the exigency of a friendship *before* friendship, or more urgently, a friendship exterior to the friend/brother. *Arché*-friendship, in the manner of the synthetic *a priori*, 'points to that which must be supposed in order to be heard ... this *preliminary consent* without which you would not hear me ... if a sort of friendship had not already been sealed, before all contacts; if it had not been avowed as the impossible that resists even the avowal ... a friendship prior to friendships ... *fundamental* and *groundless*.'[67] Derrida's conception of arché-friendship is both *a*-political and *an*-economic, but it is also the apolitical condition of all politics and the an-economic condition of all exchange, all commerce. It is the subjectless, heterogeneous spatio-temporality necessary for any configuration of homegeneity, of a world of subjects and objects and their friendly or hostile exchanges. As such it is closely related to Kant's Ideas, as a locus of heterogeneity and ir-relation that follows the model of the 'unknown = x'.

Derrida's arché-friendship is explicated in the form of the problematisation of a series of oppositions foregrounding one over the other: arché-friendship is to be sought in distance rather than proximity, non-knowing rather than recognition, dispossession and expenditure rather than appropriation and finally, the incommensurable rather than the equitable and reciprocal. Political egalitarianism based on the model of friendship or fraternity runs up against two essential and characteristic problems: the question of *number* as well as the question of *woman*: how many friends is it possible to have without rendering the idea meaningless? Can a woman ever be (just) a friend, or will she have to be addressed as 'brother'? 'The test of friendship remains, for a finite being, an endurance of arithmetic. Indeed, the friend must not only be good in himself, in a simple or absolute manner, he must be good for you, in relation to you who are his friend.'[68] Consistent with the formation of a fraternal society of friends, woman is subject to a 'double exclusion'. Apparently unable to form friendships with men, women cannot be friends with each other either. For one (male) philosopher after another, they - or rather 'we' - are entirely heterogeneous to the concept. And not only friendship and fraternity, of course, women are also heterogeneous to other requirements of an egalitarian democracy: justice, law, humanity. For Nietzsche, woman is either a slave or a tyrant, she knows nothing but love and so will never be able to respect the enemy or subscribe to the idea of equality required by political friendship. While, for Nietzsche, woman is the 'outlaw of humanity,' for Hegel she is 'the eternal irony of the community.' Many of these judgments are of course misplaced compliments, but at the same time they are bouquets that, in situating woman outside, nevertheless sustain the homogeneity of the society of brothers rather than disrupt it. Michelet, for example, considers that 'woman is ... like law beyond the law, justice beyond justice. She is "more than just." Except for the fact that she destroys, with justice, what she thus is, what she could be, what she is without being it: pure friendship.'[69] The Kantian concept of friendship is based on secrecy which also requires the restricted number of friends. It is the imperative of secrecy that renders the experience of friendship rare if not impossible for Kant. He contends that 'intelligence' is incapable of recognising a secret as such with absolute certainty. The friend can be let down by a misrecognised secret, a betrayed secret. To express this difficulty inherent to secrecy and restricted number in friendship, Kant borrows, without acknowledgement, the metaphor of the 'black swan' from Juvenal. The Kantian friend has his eyes (it's always a he) on the empty horizon awaiting the appearance of the black swan. What Kant does not know, however, is that (Derrida notes) Juvenal meant a woman by this black swan. Woman is once more related to irony in so far as she interrupts and disturbs the homeo-erotic quietude of Kantian friendship where Kant thought that he was writing about the society of brothers.

Political friendship is exclusive in so far as it is not possible to enter in the community of brothers/ friends, to be a constitutive member of the 'schematic of filiation', if one is 'other rather than the same' as the friend. Heterogeneous to the homo-fraternal schema of friendship, and its one-to-one relation, the figure of woman 'reopens the question of multiplicity, the question of the one and that of "the more than one," (of the one qua woman and the "more than one" of the feminine one and the "more than one" feminine one as well ... etc.)'[70] In conversation with Kantian practical reason, Derrida writes:

> is it possible, without setting off loud protests on the part of militants of an edifying or dogmatic humanism, to think and to live the gentle rigor of friendship, the law of friendship qua the experience of a certain

a-humanity, in absolute separation, beyond or below the commerce of gods and men? And what politics could still be founded on this friendship which exceeds the measure of man, without becoming a theologem? Would it still be a politics?[71]

By conjugating the unresolved question of number with that of woman and presenting them as the two essential limits of the totality of the history of friendship, Derrida proposes a different 'model' of friendship. This *arché-friendship* that, like Michelet's conception of woman, is 'prior to all organised *socius*, all *politeia*, all determined 'government', before all 'law', and ethical (pre)determinations. In *Politics of Friendship*, this arché-friendship is characterised by a 'non-negative neutrality', but in conversation with Jean-Luc Nancy, Derrida goes further and speaks of an 'affirmation', in reference to James Joyce's *Ulysses* and the words 'yes, yes' that end (without ending) the novel (words that are spoken by Molly Bloom as she 'comes' in masturbation), that even the 'most primordial question implies ... that "yes, yes" that answers before even being able to formulate a question, that is responsible without autonomy, before and in view of all possible autonomy of the who-subject.'[72] The black swan has appeared on the horizon, it is coming but it is not with us/with itself yet. At the doorway to this 'arché-friendship', then, stands, or lies - it is not certain, she is 'coming' - the representation of a woman, but more than one, more than two women, who cry 'yes, yes' (even when answering 'no'). In spite of its apparent structural 'non-negative neutrality', there is something strangely familiar about this arché-friendship prior to all friendships. It seems there always must be, or always will have been, at the masthead of the Democracy-to-Come that presides over the present even as it is always already disappearing backwards over the horizon into the future, is a woman who can't say no. I am aware that I am forcing this concept a little, misreading it, looking too closely at its somewhat colourful textual genealogy, but that is because there is, *perhaps*, a danger (and no doubt more than one) in this 'arché-friendship' that, like anything else, can be so easily misread.

Because it is not at all clear how one, or more than one, (and who or what institutional body) could seek, require or enforce, in 'relation to the "yes" or to the *Zusage* [acquiescing to language, to the mark] presupposed in every question ... a new (post-deconstructive) determination of the responsibility of the "subject".'[73] What are the implications of this 'responsibility of the "subject"' for some new, self-styled 'post-deconstructive' regime where that responsibility is located in the presupposition of a 'preliminary consent' to its language, its politics, its economy, its legislation, its ethics, purely through being marked by it in some way. To use a crude example, in the absence of any other economy, does every publication, every action, necessarily presuppose a preliminary consent to capitalism? What kind of 'consent' is it that has no choice in the matter, that consents even when it wants to say 'no', what kind of 'consent' can be presupposed even before the 'who-subject' is 'able to formulate a question'? What does 'consent' mean in this context? Where is *différance* if 'affirmation' is necessarily prior to every negative? Does *différance* disappear in the new 'post-deconstructive' democracy-to-come, the democracy to which it is impossible to say no? For it is precisely to the degree that the 'non-negative' is taken as affirmation that precludes the possibility of an absolute 'no', an affirmation that insists on the 'yes' prior to every 'no'. Otherwise, this infinite (in)/divisibility, this feminine 'economy without reserve,' that applies to the friend would also apply to the enemy, for as Derrida explains there is an endless perversion of one figure into its other due to the intricate logic of selectivity in friendship. The 'more-than-one' friend can become as unmanageable as the 'more-than-one' enemy feared by Schmitt, in both cases the monitoring and application of the egalitarian law is challenged and rendered almost impossible.

There is, however, yet another limit to the universalising, European law that Schmitt stresses, and that Derrida notes though without elaborating on it. There is another challenge to the whole conception of Western politics and its economy, a challenge that has seemingly become more urgent after the apparent collapse of the 'friendly enemy' that was the Soviet Union and the spectre of international communism. This universalising law, a universalism predicated historically on European Christianity, demanded and continues to demand that 'Islam would remain an enemy even though we Europeans must love the Muslims as our neighbours.' Following Schmitt's logic through, Derrida continues, 'defending Europe against Islam, here considered as a non-European invader of Europe, is then more than a war among other wars, more than a political war. Indeed, this would be not a war but a combat with the political at stake, a struggle for politics. And this holds even if it is not necessarily a struggle for democracy.'[74] Islam, then, like 'women' but in apparently a very different way, threatens the European conception of the political even as they (we) hold out, perhaps, the promise of a democracy-to-come. There are (at least) two problems, though, two problems that are mostly left implicit because Derrida does not elaborate (in fact the whole 'case' of Islam is placed in parentheses). The first concerns his scepticism that Islam is indeed free of, or heterogeneous to, the European conception of the political. Schmitt's fear holds only in so far as Islam is genuinely 'a being radically alien to the political as such, supposing at least that, in its purported purity, it is not Europeanised and shares nothing of the tradition of the juridical and the political called European.'[75] And we might add, supposing that Europe, in its purported supremacy and in its political, cultural and economic imperialism, is not Islamicised and shares nothing of the culture, science, technology, juridical and political traditions of Islam. The second, noted two hundred pages later in another parenthesis, concerns the urgency with which should be investigated 'the figure of the brother in Arabo-Islamic culture ... the "Muslim brothers".'[76] Unfortunately, Derrida does not give way to this urgency, and 'shirks' the responsibility 'without avowable justification.' (And perhaps we could add here, in parenthesis, while shirking the responsibility of taking it seriously, the example of Islamic women. Heterogeneous both to the European society of friends and the Muslim brothers, the place(s) marked out by and for Islamic women, in both an interior and exterior relation to these homo-fraternal schemas, perhaps provides a less overheated place from which to contest them than the example of the exciting imaginings of European male writers and the affirmations placed in the mouths of their female characters - as enjoyable as they are, without doubt).

Nevertheless, the spectre of the 'Muslim brothers', the spectre of the millennial threat that Europe might be 'delivered over' to Islam, a spectre that haunts the extimate figure of the 'noisy Islamic neighbour',[77] haunts the fraternal limits and hospitality of Western liberal democracies, and provides the shifting threshold of its self-loving enmity. In the romance that is not One that characterises the post-political order feared by Schmitt, but which for Derrida contains the promise of the democracy-to-come, the impetus remains murderous (if not fratricidal) as the Cold War maps are re-drawn. In the face of this post-Cold War 'deconstructive' peace that seems to consist in wars waged by Christians against or on behalf of Muslims,[78] a 'peace' that still consists in a variety of stand offs between what used to be the Occident and the Orient, it seems to me imperative that someone elaborates a more effective, radical means of non-consent (that is not necessarily resistance as understood by Derrida),[79] rather than the contrary. To do that, it seems to me, necessitates 'deconstructing', if that is possible, the conditions whereby a 'preliminary consent' is always presupposed to the (m)arché-friendship in which the global capitalist corporations determine the Other with the promise of the market friendliness and user friendliness of 'Western' products and technology. This also means that one will have to think with both Kant and Derrida against the unconditional of the *a priori* condition or that *as if* that always lays down the law (of hospitality), as Derrida says.

The experience of hospitality and forgiveness: the Kantian unconditional

Hospitality is 'cultural' rather than just ethical. 'It has to do with the *ethos*, that is, the residence, one's home, the familiar place of dwelling.'[80] The cultural is one of the structural elements of *aporia*. It is related to one type of the border limit which is closely connected to a number of 'conceptual' and 'discursive' implications.[81] The cultural presupposes the static structure but also requires an infinite experience. This is why when Derrida relates ethics to the experience of hospitality, he redefines the Kantian ethical (non-)experience in terms of an imperative opening onto the other as such. This *ethos*, or experience of being at home with self/other, redefines the scope and relevance of duty and responsibility. The aporetic unconditional turns its back to dialectics which would have legitimated 'the violence, the occupation of a non-conceptual field by the grid of a conceptual force.'[82] The dialectical confrontation is now replaced by a field of infinite substitutions, a field defined through 'analogies' already implied in the 'as' of the *as if*.

The event of decision and responsibility when involved in a field of infinite analogies presupposes an open experience now liberated from the spectacles of the concepts, the limits of the moral law and the boring contemplations of the subject of aesthetics. 'A responsible decision must obey an "it is necessary" that owes nothing, it must obey *a duty that owes nothing*, [...] a duty without debt and therefore without duty.'[83] The moral responsible decision is no longer a blind and 'technical application of a concept.' Preliminary consent, for instance, even though introduced as an *a priori* condition, is not conceptual in so far as it is not knowledge. This is consent that does not know why it says 'yes' and to what or whom it says 'yes'. It is also possible to say that this preliminary consent may never agree to consent, it may never take place. The one who replies to this *a priori* non-knowing unconditional condition 'will answer for it as if for a responsible decision.'[84] Promises, or decisions (or decisions formulated like promises, yet-to-come) must run the risk, must prove themselves in the very 'experience of the aporia,' words, that Derrida says, are 'coupled in an aporetic fashion.'[85] *Aporia* is related to passage and non-passage at the same time.

One is bound to and by duty, subject to duty because it is possible to know what ought to take place. However, if one does not know (feigned or genuine non-knowing mediated by the *as if*) there is no compelling urgency to act in the first place. Derrida thinks that it is imperative to put aside the certainties of the Kantian system of knowledge where 'each moment risks reassuring itself in order to reassure the other and to promote the consensus of a new dogmatic slumber.'[86] In this context, the laws of hospitality, formulated in Derrida's conversation with Kant's *Perpetual Peace* and *On a Supposed Philanthropic Justification for Lying* reflect a different understanding of duty, responsibility and respect, in other words a different perception of the whole Kantian ethical project that is now devoid of will and conditional laws.

If, as Kant contends, one is entitled only to the 'right of visitation' and not the 'right of residence' in the experience of hospitality, it is impossible to talk about transgression. However, outside the 'pacifying reason of Kant,' the subject is always a haunted/haunting subject, a perpetually disturbed subject who remains a stranger to peace. The foreigner is always looming at the host's door, he/she is the one who puts forward 'the unbearable question,'[87] and as such turns reason into a stranger like Klossowski's Victor in the presence of his wife Roberte. Pierre Klossowski's trilogy,[88] entitled the *Laws of Hospitality*, is an essential text to understand Derrida's experience of hospitality in his conversation with the Kantian practical reason. In Klossowski's trilogy, every man who visits Octave's house has the absolute right to court his wife Roberte. These *accidental* encounters with the guest are staged by Octave for the voyeuristic gaze of her nephew Antoine. Octave wants to see whether Roberte is going to be the same with different men when she is taken by surprise in the presence of an unexpected guest. The accidental relationship becomes an essential one when Octave, initially the host, becomes a guest in his own house. He is the guest of the visitor who is going to reveal the inactual essence of Roberte to Octave and to Roberte herself. Octave thinks that his wife Roberte has some substance, or a hidden content that can be revealed to him when he observes the way she acts in the presence of strangers. There is something in the hostess which is more than her. Something that does not belong to her even though it is with her, something that is decomposed under the gaze of the host who becomes a guest in his own house. This sort of experience seems to be based on the voyeuristic gaze, the in/sight that is coupled with absolute blindness and that is essential in every experience. This is the *droit de regards*, right of inspection, that Derrida negotiates. I have already evoked this gaze (that brings together blindness and insight) in the metaphor of the keyhole of the critical door. But experience, according to Derrida, is probably best apprehended in blindness, when it is totally non-conceptual, non-phenomenal, unable to reveal, to concede to surrender meaning or knowledge. The gaze would 'inspect' but remains unable to come out with a story, or a plot. Here again experience requires and recommends the 'protocol of silence', the law of secrecy.

In the sphere of action, or practical reason, the Kantian subject is the host/hostess of the moral law. To act according to duty places the foreigner in a condition that does not speak the same language of duty, 'the foreigner is first of all foreign to the legal language in which the duty of hospitality is formulated, the right to asylum, its limits, norms, policing.'[89] This hospitality, the descent of the moral law in the hosting practical reason of the subject is not based on a contract or pact or law and justice as right. For what he calls 'absolute hospitality, requires that I open up my home and that I give not only to the foreigner ... but to the absolute, unknown, anonymous other, and that I give place to them, that I let them come, and that I let them arrive, and take place in a place I offer them, without asking of them either reciprocity ... or even their names.'[90] Such disorder would be totally inadmissible in the Kantian architectonic in so far as the system never grows by 'external addition'.

For Kant, the absolute duty of veracity would come before Derrida's absolute duty of hospitality, this is why it is perfectly imperative for Kant not to lie to assassins who came to look for a friend staying in your house. You cannot lie even to assassins because if you do to save your friend you infringe the law of veracity. The Kantian hospitality is based on the law, like any other social relationship: '*as if* always lays down the law.'[91] Derrida wants to go a step beyond the Kantian idea of duty and follows, after Alexandre Kojève, the lead of the 'as if' to find the point of transition, passage, *aporia* in the Kantian system (the point which allows the whole philosophy of Kant to progress from pure reason to practical reason to the sphere of aesthetic judgment) but at the same time this constitutes in itself the point at which the 'apparatus of critical distinctions' trembles from within. The *as if* recalls in a sense the condition of unconditionality in the law. This is the antinomy endemic to the Law: laws are conditional but at the same time they are based on the unconditionality of the Law. Derrida wants to dig the conditional surface of the law to reach for its bases, to transgress the transcendental to the sphere of the transcendent, go back to the condition of the 'perhaps' rather than the imperative of 'you must'. He can then deconstruct the imperative of veracity in the name of the imperative of absolute hospitality in 'the name of the unconditional, even if this pure unconditionality appears inaccessible, and inaccessible not only as a regulatory idea, an Idea in the Kantian sense of infinitely removed, always inadequately approached.'[92] Derrida's aim is to prove the incompatibility of conceptual economic, political, ethical or aesthetic conditions with the requirements of an infinite or open experience. In Appendix I to *Perpetual Peace*, Kant discusses the opposition between morality and politics. 'Politics says, "Be ye wise as serpents;" morality adds, as a limiting condition, "and guileless as doves." [...] If these two qualities ought always to be united, the thought of contrariety is absurd, and the question as to how the conflict between morals and politics is to be resolved cannot even be posed as a problem.' The experience of forgiveness interrupts this complicity between morality and politics. 'Forgiveness is mad, it must remain a madness of the impossible,'[93] and as such it 'arrives, it surprises the ordinary course of history, politics and law.' Scenes of forgiveness should not be staged or summoned or presided over by the 'conditional' sovereignty of the political or the juridical law. Forgiveness does not aim at reconciliation in a Hegelian sense because it does not involve a third term. On the contrary, it is strictly limited to the guilty and the victim at the exclusion of any tertiary institution. Derrida proposes the following *aporia* that 'forgiveness forgives the unforgivable.'[94] Forgiveness is conceivable where there is absolute unforgiveness, the impossibility to forgive. The impossible introduces an element of 'transcendence', an empty concept without knowledge and without intuition, a pure contemplative and beautiful forgiveness. 'Pure and unconditional forgiveness, in order to have its own meaning, must have no "meaning", no finality, even no intelligibility. It is a madness of the impossible.'[95] The unconditional law of forgiveness is no longer dependent on the Kantian 'hypothetical imperatives', the conditional, the limited, but it is placed in the sphere of general economy. Here we can talk about Derrida's 'aporia' or 'paradox', one of its forms being the impossible communication between the guilty and the victim who literally do not speak the same language. Here is again another silent experience, one that takes place in the violent (or is it pacifying?) absence of discourse, a metaphysical experience that takes place in the dark. 'It is necessary in effect that alterity, non-identification, even incomprehension, remain irreducible. Forgiveness is thus mad. It must plunge, but lucidly, into the night of the unintelligible.'[96] If communication is established between the victim and the guilty person, then reconciliation takes place, and this is something that has nothing to do with 'pure forgiveness', a sort of '*a priori*' forgiveness. In the mad logic of Derridean *aporia* (impossible) forgiveness 'comes' with 'radical evil'. The aim is to establish 'another peace', one 'without forgetting, without amnesty, fusion, or confusion.'[97] What Derrida wants to repudiate is the conditional that comes with the restricted economy of reciprocity and exchange, the reply that comes back to the subject from the site of the other as in the opposition between punishment and forgiveness: nothing should reply to the demand of forgiveness, neither a 'you're forgiven' nor an 'I'll forgive but never forget.' It is also not clear whether the demand of forgiveness takes place at all (even though the guilty party is face to face with the victim). In this (missed) encounter that requires the quasi (non-)categories of the time and space of *différance* there might be no direct or implicit demand of forgiveness. Just like 'an-economical' and 'a-political', arché-friendship, Derrida proposes again another model of an aneconomical and unconditional forgiveness: 'beyond the exchange and even the horizon of a redemption or a reconciliation.'[98] There is, in that sense, a play between the conditional and the unconditional, an over-duty or a hyperbolic ethics that is both pre-critical and non-phenomenal. For if in the philosophy of Kant the 'pure' or the *a priori* institutes the absolute conditions of the possibility of experience even before this experience takes place, and regardless of whether or not it does take place, Derrida finds in a certain type of experience an inherent *lack of sense*, something that cannot be thought because the secret of a certain type of experience remains with the subject (understood as an irreducible singularity). Where a victim insists on bringing the guilty party before justice but in their hearts they have already forgiven them, or on the contrary if forgiveness is announced in public but in their heart the victim chooses not to grant forgiveness, in both cases we are talking about an experience that remained totally heterogeneous - 'intact, inaccessible to law, to politics, even to morals: absolute.'[99] Respecting this 'secret' is in fact a 'political' act that exceeds politics altogether, and this is what Derrida proposes to call 'democracy to come.'[100] This is for Derrida something that best answers the Kantian imperative of the 'unconditional necessity.' In the second Appendix to *Perpetual Peace*, Kant rejects secrecy on the basis that whatever is capable of publicity does not contradict itself. The experience of (impossible) forgiveness is built on contradiction and it becomes possible only in so far as it maintains this *ressentiment* as a secret. 'Every legal claim must be capable of publicity. We can call the following proposition the transcendental formula of public law: All actions relating to the right of other men are unjust if their maxim is not consistent with publicity.' Derridean experience, on the other hand, inscribes secrecy as the irreducible signifier of singularity. Where there is a secret (even when there is no secret at all) stories are not told, there is no single narrative that entraps the ethos in the domain of the other.

Derrida's encounters with the three critiques of Kant as well as other major texts (he reads through Husserl and Heidegger) seek to extend and intensify the work or the moment of the 'as if'. This would disturb the otherwise absolute peace of the Kantian system of knowledge that, in many respects, holds no surprises. For Derrida, the 'as if' would be an essential component of 'différance'. The 'as if' is no longer a pacifying device, but a point of difference analogous to Derrida's 'undecidables' or non-concepts such as 'supplement' or '*pharmakon*' that inhabit a system not as its foundation but as a necessary addition, an indispensable 'foreign body', that endlessly defers the completion of a rational discourse, a project, and necessitates a perpetual 'philosophy of the future', a philosophy that is yet to come. This position, which goes against the very essentials of Kant's metaphysics, is no longer concerned with laying foundations (*Grundlegung*) but with dissemination and expansion (*Erweiterung*).

Notes:

1 'What can I know? What ought I to do? What may I hope?' are questions asked at the end of the *Critique of Pure Reason*, trans. Mieiklejohn.(London: Everyman, 1991), p.518.

2 The essential question of 'transition' is discussed for example in Roger Daval, *La métaphysique de Kant: perspectives sur la métaphysique de Kant d'aprés la théorie du schématisme* (Paris: Presses Universitaires de France, 1951). According to Daval, Kant tried, at the end of his life, to reformulate his 'theory of possible experience' in terms of a 'real' metaphysics. He had always been unsatisfied with the *'possibilities* of *possible* experience,' (p.271) that define an overlap between 'transcendental philosophy' (which defines forms and the systematic link between them in experience) and 'metaphysics' (which departs from experience to discover its primary conditions). Metaphysics thus always exceeds experience towards a total experience that brings together the world, God and the Human being. Daval explains that 'the transcendental philosopher is happier than the metaphysician.' (p.271)

3 Kant mentions the myth of Tantalus in a letter he sent to Garve dated 1798, where he talks about a 'pain like that of Tantalus,' which he experienced when he was trying to find a way to move from 'the metaphysical foundations of natural science to physics.' See Immanuel Kant, *Philosophical Correspondence: 1759-1799.* Trans. Arnulf Zweig. (Chicago: The University of Chicago Press, 1967), p.251. In hell, Tantalus is threatened by a huge stone balanced over his head and that constantly threatens to fall and crush him.

4 Jacques Derrida, *Writing and Difference*, trans. Alan Bass (London and New York: Routledge, 1997) p.158.

5 Jacques Derrida, *Aporias*, trans. Thomas Dutoit (Stanford: Stanford University Press, 1993), p.1.

6 Jacques Derrida, *Writing and Difference*, p.167.

7 Ibid. p.162.

8 Jacques Derrida, *Points... Interviews, 1974-1994*, edited by Elisabeth Weber (Stanford: Stanford University Press, 1995), p.286.

9 This is, I think, a parody of the excessively regulated and undisturbed promenades of Kant in the streets of his native hometown according to which one can set their watch. This is a well celebrated anecdote about the life of Kant.

10 See Jacques Derrida, *Right of Inspection*, Trans. David Willis.(New York: The Monacelli Press, 1998)

11 Immanuel Kant, *Critique of Pure Reason*, p.205.

12 Immanuel Kant, *Critique of Practical Reason*, trans. Lewis White Beck (Indianapolis: Bobbs-Merril, 1956) p.6.

13 Ibid. fn 3.

14 Ibid. p.31. (*my emphasis*)

15 The objects of experience are according to Kant appearances and not things in themselves (as Hume thought), see *Critique of Practical Reason*, pp.54-55.

16 Ibid. p.44.

17 Alexandre Kojève (1902-1968) is a key figure not only in French philosophy but in the whole field of what is called post-modern thought. He is particularly famous for

his 1933-1939 lectures on Hegel's *Phenomenology of Spirit*, interpreted following the master-slave dialectic and reaching the conclusion that Hegel's system of knowledge achieved in the Absolute Spirit the end of the totality of the Western discourse on philosophy. This came to be known as the end of history thesis. Kojève's lectures were attended by prominent French thinkers, namely: Sartre, Merleau-Ponty, Eric Weil, Raymond Aron, Bataille, Blanchot and Lacan. The importance of the *as if* in the whole philosophy of Kant was already examined by German philosopher Hans Vaihinger (1852-1933) in his seminal work *Die Philosophie des Als Ob* (1911), translated as *The Philosophy of the As If* by C.K. Ogden (New York: Harcourt, Brace, 1925). It is quite possible that the fictionalism of Vaihinger exerted a major influence on Kojève's reading of Kant. After finishing his *Introduction to the Reading of Hegel*, trans. James H. Nichols. (Ithaca and London: Cornell University Press, 1980) Kojève thought that there was nothing left for the modern philosopher except repeating what has already been done and said by Hegel's philosophy. For that matter he wrote his *Essai d'une histoire raisonnée de la philosophie païenne* in three volumes (published by Gallimard in 1968, 1972 and 1973). In these volumes, Kojève wanted to show how Western philosophy from Plato to Kant was wrestling with the relationship between Time and the Concept. All previous attempts failed to equate Time with the Concept. This has only been realised and perfected in the philosophical system of Hegel. When Kojève wanted to publish his volume on *Kant*, he lost the manuscript that was published posthumously just like Volumes II and III of the *Essai*. Kojève's reading of Kant is based on the theses of Hans Vaihinger even though Kojève never makes any direct reference to him. I still believe that Derrida's Kant, like his Hegel, is to be sought in the work of Alexandre Kojève; hence the direct link that I'm making between Kojève's reading of Kant and the centrality of the *as if* in Derrida's Kant.

18 According to Kojève the whole history of philosophy is divided into two major periods: philosophical discourse from Plato to Kant, and the philosophical discourse that begins with Hegel. It is Kant who came the closest to the major tenet of Hegelian philosophy, namely, that 'Time is the Concept'. That equation defines the dialectical method as the only way to reach knowledge as 'self-consciousness' and as such nothing outside human consciousness provides a 'given objective reality'. The Hegelian discourse is the discourse that speaks about itself while it speaks about everything else in the world. The Kantian discourse on the other hand is a discourse that speaks about everything in the world without contradicting itself. It does not thus reduce the world to self-consciousness. Kojève explains that 'Kant was the first to see [...] that time is what makes the actual exercise of thought possible. In other words, we can use our eternal concepts only provided that we relate them to time as such - that is provided that we "schematise" them.' (*Introduction to the Reading of Hegel*, p.127)

19 Immanuel Kant, *Critique of Pure Reason*, p.202.

20 Ibid. p.215.

21 The conclusion of the *Critique of Practical Reason* is quite disturbing (see p.166). The subject of practical reason is placed between 'the starry heavens above' itself and the 'moral law within' itself. In the infinite extension of the cosmos, the Kantian subject of the moral law is annihilated. But in the infinite extension of the 'invisible self' the subject's value and worth is re-established in its direct communication with the whole cosmos. But in this position, the subject of the moral law is constantly interpellated by that which never replies to its desire. We already know, at least since

Althusser and Lacan, that interpellation is based on the absolute silence of the other, the other that never replies to anything. So it is the subject of the moral law itself that interpellates itself on behalf of the other, or in place of the other. In the third *Critique*, the beautiful object exists regardless of the subject of the aesthetic experience. The non/existence of the beautiful does not concern the subject's existence. The aesthetic experience is based on a totally detached and pure contemplation of the beautiful. This is again an essentially silent experience.

22 Alexandre Kojève, *Kant* (Paris: Gallimard, 1973), p.16. *My translation.*
23 Immanuel Kant, *Critique of Pure Reason,* p.213.
24 Immanuel Kant, *Critique of Judgment,* trans. Werner S. Pluhar (Indianapolis and Cambridge: Hackett, 1987), p.162.
25 Ibid. p. 167.
26 Jacques Derrida, *The Truth in Painting,* trans. Geoffrey Bennington and Ian McLeod (University of Chicago Press, 1987), p.43.
27 Ibid. p.46.
28 Ibid. p.55.
29 See in particular Jacques Derrida, 'Economimesis' in *Diacritics 11*, (1981) pp.3-25
and '*Parergon,*' in *The Truth in Painting*.
30 Jacques Derrida, 'Economimesis', p.4.
31 Ibid. p.5.
32 Ibid. p.6.
33 See Kant's *Critique of Judgment*, pp.201-207.
34 Jacques Derrida, 'Economimesis', p.7.
35 Ibid.
36 Ibid. p.6.
37 Ibid. p.9.
38 Ibid. p.10.
39 Ibid. p.14
40 Jacques Derrida, *The Truth in Painting,* p.41
41 Jacques Derrida, 'Economimesis', p.17.
42 Ibid. p.21.
43 Ibid. p.22.
44 Ibid.
45 See *The Truth in Painting,* p.39.
46 See Eric Weil, *Logique de la philosophie* (Paris: Vrin, 1950). Weil thinks the whole history of Western philosophy in terms of alternation between the 'coherent discourse' and the moment of violence. The coherent discourse is a unique discourse of moral perfection. The 'logic of philosophy' operates in the context of contradiction that identifies meaning (or the philosophical discourse) only from the point of view of non-meaning (that is violence or the violence of the ineffable). Unlike Kant, Weil thought that the choice of the coherent discourse, that understands and posits itself as non-contradiction, is not absolute. Following Hegel's basic understanding that reason involves itself in a conflict with the world, Weil notes that, since it is part of the world, reason is also and essentially in conflict with itself. It is possible that reason may reach a point where it understands its own irrationality, hence it becomes possible to accommodate violence within the field of philosophical thought rather than attempt to

evacuate all manifestations of violence from the philosophical discourse altogether. The 'other' of reason is not the world but rather reason's refusal of the world, its retreat into non-being. Kant neutralises the violence of reason in the alliance between intuition and concepts. The diversity of the thought object (in concepts) and the given object (in intuition) ultimately comes under the unifying principle of the Idea. By limiting the function of reason to ordering and arranging concepts rather than creating their form, Kant proves that his architectonic system of knowledge does not entirely rely on one particular faculty whose faltering or retreat would cause the total collapse of the whole system: 'the unity of the end, to which all the parts of the system relate, and through which all have a relation to each other communicates unity to the whole system, so that the absence of any part can be immediately detected from our knowledge of the rest; and it determines *a priori* the limits of the system, thus excluding all contingent or arbitrary additions.' (*Critique of Pure Reason,* p.532)

47 Immanuel Kant, *Critique of Pure Reason,* p.544.
48 Jacques Derrida, *Politics of Friendship,* trans. George Collins (London and New York: Verso, 1997) p.273.
49 Jacques Derrida, *Aporias,* p.17.
50 Ibid. p.16.
51 Ibid. p.8
52 Immanuel Kant, *Critique of Pure Reason,* p.208.
53 Immanuel Kant, *Critique of Practical Reason,* p.19.
54 Ibid. p.86.
55 Jacques Derrida, *Politics of Friendship,* p.68.
56 Ibid.
57 Immanuel Kant, *Critique of Pure Reason,* p.519
58 Ibid. p.520.
59 Jacques Derrida, *Aporias,* p.15.
60 Immanuel Kant, *Critique of Pure Reason*, p.423
61 Jacques Derrida, *Writing and Difference*, p.95.
62 Gilles Deleuze, *Difference and Repetition*, trans. Paul Patton. (London: The Athlone Press, 1994.), p.86.
63 Jacques Derrida, *Writing and Difference*, p.275.
64 Ibid. p.162.
65 Jacques Derrida, *Politics of Friendship*, p.32.
66 Ibid. p.83.
67 Ibid. p.236. (my emphasis)
68 Ibid. p.21.
69 Ibid. p.239.
70 Ibid. p.209.
71 Ibid. p.294.
72 Jacques Derrida, *Points ... Interviews, 1974- 1994*, p.261.
73 Ibid. p.268.
74 Jacques Derrida, *Politics of Friendship,* p.89.
75 Ibid.
76 Ibid. p.289.
77 See Jacques-Alain Miller, 'Etimité', *Prose Studies 11* (1988), pp.125-6 on the *jouissance* that grounds the Other's alterity: 'we may well think that racism exists

because our Islamic neighbour is too noisy when he has parties ... [but] racist stories are always about the way the Other obtains a "plus-de-jouir".'

78 The event of the so called gulf War, for example, is a powerful, spectacular, and tragic condensation of these 'deconstructions' (i.e. deconstructions of various social, historical, economic, technical and military texts). See Derrida in *Points,* p.356.

79 Jacques Derrida, *Resistances of Psychoanalysis,* trans. Peggy Kamuf, Pascale-Anne Brault and Michael Naas (Stanford: Stanford University Press, 1998)

80 Jacques Derrida, *On Cosmopolitanism and Forgiveness,* trans. Mark Dooley and Michael Hughes (London and New York: Routledge, 2001), p.16.

81 In *Aporias,* Derrida talks about three types of aporetic border limits: 1) *aporias* that separate 'territories, countries, nations, states, languages and cultures,' also called 'anthropological cultural borders;' 2) *aporias* that separate between 'domains of discourse' also called 'problematic closure;' and 3) borders between concepts, also called 'conceptual demarcations'. (p.23).

82 Jacques Derrida, *Points ... Interviews, 1974-1994,* p.76.

83 Jacques Derrida, *Aporias,* p.16.

84 Ibid. p.17.

85 Ibid. p.19.

86 Jacques Derrida, *On the Name,* trans. David Wood, John Pierre Leavey and Ian McLeod (Stanford: Stanford university Press, 1995), p.15.

87 Jacques Derrida, *Of Hospitality,* trans. Rachel Bowlby (Stanford: Stanford University Press, 2000), p.5.

88 Pierre Klossowski, *Roberte ce Soir and the Revocation of the Edict of Nantes,* trans. Austin Wainhouse (London: Boyars, 1989). *Le Souffleur,* third book in the trilogy, has not yet been translated into English.

89 Jacques Derrida, *Of Hospitality,* p.15.

90 Ibid. p.25.

91 Ibid. p.123.

92 Ibid. p.149.

93 Jacques Derrida, *On Cosmopolitanism and Forgiveness,* p.39.

94 Ibid. p.32.

95 Ibid. p.45.

96 Ibid. p.49.

97 Ibid. p.50

98 Ibid. p.38

99 Ibid. p.55.

100 Ibid.

3
The End is Here

Geoffrey Bennington

Kant explains that the determinative judgment cannot present an antinomy, because it is not autonomous, gives no law.[1] But when we come to the reflective judgment, where the law is not given, but where the judgment seeks the law, judgment must follow *maxims* in order to guide itself, and these maxims can enter into conflict with each other, giving rise to the possibility of an antinomy, and thereby a dialectic, calling for a critique. Exploring empirical nature beyond what is determinatively legislated by the categories of the understanding, we are led to invoke the maxim according to which every natural product must be possible according to *mechanical* causality. But sometimes, also, especially when faced with organisms, the maxim according to which that part of nature (but perhaps too nature in general, taken by analogy with the organisms it contains) can be explained only according to final causality, causality by purposes or ends. Kant's presentation can give the impression that this antinomy is straightforwardly resolved (by the end of §71, and even in §70, i.e. as soon as it is presented, so that the antinomy would simply disappear immediately it is brought to light) by insisting on the fact that we are dealing here merely with *maxims*, i.e. regulative principles for our investigation and not constitutive principles of the objects of that investigation. There would be an obvious contradiction involved in maintaining that an object was *objectively* caused by both natural mechanism *and* final causality (a technics of nature), but not in appealing, as a principle for *judging* nature (without claiming dogmatically that this gave rise to objective knowledge) on the one hand to the maxim of mechanical causality (I should judge according to this maxim *as far as possible*, for only this maxim sets me on the road to *knowledge*, even if this knowledge is not determinative), and, on the other, to the maxim of final causality (when the first maxim no longer serves, I must judge some natural objects, especially organisms, and even nature as a whole, according to a quite different causality, i.e. in terms of ends).

Kant's argument here is extremely delicate. If we were to maintain these two principles dogmatically (making them determinative), we should indeed have an antinomy, in that these two principles are in contradiction with each other. But, says Kant, this antinomy would not be an antinomy *of judgment*, because in making these principles determinative of objects, we would have provoked a contradiction in the very legislation of reason with respect to nature, and this contradiction would allow for no resolution, for the legislation of human reason cannot *determine* objects of nature in so far as they are empirical. We do certainly prescribe laws to nature, following transcendental logic, but these laws cannot exhaustively determine nature as a field of empirical investigation in which objects as *singular cases* remain in part contingent with respect to the legislation of reason.

So it cannot suffice to insist that we are dealing with *maxims*, regulative principles for a reflexive judgment about empirical nature, in order to *resolve* the antinomy, because it is precisely on the level of the maxims that there is an antinomy of *judgment* (rather than of rational legislation itself). And yet Kant, at the end of a paragraph which presents itself as a simple preliminary or preparation for the solution of the antinomy (§71: ' *Vorbereitung zur Auflösung obiger Antinomie*'), says this:

> Hence all semblance [*aller Anschein*] of an antinomy between the maxims of strictly physical (mechanical) and teleological (technical) explanation rests on our confusing a principle of reflective judgment with one of determinative judgment, and on our confusing the autonomy of reflective judgment (which holds merely subjectively for our use of reason regarding the particular empirical laws) with the heteronomy of determinative judgment, which must conform to the laws (universal or particular) that are given by our understanding.[2]

But Kant has already explained that an antinomy of judgment can arise only to the extent that the maxims of judgment *are just* maxims of judgment (and not determinative principles of objects). The antinomy of judgment results, precisely, not from any confusion of autonomy and heteronomy, but *insofar as judgment is autonomous*. So it cannot be resolved simply by recalling that autonomy. The appearance of a legislative antinomy (an insurmountable contradiction) is dissipated by recalling the maxim-status of both mechanical and purposive principles: it remains to resolve the properly *judgmental* antinomy that results from this, and this is merely prepared by removing any appearance of legislative antinomy.

But then, where exactly is the antinomy that remains to be solved? From the first presentation of the antinomy in §70, Kant appears to suggest that the coexistence of the two maxims (mechanical and final) is fundamentally peaceful. This peace of judgment about nature does not result from equality of the two maxims, however, but rather the subordination of one of them to the other, in the name of knowledge:

> If I say that I must judge [*beurteilen*] all events in material nature, and hence also all the forms that are its products, in terms of merely mechanical laws as to [how] they are possible, then I am not saying that they *are possible* in terms of mechanical laws *alone* (i.e. even if no other kind of causality comes in). Rather, I am only pointing out that I *ought* [*ich soll*] always to *reflect* on these events and forms *in terms of the principle* of the mere mechanism of nature, and hence ought to investigate this principle as far as I can, because unless we presuppose it in our investigation [of nature] we can have no cognition of nature at all in the proper sense of the term [*keine eigentliche Naturkenntnis*]. But none of this goes against the second maxim - that on certain occasions, in dealing with certain natural forms (and, on their prompting, even with all of nature), we should probe these and reflect on them in terms of a principle that differs entirely from an explanation in terms of the mechanism of nature: the principle of final causes. (§70)

It is not, then, a matter of putting the two maxims together and then choosing one or the other arbitrarily; in the perspective of knowledge, the principle of mechanical causality (in harmony with everything in the understanding that is properly legislative with respect to nature) comes first, and one remains with it as long as is possible, passing to the other maxim only when the mechanical explanation falls short (faced, for example, with organisms). And yet (and this is where the antinomy will find its place), the punctual occasions on which one appeals to the purposive principle of judgment also serve as a pretext or motif for judging, similarly, nature as a whole (so that nature would be *fundamentally* purposive, final), which cannot fail to bring about a conflict between the two maxims which henceforth try to apply to the same objects at the same time. This antinomy results from the abandonment of any *dogmatic* appeal to knowledge, leaving open a free competition between the two maxims of judgment.

We do not know, therefore, if mechanical causality is sufficient to account for everything that is in nature, and we do not know this to the extent that natural particularities and their particular laws are, for us, empirical, and therefore, at least in part, contingent. So we know that we cannot *wholly* know nature according to mechanical causality, in spite of the infinite field opened to judgment according to this principle, in the scientific investigation of nature. We know that, *for us*, mechanical causality does not account for everything - for example, organisms.³ We could simply leave things at that (and there would be no antinomy); if our investigation of nature is directed towards the discovery of scientific knowledge, we follow the mechanical maxim as far as possible, and the purposive maxim for 'organised' entities, without further elaborating the 'speculative' question of knowing whether (without yet making it into a determinative principle) this last maxim does not signal towards an inclusive comprehension of nature as such, which would reverse the hierarchical order of the maxims to the profit of the mechanical one. The maxim tells us to judge, on occasion, *as if* nature involved a final causality, and, for the purposes of investigating nature, we can, and we even must, limit ourselves to this subjective status of the maxim without doing any more: but we *can* also wonder whether nature's invitation to judge it according to a purposive maxim, while rendering any *theoretical knowledge* impossible, does not lead us to go further:

> Now we could leave this speculative question or problem quite undecided and unsolved. For if we [remain] within the bounds of mere cognition of nature, the above maxims are sufficient for us to study nature to the extent of our human powers, and to probe its most hidden secrets. So [if in fact we try to do more than this,] it must be that reason has a certain suspicion, or that nature gives us a hint [*Wink*], as it were, that if we use the concept of final causes we could perhaps reach beyond nature and connect nature itself to the highest point in the series of causes. Why not stop our investigation of nature (even though we have not yet advanced far in it), or at least suspend it for a while, and try first to find out where that stranger [*Fremdling*] in natural science, the concept of natural purposes, may lead us? (§72)

Suspending scientific research in this way, in the name of speculative reason, does not lead us to fall back into the dogmatism of taking a subjective maxim to be a determinative principle, but rather makes of it a question, a problem which, as Kant says, opens 'a wide field for controversy' (§72). And these arguments have indeed taken place in the tradition: it has been affirmed either (1) that the technic of nature (its at least apparent operation by purposive causality) is not intentional, and therefore it is not really a purposive causality, 'that this ability is basically quite identical with the mechanism of nature, and that we have falsely interpreted the contingent agreement of that ability with our concepts and rules of art, namely, as a special kind of natural production, whereas in fact it is merely [the result of] a subjective condition under which we judge that ability' (§72); or, (2) that it is intentional, in which case there really is a purposive causality. At the risk of confusing the reader, Kant calls the first of these the system of idealism (in the sense that purposive causality is only an idea), and the second, the system of realism.

Each of these two ways of tackling the problem divides into two. On the side of 'idealism' in this rather specialised sense, we find opposed to Epicurus (and Democritus) on the one hand, and Spinoza, on the other:

> The *idealistic* interpretation of purposiveness (I always mean objective purposiveness here) then interprets the natural determination [that gives rise] to the purposive form of its products either as *causalistic* or as *fatalistic*. The causalistic principle refers matter to the physical basis [responsible] for its form - the laws of motion; the fatalistic principle refers it to the *hyperphysical* basis of matter and of all of nature. The system that espouses the *causalistic* interpretation - it is attributed to Epicurus or Democritus - is so manifestly absurd, if taken literally, that we must not let it detain us. But it is not so easy to refute the system that espouses the fatalistic interpretation. (Its author is said to be Spinoza, even though it is to all appearances much older than that.) This system appeals to something supersensible, which therefore our insight cannot reach. What makes the refutation of this system so difficult is the fact that its concept of the original being is quite unintelligible [*nicht zu verstehen ist*]. (§72)

The 'absurdity' of the Epicurean system (Democritus will not reappear, and the question of eventual differences between them is not raised at all), here apparently dismissed out of hand, is a little later, in a way entirely characteristic of Kant's treatment of Epicurus throughout his work, given a fuller and more complex explanation:

> The systems that defend the idealistic interpretation of final causes in nature are of two types. Some of them, while granting the principle of these final causes a causality in terms of laws of motion (where this causality is responsible for the purposive existence of natural things) deny that it follows intentions: they deny that intentions determine it to produce [things] purposively, i.e. that a purpose is the cause. This is how Epicurus explains [the purposiveness in nature]. He completely denies the distinction of a technic of nature from mere mechanism. Instead he adopts blind chance to explain not only [nature's] technic, i.e. why [nature's] products harmonise with our concepts of a purpose, but even nature's mechanism, i.e. how the causes of this production are determined to this [production] according to

laws of motion. Hence nothing has been explained, not even the illusion in our teleological judgments, so that the alleged idealism in them has by no means been established. (§73)

The rejection of Epicurus is, as always, more complex than it appeared at first sight.[4] What is the basis of the refutation here? Not, as might have been expected, that Epicurus simply denies all purposive causality in the name of mechanism alone (which would suffice to motivate rejection on the grounds of dogmatism), but rather the way he understands mechanical causality itself as being based on *chance*. According to Epicurus, as read by Kant, the only causality is chance, which removes from the start any chance of understanding anything whatsoever. The appearance of purposive causality is thus 'explained' by the reality of a mechanical causality which is not even causal. So Epicurus, brought in to argue that apparent purposive causality in nature is not the result of an intention, says too much for Kant's needs, in that he refuses even the principle of non-intentional mechanical causality, thus making the question of causality in general fall *below* the very opposition between intentionality and non-intentionality, into pure chance, *explaining* nothing, but absurd by the very fact of invoking absurdity (chance) as a principle for explaining anything at all.

This means that chance remains in an excessive and eccentric position with respect to the requirements of Kant's demonstration. In order to fill this slot in his matrix (non-intentional/idealist), Kant did not need a doctrine as radical as that of Epicurus, which, presented as he presents it, is strictly speaking not even a mechanistic dogmatics. Unless (and this is the suspicion that guides our reading of the antinomy), unless in Kant's logic mechanism without purposive causality be doomed precisely to the abyss of chance, in which case, as always, Epicurus, excessive with respect to the position that assigns him in the demonstration attempted here, will not really be dismissed at all, but will continue to prowl around the antinomy as what we might call its negative resource.

Recall Kant's procedure thus far: the antinomy of judgment results from the possibility for reason to appeal to two incompatible maxims in its consideration of nature: and this antinomy is only an antinomy *of judgment*, rather than a contradiction in the very legislation of reason to the extent that we are indeed dealing with *maxims* (regulative principles). In the perspective of the investigation of nature (from the point of view of natural science), the coexistence of these two maxims is not a problem so long as one gives a certain priority to mechanical explanation, following it as far as possible, before appealing to the purposive maxim only at the moment at which the other maxim no longer explains anything (as we shall see, this is the moment of *contin-*

gency). But, following the (natural) movement of speculation, one can suspend this priority of the mechanical maxim and give a certain priority to the mechanical maxim, on the pretext that natural contingencies (seen from the point of view of mechanism) perhaps give us a clue to a more encompassing natural purposiveness to which our reason cannot remain indifferent, and which would be the proper question of philosophy as transcendental. In the tradition there are four principal ways of dealing with this problem of at least apparent natural purposiveness (for no one has yet denied that there is at least an *apparent* purposiveness in at least some natural objects): all four sin through dogmatism, but Epicurus' is absurd, for not only does it attempt to reduce purposiveness to mechanism (which in itself is not so different from what the natural scientist must do if he wants to reach true *knowledge* of nature), but it also reduces mechanism itself to chance. Our suspicion is that this is precisely the Kantian fate of any mechanistic explanation as such (and thereby of all *knowledge* of nature in the theoretical sense, and ultimately of all determinative judgments), if it does not subordinate itself to the purposive maxim, which by the same token becomes much more than a merely 'subjective' maxim, and which, moreover, disturbs all the oppositions on the basis of which Kant is trying to think here, starting with the oppositions between the constitutive and the regulative, the determinative and the reflective, the contingent and the necessary, and others too. In this perspective, the position of Epicurus will provide a negative ('materialist') truth of Kant's thought.

Having dismissed the four traditional ways of replying to the question of natural purposiveness,[5] Kant must motivate the properly critical explanation of the antinomy (and even its critical presentation, because we are still waiting to find out precisely in what way this is truly an antinomy), and this he attempts in §74. in order to be justified in using *dogmatically* (for a determinative judgment) the concept of a thing as natural purpose (i.e. the concept of something given to us as part of a nature subject to a natural causality), we should have to be in a position to establish the objective reality ('objective', as always in Kant, according to the conditions of possibility of an experience *for us*) of this concept. One might be tempted to think that this concept *must* be objective, in that it undeniably comes to us in a context of empirical conditions, which must be subordinated to the laws of the understanding in general, giving the principle required for subsumption. But one cannot *abstract* it from experience (i.e. produce it as a concept by abstraction from the singular conditions under which it manifests itself in given empirical situations): for it is a concept possible only as a rational principle of the judgment we bring to bear on the object in the first place. This amounts to saying that we can never *see* a natural purpose or end as such (we shall see in a moment that what we see is always a *contingency*: if the end is here, we can't *see* it), but we can *judge* a given object as being the result of a causality other than mechanistic. But judging it this way, according to a principle which is indeed rational, but whose objective validity remains indemonstrable, we can no longer proceed by subsumption and determinative judgment. So the principle must remain regulative for a reflective judgment, and thus subject to a merely (but radically) *critical* judgment, i.e., according to the position of judgment as such, a treatment that will never be able to advance beyond critique to doctrine (this radically critical position being the position of judgment when truly judgmental (i.e. reflective) as described in the opening pages of the introduction to the third *Critique*.)

So far as the judgment exercised according to this principle necessarily takes place on the basis of a natural datum (what we judge to be a natural purpose - an organic being - is indeed found *in nature*), it appears to involve a contradiction, which will be the formal measure of our inability to subsume it under an objectively established concept giving rise to determinative judgments (and thereby to objective knowledge). For, to the very extent that the object in question is found in nature, as *natural* purpose, it must, necessarily, involve *necessity*,[6] whereas, as natural *purpose*, it involves a *contingency* with respect to those same laws. So the real antinomy lies here: it is not a matter of simply invoking the availability of two maxims of investigation one of which takes over from the other when the first falters, for the concept guiding the maxim of purposive judgment itself appears to be split between two contradictory suppositions, that of necessity and that of contingency. This antinomy (within the very concept of natural purpose) can only be resolved, according to Kant, by placing 'purpose' and 'nature' at radically different levels, which has the consequence that the concept of natural purpose can in principle never be objectively established:

> As a concept of *natural product* it contains natural necessity, and yet, as concept of that same thing as a purpose, it contains at the same time a contingency (relative to mere laws of nature) of the form of the object. Hence, if this is not to be contradictory, then the concept must contain not only a natural basis that makes the thing possible, but also a basis that makes possible nature itself and its reference to something that is not empirically cognisable nature (but is supersensible) and hence is not cognisable for us all, [a reference] by which we can judge the [object of the] concept in terms of a causality other than that of natural mechanism when we try to decide on its possibility. (§74)

What is contingent to the eyes of mechanical causality, as revealed by the form of organized beings, then, refers us not only to a different maxim to guide our research, but beyond nature as such, or at least to a thought of a totality of nature as such, as grounded in something non-natural and unknowable. Our inability to get to the end of our subsumptive determinative judgments according to mechanical causality, the fact that we stumble over contingencies (objects whose indubitable organisation escapes our mechanical explanations) does not allow us to posit a purposive causality as *objective* (because we understand it not at all), but obliges us to think of the possibility of nature in general, the sphere of mechanical causality itself, as not falling under the law of the same mechanical causality that in general, and perhaps entirely, reigns within it.

The antinomy, then, resides in the fact that faced with organized beings we cannot appeal simultaneously to both causalities, and its resolution in the fact of referring purposive causality (which had yet emerged *in* nature in the form of organized beings, contingent with respect to mechanical causality) to the unknowable (hence super- or at least extra- natural) domain of the supersensible. The concept of natural purpose therefore remains forever *problematic*, and can never give rise to dogmatic responses, be they positive or negative. The concept of a purposive causality indeed exists objectively (human art and technique give us the example), just as does that of a natural mechanical causality: what can never attain to such objective status (whence the crucial place of the teleological judgment for Kant's system as a whole)[7] is the concept of a *natural* purposive causality, for such a concept can neither be drawn from experience (by abstraction, as we were saying above), nor posited as necessary for an experience to be possible. Such a concept remains forever problematic, for even if, *per impossibile*, I managed to show that some natural objects were the intentional products of a divine artistic understanding, I would thus simply withdraw them from the domain of nature, whereas the problem was that of understanding how they were possible *as natural products*. We can thus preserve the naturality of nature only by invoking in merely problematic fashion a concept the (positive or negative) objectivity of which will never be established. Nature *is wanting* this strange concept of a nature other than properly natural nature, this phantom nature of which we will never know anything other than that we need it. This structure is none other than that of transcendentality itself.

The fact that this concept is fundamentally problematic, then, does not at all mean that we could do without it. The *problematic* concept of natural purpose is in a certain sense necessary. In what sense? In that it is *necessary for necessity*. We saw above that the study of nature in view of *knowledge* must lean toward the maxim of judgment according to mechanical causality, a judgment which is perfectly in accord with the necessary, determinative character of the laws of nature (even if this law be in the event empirical). But

Kant's movement of thought, which consisted first in 'suspending' this investigation in order to respond to the speculative, transcendental, call of the other maxim, results in our being unable, at least when faced with organisms, not to appeal simultaneously to both causalities, and to refer the second to the unknowable supersensible. Now this ('subjective', regulative, problematic) referring of purposive causality outside nature as such returns, after the suspension of scientific activity, as indispensable to its progress, and even to possibility as such.

For, as Kant says in §75, the fact of making the concept of a natural purposiveness merely a principle of my judgment (a result of the particular, limited constitution of human reason) only confirms the necessity of this concept which essentially escapes from natural necessity: 'We find it completely unavoidable to apply to nature the concept of an intention, so that even for our empirical use of reason this concept is an absolutely necessary maxim.' This necessity, insofar as it concerns organized beings taken singly, cannot fail, as we have seen, to refer us to a thought of the whole of nature. Now Kant, having established (against the apparent movement of the beginning of the antinomy, which appeared to concede priority, so far as knowledge is concerned, to the maxim of mechanical causality) that we must necessarily invoke the purposive maxim for any knowledge of organized beings, wants to move to the totality without letting go the question of knowledge (the necessity for knowledge of the purposive maxim in the case of particular beings must lead us to try it out on nature as a totality), but without suggesting that the question is still situated at this level.

Whence a paragraph that must take off from the ground of knowledge then to go on beyond:

> Now, obviously, once we have adopted such a guide for studying nature and found that it works, we must [*müssen*] at least try this maxim of judgment on the whole of nature too, since this maxim may well allow us to discover many further laws of nature that would otherwise remain hidden to us since our insights into the inner [nature] of its mechanism is so limited. [Do not, however, imagine that that is the principal reason for performing that extension.] But while the maxim of judgment is useful when applied to the whole of nature, it is not indispensable there, since the whole of nature is not given to us as organized (in the strictest sense of *organized* as given above). But when we deal with those products of nature that we can judge only as having intentionally been formed in just this way rather than some other, then that maxim of reflective judgment is *essentially necessary* [trans. mod.: *wesentlich notwendig*, my emphasis] if we are to acquire so much as an empirical cognition of the intrinsic character

of these products. For we cannot even think them as organized things
without also thinking that they were produced intentionally [*mit Absicht*].
(§75)

So the purposive maxim leads us, on the basis of its grounding at the
level of knowledge, to ask the question of nature as a whole. This question
can no longer be strictly situated at the level of empirical knowledge (the
maxim can also serve as a maxim for knowledge, but does not essentially enter
into the thought of nature as a whole). But it nonetheless follows that the
purposive maxim has revealed itself to be *necessary* for part of nature, i.e.
organized beings. This necessity of a purposive thinking thereby also necessitates the thought of a certain *contingency* in nature (thought as a mechanism). But if nature is thereby not thinkable (for us) as integrally necessary,
nature as a whole must *itself* be considered as contingent, and must therefore,
still for us, be thought of as the work of an intelligence outside nature:

> That is also why those natural things that we find possible only as purposes
> constitute the foremost proof that the world as a whole is contingent [*den
> vornehmsten Beweis für die zufälligkeit des Weltganzen*], and are the sole
> basis for a proof that holds both for a common understanding and for the
> philosopher: that this whole [*der Welt*] depends on and has its origin in a
> being that exists apart from the world and (given how purposive these
> forms are) is moreover intelligent. Hence these things are the sole basis for
> proving that teleology cannot find final answers to its inquiries except in a
> theology. (Ibid.)

So, by explicating what is merely a maxim of the faculty of reflective
judgment, Kant has sent us off beyond nature as such, towards God. But,
according to a movement which is none other than that of the becoming-transcendent of the transcendental, this movement runs the risk of carrying
us much too far. The thought of a purposive causality in nature cannot but
send us beyond nature to God: but it will never *demonstrate* the existence of
God, which remains here, at least, a purely subjective necessity for our limited
faculty of judgment. We will never be able to prove the existence of God in
this way because, as Kant recalls, we never *see* natural purposes as such, but
only certain objects which we cannot even conceive without judging according to the thought of a purposive causality.

All teleology, which thus finds its end in theology, is radically *subjective*. What does this mean here? That for human reason, which is *ex hypothesi* limited with respect to other possible rational beings, we cannot do without the purposive maxim (nor, therefore, its theological consequence), but that the limited nature of the reason that makes this maxim necessary prevents by the same token any objective proof of it. Any such objective proof (which would establish that the purposive causality is constitutive of the object, and not merely regulative for the judgment we are in a position to bring to bear on the object) would come down to demonstrating that the maxim in question was necessary not merely for us, but also for superior intelligences. We can sense the impossibility of any such demonstration: to the very extent that human reason is limited, any conception of a reason which would go beyond those limits is itself limited by the limits it would wish to transgress, according to the very logic of transcendality, the structure of the *Grenze*[8] - the limits of human reason are transgressed only to the extents that *limits* are transgressed, limits which by definition hold us short of what any such transgression would wish to accomplish. This is abundantly clear in the 'examples' Kant gives in §76, and especially in the thought that it is *possible* for us to imagine a rational being for whom the distinction between possibility and actuality would not hold, so that we still and always need the modality of the possible in order to produce the thought of its demise. The thought of the possible absorption of the possible into the necessary is *necessarily (for us) (merely) possible*, confirming thereby a structural *impossibility*. One can cross the limits of human reason only the better, (im)possibly, to trace them: any 'objective' truth must find its circumscription here, and everything that is not there susceptible to objective proof (including the very objectivity of that objectivity) will never be so. So it is not simply that one is condemned to appeal to the purposive maxim because of a negative limit from which superior intelligences would not suffer, because the very idea of such intelligences is only *positively produced by* the structure of that limit itself (and so the infinite is finite). The limit produces both the limited and what is beyond it, but what is beyond it *is beyond it* by the very fact of that limit. Reason thereby produces itself as understanding (at home within the limit, grounding an 'objectivity' entirely subordinated to it) *and* as reason (the limit *itself*) as two-faced frontier which folds its external face back towards the inside (that's the transcendental), whence it never ceases to re-externalise itself, to find itself turned around, in a fundamental, unbelievable disorientation. This is what Kant says literally, but almost apologetically,[9] in the comment that constitutes §76:

> Reason is a power of principles, and its ultimate [*äussersten*] demand [for principles] aims at the unconditioned. Understanding, on the other hand, always serves reason only under a certain condition, one that must be given [to us]. But without concepts of the understanding, to which objective reality must be given, reason cannot make objective (synthetic) judgments at all. As theoretical reason it has absolutely no constitutive principles of

its own, but merely regulative ones. Two points emerge from this. First, if reason advances to where understanding cannot follow [i.e. to where reason is most properly *itself*], it becomes transcendent [*überschwenglich*, excessive, exalted], displaying itself not in objectively valid concepts, but instead in ideas, though these do have a basis (as regulative principles). But, second, since the understanding cannot keep pace with reason, while yet it would be needed to make [ideas] valid for objects, it restricts the validity of those ideas of reason to just the subject, yet in a universal way, i.e. [as a validity] for all subjects of our species. In other words, understanding restricts the validity of these ideas to this condition: that, given the nature of our (human) cognitive ability, or even given any concept we can form of the ability of finite rational being as such, all thinking must be like this and cannot be otherwise - though we are not asserting that such a judgment has its basis in the object. (§76)

All Kantian frontiers are trembling here. On the basis of the apparently anodyne antinomy of the faculty of teleological judgment (mechanism or purposiveness), Kant, having apparently defused the antinomy by appealing to the merely subjective character of the maxims in question, has now, by pushing at the very subjectivity of the purposive maxim, exceeded nature as a whole and grounded its possibility in a principle of subjectivity so radical that it carries away with it any 'objective' definition of objectivity itself. The objectivity of the objective is given by a principle that can never achieve the objectivity it radically undermines, and the supposed 'subjectivity' of which in principle precedes the very distinction between the subjective and the objective. The understanding (and thereby any use of the faculty of determinative judgment) is in the rather hapless service of a reason which is only the exposure of that understanding to its own frontier, where its finitude is denounced before a principle of excess which is none other than the supposedly regulative principle of reflective judgment. As rational (excessive), reflective judgment (always, remember, in search of its law), 'grounds' the understanding in an 'objectivity' strangled by the 'subjective' finitude of a reason which is nothing other than its turning itself inside or outside towards an absolute exteriority.

Two apparently opposing consequences flow from this. *On the one hand*, Kant can point to a relative *self-sufficiency* of human reason, grounded in the resemblance between what is objective and what is subjective but necessary to the subject in order to have objects. 'Now if', say Kant in §75,

> Now if this proposition, which is based on an indisputable [and] necessary maxim of our judgment, is perfectly satisfactory for all speculative and

practical uses of our reason from every *human* point of view, then indeed I would like to know [*so möchte ich wohl wissen*] just what we have lost if we cannot also prove it for higher beings, i.e. prove it from pure objective bases.

But the implied rhetorical question in 'indeed I would like to know', and the satisfaction or complacency it can indicate, also invite, *on the other hand*, a more literal reading: I *would* like to know, I would *really* like to know, but all I have said shows that I can never know, but at best *judge*. Human reason, complacent there, is here rather miserable. What is wanting here will never be the object of a theoretical knowledge for us, by the very fact that it is wanting. But it is precisely this indeterminative wanting that is the principle of judgment *qua* reflective, i.e. as characterised *by* what is wanting (the law for the case). The self-sufficiency of human reason is therefore grounded in its radical insufficiency as understanding, its deficit of objectivity that thus becomes the reason of (human) reason itself.

Nothing in the remainder of the *Critique* resolves this situation. God, called for by this very structure, merely confirms it as wanting. For as the long discussion of the possible proofs of the existence of God in the 'Methodology of Teleological Judgment' (§79-91) shows repeatedly, God cannot be an object of knowledge, and can at best be approached by means of an analogical process that brings us to a point of absolute heterogeneity between God and us, but that Kant nevertheless claims results in 'not the slightest loss' to our ability to cognise God's relation to us and to the world (§90, n.69). God is the *end* of teleology, the *telos* radically cut from that of which it is the end according to a general logic I have laid out elsewhere as the truth of teleology as such.[10] The only way to reach the end, in teleology, is to accept radical separation from the end, and so never reach it. This means that the end is not *there*, but *here*; this is the end of the end, before the end: to try to get to the end by seeking to know what God is in Himself, says Kant in the same note, is to show an inquisitiveness, a presumption [*Vorwitz*], that is, precisely, *endless*, pointless, *zwecklos*. Which is also why critique, revealed as most properly itself in reflective judgment, *remains* critical in every sense, unable to progress to doctrine, the prescribed *telos* of critique itself. The end is here, before the end, before the Law, in the tension of a *promise* of the end that will never reach its end: have faith in the promise of the Law (§91, n.90). The end is here, before the end, endless.

Notes:

1 This paper an adapted translation of part of the final chapter of my book *La frontière kantienne* (Paris: Galilée, 2000)

2 Immanuel Kant, *Critique of Judgment*, trans. Werner S. Pluhar (Indianapolis: Hackett, 1987). All references are to this translation, which I have occasionally altered a little in the interests of literal accuracy. Any judgment on Pluhar's very active and interpretative translation might bear in mind Paul de Man's comment: 'Just try to translate one single somewhat complex sentence of Kant, or just consider what the efforts of entirely competent translators have produced, and you will soon notice how decisively determining the play of the letter and the syllable, the way of saying (*Art des Sagens*) as opposed to what is being said (*das Gesagt*) ... is in this most unconspicuous [*sic*] of stylists', 'Phenomenality and Materiality in Kant', in *Aesthetic Ideology* (Minneapolis: University of Minnesota Press, 1996), p.89. The type of 'materialism' at stake in De Man's reading of Kant bears a complex relation to that being sought here via Epicurus, and is the object of work in progress.

3 The fact that the teleological judgment is so much less well read than the aesthetic judgment is no doubt principally due to the fact that Darwinism is thought to have solved the problem that Kant is grappling with here, and produced a properly determinative account of the appearance of purposive causality. However compelling the Darwinian account in general, and however triumphalistic some of its proponents in their disdain for philosophical questioning in general (see especially the work of Richard Dawkins, with its almost pathologically symptomatic contempt for philosophy and philosophers), the displacement of the question of purpose to the level of the gene leaves the Kantian transcendental questions relatively untouched.

4 This is also true of the treatment of Epicurus in the Antinomies of both first and second *Critiques*, in the essay 'Idea for a Universal History with a Cosmopolitan Purpose', and even the pre-critical *Theory of the Heavens*: I discuss these examples in some detail in *La frontière*.

5 Epicureanism is 'absurd', as we have seen; Spinozism 'unintelligible', in that it gives rise to the thought of a 'blind necessity' which will be the pendant of Epicurus' 'blind chance'; hylozoism is insufficient, because in attributing the quality of life to matter one is making a simple category error about the concept of matter, and moreover getting into a vicious circle (we suspect on the basis of the existence of organized beings that nature as a whole is perhaps organized in the same way, but hylozoism explains this purposiveness in the detail of nature by presupposing in the global purposiveness the point it was to explain); and theism also sins by dogmatism, because it would first be necessary to prove the impossibility of an exhaustive explanation based on mechanism alone before being justified in positing determinatively the existence of a superior understanding outside nature.

6 As made clear at the beginning of *The Metaphysical Principles of Natural Science*.

7 Kant asserts that the aesthetic judgment belongs 'essentially' to a critique of judgment (Introduction, §VIII), whereas teleological judgment 'is only reflective judgment as such proceeding according to concepts', and, to that extent, belongs 'as regards its application' to the theoretical part of philosophy, and is therefore not clearly situated in the critical setup. But it is precisely this impure position of the teleological judg-

ment that gives it its special *critical* position, to the extent that it threatens the whole coherence of the theoretical part of philosophy in a way the relatively contained aesthetic judgment does not. Teleological judgment is the frontier between the theoretical and the practical, the scientific and the theological, and that frontier is a place of contamination rather than of separation. To this extent, the Analytic of the Sublime, which has attracted so much recent interest, is in principle a less promising place to begin a 'deconstructive' reading of Kant than the teleological judgment.

8 See my detailed discussion of Kant's famously obscure distinction between *Grenze* and *Schranke* in 'De la fiction transcendentale', in Michel Lisse, ed., *Passions de la littérature: pour Jacques Derrida* (Paris: Galilee, 1996), pp.141-60.

9 'The following contemplation would greatly deserve elaborate treatment in transcendental philosophy; but here I insert it only as a digression intended for elucidation (not as a proof of what I have set forth here).' (§76)

10 See my 'Almost the End', in *Interrupting Derrida* (London, Routledge, 2000).

4
Apocalyptic Imagination

Gary Banham

> ... what the *nature* of the highest being (objectively) is can be entirely unfathomable to us and indeed can be posited entirely beyond the sphere of all theoretical knowledge we are able to attain, and yet this concept can nevertheless maintain (subjective) reality *in a practical respect* (to a way of life); only in relation to this reality can an *analogy* of the divine intellect and the divine will with that of man and his practical reason be assumed, whereas theoretical considerations of the relation between the divine and the human reserve no place for analogy.[1]

> One ought as well to reconstitute a tradition or genealogy ...of this thematics of the ghost in the nineteenth century, at least, from Kant (not only the Kant interested in Swedenborg, but the thinker of the transcendental imagination and thus of all the conceptual third terms that the fantastic introduced between the sensible and the intelligible, which are so many propitious places for spectrality)...[2]

There is no direct discussion by Derrida of *The Critique of Pure Reason* (at least to date). This might be thought a surprising absence were it not for the fact that a key reading already exists in the works of Heidegger. In *Kant and the Problem of Metaphysics* Heidegger set out a reading of *The Critique of Pure Reason* that remains controversial, a reading in which he suggests that the transcendental imagination, a power allegedly located on the side of sensibility and hence set against the order of the intelligible, is in fact the root stem of both poles of reason.[3] While Heidegger's interpretation is in many respects violent, it has succeeded in making clear that the role of the transcendental imagination in Kant's account of the transcendental deduction of the pure categories of understanding and the schematism is, to say the least, intricate and in need of much consideration.[4] The liminal role of the imagination suggests that the separation between the sensible and the intelligible in Kant is less clear cut than many of his formulations might suggest and its connection to the account of time in the First *Critique* helps to make clear why Heidegger claims in *Being and Time* that Kant is 'the first and only person who has gone any stretch of the way towards investigating the dimension of Temporality'.[5]

In this piece I wish to set out three levels of Derrida's marginal response to this Heideggerian reading of Kant. The first level will concern a couple of direct statements about this reading. These are strategically placed in the midst of quite dense textual frameworks but they question aspects of Heidegger's reading in the process of unsettling the Heideggerian account of the 'history' of metaphysics. The second level concerns Derrida's own most explicit text on the Kantian project of critique, 'On A Newly Arisen Apocalyptic Tone In Philosophy'. Whilst this latter text does not directly address the enquiries of *The Critique of Pure Reason* it does respond in an intriguing manner to some very late texts of Kant and in the process provides an oblique response to Heidegger's reading of Kant. The third level will be presented as a marginal aspect of *Specters of Marx* in which Kant will emerge as a third beside Heidegger and Marx.

Marginal writing: displacing Heidegger's reading of Kant

Heidegger's account of the key nature of Kant's breakthrough in relation to thinking temporality is immediately qualified in *Being and Time*. Repeating the qualifications of Husserl (first set out in the *Logical Investigations*) Heidegger suggests that Kant 'took over Descartes' position quite dogmatically'[6] on the question of the nature of subjectivity. Despite this *Kant and the Problem of Metaphysics* maintains and strengthens the view that Kant's account of temporality presents a radical breakthrough. However, in '*Ousia* and *Grammé*' Derrida sets next to each other the understandings of Kant given in *Being and Time* with those presented in *Kant and the Problem of Metaphysics*. Derrida suggests that in the course of presenting an account of Hegel in *Being and Time*, Heidegger shows him to have described time and space as having a pure form and thus being 'non-sensuous sensuous'. On the basis of this account of Hegel Derrida poses the following question: 'Heidegger does not relate the Hegelian concept to its Kantian equivalent; it is well known that he considered Hegel to have covered over and erased Kant's audaciousness in many respects. Are we not justified here, *Heidegger notwithstanding*, in placing Kant in the *direct line* which, *according to Heidegger*, leads from Aristotle to Hegel?'[7]

This question implicates Heidegger's reading of Kant in the 'history' of metaphysics by showing that, despite Heidegger's claim of a 'radical break' with Kant, Kant's thought of temporality (at least in terms of the thought of pure form) is reproduced by Hegel. This point is then accentuated by Derrida when he remarks that Hegel's statement in section 258 of the *Encyclopaedia*, that time is the same principle as the unity of self-consciousness, is repeated in the analysis of self-affection presented in *Kant and the Problem of Metaphysics*. Since Heidegger claimed in *Being and Time* that Kant took over from Descartes his account of subjectivity, this claim of a unity between self-affection and temporality has to be stated by Heidegger to be something that Kant does not expressly see 'as such for himself',[8] but could not Hegel add the same reservation?

Having aligned Heidegger's reading of Kant with Hegel's account of time Derrida goes on to mention that Heidegger 'repeats' Kant's gesture in *Kant and the Problem of Metaphysics*, in the sense of preparing a fundamental ontology that undertakes a 'destruction of metaphysics' that remains within metaphysics. Derrida supports this by bringing out that Kant's discussion of time in the Transcendental Aesthetic repeats Aristotle's *Physics*: 'Whatever elements of the transcendental imagination that seem to escape the domination of the present given in the form of *Vorhandenheit* and *Gegenwärtigkeit* doubtless have been foreshadowed in *Physics IV*.'[9] The foreshadowing of Kant by Aristotle would turn on something of the utmost importance to Derrida; a thinking of time that transcended the privileging of the present. Derrida makes this explicit by citing from *Kant and the Problem of Metaphysics* Heidegger's claim about the 'radicality' of Kant's thought. Citing Derrida's citation we discover that according to Heidegger Kant has transcended the thinking of presence:

> pure intuition, which is the subject of the transcendental aesthetic, cannot be the reception of something 'present' (*Gegenwärtigen*). Pure intuition which, as receptive, gives itself its object is by nature not relative only to something present (*ein nur Anwesendes*), and least of all of a being actually given.[10]

If this thinking of time on the model of the 'now' and hence as 'presence' is superseded by Kant, and if this supersession is anticipated by Aristotle, then it is still the case that the 'repetition' between them remains (and this includes for Heidegger according to Derrida) within metaphysics itself which constantly steps beyond itself. The closing reason for this thought can even be given in the quote just cited. Heidegger, who took pains constantly and in a number of texts to distinguish 'presencing' [*Anwesen*] from 'presence' as 'now' [*Gegenwärtigen*], nonetheless assimilates these terms in claiming a radicality for Kant who is perceived as thinking a time beyond them both. This assimilation is specifically marked by Derrida who thereby suggests a limit not just to Heidegger's reading of Kant but to his thought of 'presence' in general.

If the account of *Kant and the Problem of Metaphysics* given in '*Ousia and Grammé*' has some very general implications it will not be possible to set them out from an analysis of its pages alone. Before moving on to looking at Derrida's own elliptical response to Kant it is worth adding a footnote to this result from '*Ousia and Grammé*'. Writing in another essay Derrida mentions again the closeness of Hegel and Kant on the topic of transcendental imagination as it is here that 'all the Kantian oppositions regularly criticised by Hegel are confused and negated.'[11] Since it was a contention of Heidegger's that this thought of Kant's was suppressed or ignored by Hegel the presence of this motif both within Hegel's aesthetics and his philosophy of spirit would mark the site of a potential investigation of the extent of Hegel's belonging-with Kant rather than being simply set against him.

Derrida, Kant and the apocalypse

Twelve years after these intricate responses to Heidegger's reading of Kant in the context of a piece that seeks to complicate the movements of *Being and Time*, Derrida turns to writing one of the few texts that involve his own type of response to Kant. Rather than focus on *The Critique of Pure Reason*, however, and produce some kind of account of transcendental imagination or the schematism, Derrida turns instead to some very late texts of Kant's in which Kant is polemically responding to a certain interpretation of Plato. The interpretation to which Kant is responding based itself on a reading of Plato's letters and it is thus not surprising that one of the contexts for this piece by Derrida is in relation to *The Post Card*, a work invoked on a number of occasions within the pages of 'On A Newly Arisen Apocalyptic Tone in Philosophy'. Invoking the relation to *The Post Card* will locate this response to Kant in relation to the reading of Lacan attempted there as well as continuing, albeit obliquely, the response to Heidegger's reading of Kant.

The stakes of Kant's polemical essays can be said to reside not just in defence of the Plato of the dialogues against the Plato of the letters but also in terms of a relationship to the divine through an analogy that occurs in the area of practical reason by contrast to the attempt to present the divine theoretically. The first epigraph of this piece states this clearly and is representative of many passages from these essays in so doing. Hence these essays present in condensed form a justification for the legislative domains of theoretical and practical philosophy but within them is also contained a discussion for the conditions of an 'eternal peace' that will emerge from the process of critique in the essay entitled 'Announcement of the Near Conclusion of a Treaty for Eternal Peace in Philosophy'. It is worth citing the conditions for this peace emerging according to Kant before turning to some of the protocols of Derrida's response. Kant, in naming the conditions for such peace refers clearly to what he takes to be the cause of trouble, a cause attributable to what he elsewhere terms an *evil spirit*:

> *Lying* ("from the father of lies, through which all evil has come into the world") is the actual foul spot on human nature…The command *you ought not to lie* (even if it were done with the most pious intentions), inwardly incorporated as a principle into philosophy conceived as a doctrine of wisdom, would alone be able not only to bring about eternal peace in philosophy but also to secure it for all time to come.[12]

In stating this opposition to lying, an opposition outlined in detail elsewhere by Kant[13], we are referred to the Fourth Gospel and St Paul's letter to the Romans for support for the idea that lying is the source of all that is evil. Elsewhere, in another essay on the question of 'peace', Kant conjoins with lying the keeping of secrets as a premise for that which is insupportable in conduct and must lead to war.[14] If lying and secrecy are the basis of war and evil then truthfulness and openness must be the basis of peace. We have seen that Kant's prohibition on lying lies at the heart of his account of what constitutes evil and with this evidently comes a strict obligation towards truth. Since philosophy lost its original meaning it has been used as a name by those who wish to place everything in obscurity.[15] Derrida notes:

> While still remaining in the Kantian axiomatic, as it were, we can already infer from this that no harm would have happened [*arrivé*], no mystagogic speculation would have been credible or efficient, nothing or no one would have been dethroned [*détonné*] in philosophy without this errance of the name far from the thing, and if the relation of the name philosophy to its originary sense had been insured against every accident.[16]

That this is clear from Kant himself is the basis of the treatment of 'transcendental illusion' in the First *Critique*. Indeed, in the preface to the first edition of *The Critique of Pure Reason* Kant refers to the 'peculiar fate' of reason being that 'in one species of its cognitions it is burdened with questions which it cannot dismiss, since they are given to it as problems by the nature of reason itself, but which it also cannot answer' and that the 'battlefield of these endless controversies is *metaphysics*.'[17] The ground of these controversies seems therefore to reside within the nature of reason itself, also termed by Kant a 'natural and unavoidable illusion,'[18] and whilst critique allows us a means at hand to prevent these illusions from overpowering us it cannot destroy them. Hence it would seem to be a 'lie', or at least an overstatement, to think that peace is finally brought to philosophy by critique.

The separation of thing from name is another way of thinking the distinction between appearance and thing-in-itself, as the difference between them is what is not understood by those who dogmatically assert knowledge where it cannot be had and in so doing fall into illusion. The illusion *par excellence* occurs through taking the supersensible to be sensible and thus thinking in terms of ghosts.[19] A prime place where this is done is in apocalyptic writings, writings referred to by Kant in a number of places.[20] In the polemical texts replying to Schlösser that Derrida mentions Kant clearly assimilates Schlösser to the writers of apocalyptic works. In doing so Kant denounces the lies of Schlösser, assimilates him to the father of lies, assures us of the illusion to which Schlösser has succumbed.

This enables us however to return to the Heideggerian view of the transcendental imagination. For if we read the transcendental imagination in Heideggerian vein as that which cannot be assimilated to the sensible or the intelligible but must instead be seen as the stem of both, then there is a 'ghost' here at work in the very basis of reason as this principle of imagination must partake of the sensible and the intelligible, must transcend both through having a form that neither encompasses and thus it must be at stake in the vision Kant does allow of the divine, a vision whereby the divine is presented as precisely that which makes occur through sight, through intellectual intuition, that way of making that is divine itself.[21] This would indeed be the root of genius.

> One does not know (for it is no longer of the order of knowing) to whom the apocalyptic sending returns; it leaps [*saute*] from one place of emission to the other (and a place is always determined *starting from* the presumed emission); it goes from one destination, one name, and one tone to the other; it always refers [*renvoie*] to the name and to the tone of the other that is there but as having been there and before yet coming, no longer being or not yet there in the present of the *récit*.[22]

An apocalyptic tone is the tone of one who would seem to be a genius, some one who displays matters in an *aesthetic manner* rather than a logical method.[23] This tone is all about a type of semblance, a form of 'passing off' dross for gold (and Kant refers at the beginning of his essay on the 'apocalyptic tone' to alchemists [24]).

This is the point at which Derrida raises the stakes of the transcendental question, a raising of the stakes connected to his suggestion that Heidegger's account of Kant is insufficient: 'if the apocalypse reveals, it is first of all the revelation of the apocalypse, the self-presentation of the apocalyptic structure of language, of writing, of the experience of presence, in other words, of the text or of the mark in general: *that is, of the divisible* envoi *for which there is no self-presentation nor assured destination.*'[25]

The condition of transcendental thinking is that there is error and that this error is fundamental to the nature of thinking. Uncovering this possibility of error leads to that which is liminal in the transcendental itself, which Heidegger suggests is given in the transcendental imagination. By contrast to this suggestion Derrida raises the point of the problem of the presentation in language of the problem of presentation itself. Derrida's term for this raising of the stakes of the question of the transcendental is *envoi*, a translation of Heidegger's *schicken*. The stakes of Derrida's translation of this term from Heidegger in terms of a response to Kant and Heidegger are high. In *Time and Being* Heidegger writes:

> A giving which gives only its gift, but in the giving holds itself back and withdraws, such a giving we call sending. According to the meaning of giving which is to be thought in this way, Being - that which gives It gives - is what is sent ...The history of Being means destiny of Being in whose sendings both the sending and the It which sends forth hold back with their self-manifestation.[26]

A sending in which that which is sent is simultaneously held back. This sending that prevents a security of destination is nonetheless according to Heidegger that which is destined. The holding-back of that which is sent is further described by Heidegger as 'the fundamental characteristic of sending' and this fundamental characteristic to be what we term the 'history' of metaphysics. Which would be as much as to say that history is a concealing/sending.

The place of Kant within this history is revised in the 'seminar' Heidegger gives on *Time and Being* in which the reference to *Kant and the Problem of Metaphysics* is given a twofold inflection. Heidegger here states that the finitude spoken of in this work is no longer the finitude he is speaking of as in the earlier work finitude was thought in relation to infinity whereas now: 'The new concept of finitude is thought in this manner - that is, in terms of Appropriation itself, in terms of the concept of one's own'.[27]

Since finitude is thought now not in relation to infinitude it is released from the proximity to Hegel that Derrida discerned in *Kant and the Problem of*

Metaphysics. Set aside from this and placed within the frame of the thought of destinal sending it is released, however, into a further errancy. It is within this errancy that Derrida tracks finitude in terms of the translation of *schicken* to *envoi*. This sending which has no destinal arrival is what complicates the possibility of discerning the difference between the semblance of apocalypse and the truthful presentation of a voice. To twist this reading of 'Apocalyptic Tone' to a place where it can come back into contact with a thought that is Derrida's because of and against Heidegger and Kant it will suffice to cite the destruction of apocalypse with which Derrida's text concludes:

> an apocalypse without apocalypse, an apocalypse without vision, without truth, without revelation, *envois* ... addresses itself without message and without destination, without sender or decidable addressee, without last judgment, without any other eschatology than the tone of the 'Come', its very difference, an apocalypse beyond good and evil, 'Come' does not announce this or that apocalypse: already it resounds with a certain tone; it is in itself the apocalypse of apocalypse....[28]

Here the thought of an apocalypse takes off from the translation of *schicken* but does so in relation to the reduction of eschatological thinking. What makes this possible is a retrieval of a thought of time from the other side of Heidegger's own thinking, a retrieval which in conclusion I aim to show releases the possibility of a futural role for Kant beyond that envisioned by Heidegger's reading.

Eschatology, spectrality and a futural Kant

The most significant recent reference to Kant is in the second epigraph to this piece, taken from a footnote in *Specters of Marx*. Here Derrida indicates that Kant's thought of transcendental imagination is spectral, an indication that is further supported by his remark in *Mémoires: For Paul De Man* that the phantom is the figure for the working of 'what Kant and Heidegger assign to the transcendental imagination'.[29] This reference to the phantom's connection with work is in fact an indication of how we need to look at the encounter between Kant and Heidegger in *Specters of Marx*. Whilst it would be conventional to expect that the notion of 'work' would be connected either to Marx or to Freud (given the use of the expression 'work of mourning' in the subtitle of this text), it will be my contention that the type of work in question is key to understanding a relation between Heidegger and Kant in this text.

In the 'exordium' to *Specters of Marx* Derrida discusses 'ethics itself' as involving 'a trace of which life and death would themselves be but traces and traces of traces' and that this would be the condition of 'dignity', 'that unconditional dignity (*Würdigkeit*) that Kant placed higher, precisely [*justement*], than any economy, any compared or comparable value, any market price (*Marktpreis*).'[30] This reference to Kant occurs in an exordium where Derrida also refers an 'experience' of the past as 'to come'[31] and if Derrida can towards the end of this text declare that 'Marx has not yet been received,'[32] is not this declaration one that relates to the fundamental thought of time that would lead us to think that receiving is not guaranteed and thus might suggest that Kant has also not yet been received? There are numerous indications within this text that Kant is at work in the thinking presented. The reference early on to the '*non-sensuous sensuous*' of *Capital* [33] can only bring to mind the same phrase brought out from Hegel's *Encyclopaedia* in '*Ousia* and *Grammé*' where it was also restored to its repetition not just of Aristotle but of Kant too. If this reference involves a relation to temporality in terms of an involvement with the 'history' of metaphysics, it is also at work in economic relations themselves and is so paraphrased by Derrida citing Marx later in the work when, in referring to the section of *Capital* that concerns the 'fetishism of commodities', Derrida brings out from the German text reference to 'a *sensuous non-sensuous* thing, sensuous but non-sensuous, sensuously supersensible [*verwandelt er sich in ein sinnlich übersinnliches Ding*].'[34] In order to mark the Kantian reference of this phraseology Derrida refers to a 'ghostly schema' here [35] and goes on to note the repetition at this point of the Hegelian reading of Kant already discussed in 'The Pit and the Pyramid',[36] although without here connecting this to the parallel passages in '*Ousia* and *Grammé*' with the effect there discerned on the Heidegger of *Being and Time* and *Kant and the Problem of Metaphysics*. Since this double inscription of *Margins of Philosophy* in *Specters of Marx* has consequences as much for Heidegger as it has for Marx let us turn now back to some of the aspects of the account of Heidgger in *Specters of Marx* that will enable a futural release of Kant.

In setting out a partial response to Heidegger's *The Anaximander Fragment* Derrida points out that in this work Heidegger depends on an account of the present (*Anwesend*) as dependent upon absence, a dependence which involves non-contemporaneity with itself at the heart of presence as in the following passage: 'What is for the time being present, what presently is, comes to presence out of absence. This must be said precisely of whatever is truly present, although our usual way of representing things would like to exclude from what is present all absence.'[37] Violently retranslating *diké* as justice despite all the precautions suggested to the contrary within this text by Heidegger, Derrida questions not the spacing of presence produced by this thought of absence as constitutive of presence (rather this 'spacing' is *difference*), but instead questions the motif of gathering by which Heidegger implicitly restores the unity ruptured in *Anwesen* through a thought of the Same.

If *Specters of Marx* restores Marx to metaphysics in bringing out an ontology in Marx that accords with Hegel and Heidegger then does not the thought of a 'dignity' which is beyond market-price and that is referred directly to Kant open a space that is that of 'ethics itself'? In *The Anaximander Fragment* Heidegger places his own thinking under the sign of 'eschatology' [38] through anticipation of 'the former dawn in the dawn to come,' and Derrida at the conclusion of his 'Apocalyptic Tone' refers to this word 'come' as the basis for his 'apocalypse of apocalypse'. Within *Specters of Marx* Derrida restores to Marx a thought of eschatology, which he separates there from the notion of teleology in terms of the resources of the former having to be grasped through the figure of the ghost.

If in passing Derrida can write in *Mémoires: For Paul De Man* that the figure of the phantom is the working of the transcendental imagination we should conjoin this with his reading of the appearances of 'world-historical necromancy' in the pages of Marx's *Eighteenth Brumaire*:

> Marx intends to distinguish between the spirit (*Geist*) of the revolution and its spectre (*Gespenst*), as if the former did not already call up the latter, as if everything, and Marx all the same recognises this himself, did not pass by way of differences *within a fantastics as general as it is irreducible*. Far from organising the good schematics of a constitution of time, this other transcendental imagination is the law of an invincible *anachrony*.[39]

If there is here a different transcendental imagination that 'is' the law of anachrony then surely this is recognisable on the model of the reading of Heidegger's *The Anaximander Fragment*? This other transcendental imagination relates, as Heidegger also suggests in *On Time and Being*, to the thought of finitude first presented in *Kant and the Problem of Metaphysics* but freed now from the relation to the infinite in order for its finitude to be thought in terms of its own.

This thought of the 'own' of finitude that is separated from a relation to the infinite would be a transcendental imagination no longer set out as the 'order' of an experience but rather as the basis for that which would grant both order and disorder. If this would exceed not just the boundaries of *Kant and the Problem of Metaphysics* but even *The Critique of Pure Reason* there is still no guarantee that it exceeds Kant himself. In the 'Critique of Aesthetic Judgment' Kant refers to the 'transcendental aesthetic of judgment' [40] and explicates a free law of the transcendental imagination on the basis of this transcendental aesthetic, a different type of transcendental aesthetic to the restrictive one set out in *The Critique of Pure Reason*. This aesthetic includes different accounts of space and time, including the notion of the beautiful as enforcing a 'lingering' akin to the 'lingering' of absence within presence set out in *The Anaximander Fragment* and a collapsing of spacing precisely within the mathematical sublime (sections 25-7). While this latter account is assimilated precisely by Derrida to a thought of finitude measured in relation to the infinite, perhaps another transcendental imagination is also at work which will allow a differential reading that does not repeat the gesture of *Kant and the Problem of Metaphysics* but rather respects the 'dignity' beyond market price that can emerge from an imagination that does not simply provide order but also generates disorder?[41]

Lest this invocation of a saving of Kant from the standpoint of a reading of the Third *Critique* seem now conventional let us also in conclusion suggest a reason for thinking the First *Critique* itself otherwise. The fundamental thought of Kant is not governed by logic unless we think this as ana-logic. Rather than simply trusting in setting out in the 'transcendental logic' a notion of reason that can be freed from all alien importations Kant instead laboriously sets out a means by which reason might be discovered through elaborate and key uses of analogy. The very notion of 'teleology' in Kant is nothing separate from this as Kant describes organisms as based on self-parasitism and the generalization of grafting.[42] Such a generalized logic of life as itself ana-logical and grounded on prostheses is repeated within the account of fetishism analysed at great length in *Glas* and exploited in the analysis of Marx in *Specters of Marx*. Could it not be that this side of Kant, a side never yet analysed by Derrida *and emergent from the teleology of his work* mirrors that which Derrida releases as the eschatology of Marx? Perhaps beyond the apocalyptic side of Kant and the limited finitude trusted to in *Kant and the Problem of Metaphysics* there emerges a Kant who is not confined within the infinitude of metaphysics but emerges beyond the confines of *The Critique of Pure Reason* on the basis of another transcendental imagination as a spectral sign of futurity.

Notes:

1 Immanuel Kant, 'On A Newly Arisen Superior Tone In Philosophy', in Peter Fenves (ed. and trans.), *Raising the Tone of Philosophy: Late Essays by Immanuel Kant, Transformative Critique by Jacques Derrrida* (Baltimore and London : The Johns Hopkins University Press, 1993). This volume also includes a number of other Kant texts and Fenves' translation of Derrida's essay first delivered in 1980 and originally published in 1981, 'On A Newly Arisen Apocaplytic Tone in Philosophy'. Kant's essays will be cited by conventional reference to Akademie pagination, here Ak. 8:399

2 Jacques Derrida, *Specters of Marx: The State of the Debt, the Work of Mourning, & the New International*, trans. Peggy Kamuf (New York and London: Routledge, 1994), p.190.

3 Martin Heidegger, *Kant and the Problem of Metaphysics*, trans. Richard Taft (Bloomington and Indianapolis Indiana University Press, 1990).

4 For interpretations of the First *Critique* that oppose Heidegger's account of the transcendental imagination and yet whose intricacy is partially dependent on this response to Heidegger see Beatrice Longuenesse, *Kant and the Capacity to Judge: Sensibility and Discursivity in the Transcendental Analytic of The Critique of Pure Reason*, trans. C.T. Wolfe (Princeton and Oxford: Princeton University Press,1998) and Wayne Waxman, *Kant's Model of the Mind* (New York: Oxford University Press, 1991). In another place I intend to engage these readings in a lengthy discussion.

5 Martin Heidegger, *Being and Time,* trans. John Macquarrie and Edward Robinson (Oxford: Basil Blackwell, 1962), p.23.

6 Ibid. p.24.

7 Jacques Derrida '*Ousia* and *Grammé*: Note On A Note From *Being and Time*' in Jacques Derrida *Margins of Philosophy*, trans. Alan Bass (Brighton: The Harvester Press, 1982), p.44.

8 Martin Heidegger, *Kant and the Problem of Metaphysics,* p.134.

9 This association of Kant with Aristotle is paralleled by an association of the transcendental imagination with the *pharmakon* in Derrida's reading of Plato. See Jacques Derrida 'Plato's Pharmacy' in Jacques Derrida, *Dissemination,* trans. Barbara Johnson (London: The Athlone Press, 1982), where Derrida declares that the *pharmokon* is '*analogous*' to transcendental imagination in passing beyond the opposition of sensible and intelligible, p.126.

10 Jacques Derrida, '*Ousia* and *Grammé*', p.50, compare the translation of Richard Taft, *Kant and the Problem of Metaphysics*, p.122.

11 Jacques Derrida, 'The Pit and the Pyramid: Introduction to Hegel's Semiology' in Jacques Derrida, *Margins of Philosophy, p.79.*

12 Ak. 8: 422

13 For the most forthright presentation of this view see Immanuel Kant , 'On A Supposed Right to Lie Because of Philanthropic Concerns', in Immanuel Kant *Grounding for the Metaphysics of Morals* (Indianapolis and Cambridge: Hackett Publishing Company, 1981).

14 Kant begins *Toward Perpetual Peace: A Philosophical Project* with a preliminary article forbidding 'secret reservations' (Ak. 8: 343) and closes the discussion with the

statement of the transcendental concept of public right, a statement requiring publicity for conditions of right (Ak. 8:385) and yet in the process of setting out his articles also includes a 'secret article for perpetual peace' (Ak. 8: 368-70). Derrida writes: 'A reflection on the Kantian ethics and politics of friendship should in fact organise itself around the concept of secrecy' in Jacques Derrida, *Politics of Friendship,* trans. George Collins (London and New York: Verso, 1997), p.257. Kant's discussion of friendship is given at Ak.6: 469-73 and see also the account given here of war at Ak.6:354.

15 Immanuel Kant, *Critique of Judgment,* Ak.8: 389. Compare here Heidegger's account of the way in which philosophy itself emerges from a relationship to 'friendship' and 'war' as investigated by Derrida: Jacques Derrida, 'Heidegger's Ear: Philopolemology (*Geschlecht* IV)', in J. Sallis (ed.), *Reading Heidegger: Commemorations* (Bloomington and Indianapolis: Indiana University Press, 1993), trans. J. P. Leavey Jr. I would like to thank Joanna Hodge for drawing this essay to my attention.

16 Jacques Derrida, 'Apocalyptic Tone', p.126.

17 Avii-viii.

18 A422/B450.

19 In justifying the notion of an intelligible world Kant states that even the most common understanding 'is very much inclined to expect behind the objects of the senses something else invisible and active of itself – but it spoils this again by quickly making this invisible something sensible in turn, that is, wanting to make it an object of intuition, so that it does not thereby become any the wiser'. Ak 4: 452.

20 Derrida mentions the reference Kant makes to the Book of Revelations in *Religion within the Limits of Reason Alone* but fails to mention the reference in *The Final End of All Things*, a text that Derrida does not in fact discuss at all. For an analysis of it see G. Banham, *Kant and the Ends of Aesthetics* (London and New York: Macmillan and St. Martin's Press, 2000), Chapter 10.

21 Kant describes this working of the divine at Ak. 5: 405-10 and also states later in the same work that 'physical teleology on its own, if it proceeded consistently instead of borrowing, unnoticed, from moral teleology, could not provide a basis for anything but a *demonology*' (Ak. 5: 444).

22 Jacques Derrida, 'Apocalyptic Tone', p.156.

23 For a justification of the architectonic of Kant's *Critique of Aesthetic Judgment* that suggests this division between *aesthetic manner* and logical method is not pertinent in Kant at all and disputes Derrida's dislocation of this architectonic see G. Banham, *Kant and the Ends*, Chapter 3.

24 Ak. 8:389.

25 Jacques Derrida, 'Apocalyptic Tone', p.157.

26 Martin Heidegger, 'Time and Being' in Martin Heidegger, *On Time and Being,* trans. Joan Stambaugh, (New York and London : Harper Torchbooks, 1972), pp.8-9.

27 Martin Heidegger, 'Summary of A Seminar On The Lecture "Time and Being"' in Martin Heidegger *On Time and Being*, p.54.

28 Jacques Derrida, 'Apocalyptic Tone', p.167. Compare this with the notion of the 'holocaust of the holocaust' in Jacques Derrida, *Cinders*, trans. Ned Luckacher, (Lincoln and London: University of Nebraska Press, 1991).

29 Jacques Derrida, *Mémoires: For Paul De Man*, trans. Jonathan Culler and E. Cadava, (New York: Columbia University Press, 1986), p. 64.

30 Jacques Derrida, *Specters of Marx*, pp.xviii and xx.

31 Ibid. p.xix.
32 Ibid. p.174.
33 Ibid. p.7.
34 Ibid. p.150. It is essential here to refer to the German text as English translations seem all to 'conjure away' this reference in Marx to '*sinnlich übersinnliches*' in favour of a mere reference to 'transcendence'. For a classic example see the famous translation by Samuel Moore and Edward Aveling, edited by Frederick Engels, 1887, reprinted 1954: Karl Marx, *Capital: A Critique of Political Economy Volume 1* (London: Lawrence and Wishart), p.76.
35 Jacques Derrida, *Specters of Marx*, p.150.
36 Ibid. p.155.
37 Martin Heidegger, 'The Anaximander Fragment', in Martin Heidegger, *Early Greek Thinking*, trans. David Farrell Krell and David Capuzzi (San Francisco and London: Harper & Row, 1975), p.37.
38 Ibid. p.18.
39 Jacques Derrida, *Specters of Marx*, p.112.
40 Ak. 5: 269.
41 Jacques Derrida, *The Truth in Painting*, trans. G. Bennington and I. McLeod, (Chicago and London: The University of Chicago Press, 1987). A response to this work which focuses precisely on the relationship between finite and infinite is provided by Simon Malpas, 'Framing Infinities: Kantian Aesthetics After Derrida' in Andrea Rehberg and Rachel Jones (eds.), *The Matter of Critique: Readings in Kant's Philosophy,* (Manchester: Clinamen Press: 2000).
42 For a lengthier account of this argument and some of its consequences see G. Banham, 'Teleology, Transcendental Reflection and Artificial Life' in *Tekhnema: Journal of Philosophy and Technology* 6.

5
After *parerga*: Kant, Derrida and the Temporality of Judgment

Jonathan Lahey Dronsfield

> Denke ich mich und was immer Zweites dazu -
> und wär es die Landkarte von Griechenland -
> so sehe ich wie durch ein Fenster in mich hinein.[1]

I

In what sense does philosophy have a history such that we can meaningfully say Kant 'after' Derrida, what conception of history is presupposed by such a title? On the one hand, 'after' seems not to imply that philosophy has no history, not if Derrida's work can be construed as an historical development of Kant's. On the other, 'after' implies a 'today', or at least a time which is not simply that of Kant's, such that Kant can be read otherwise now than before Derrida. This suggests that philosophy can be understood to be a finite set of texts (or, in another perhaps conceptually distant, philosophical idiom, problems) present to us now, each in their own way a means of access to philosophy and its tradition, but each in the same way accessible, at least in principle, to us today. But if these texts (or problems) comprise the very structure of our thinking about the world, there is an important sense in which they do not change with time, or at least not such that we can *tell* that they do. We associate problems (and texts) with 'Kant', with 'Derrida', but it is precisely because these proper names are responses to problems and texts inherited by them, and, if you will, brought about by them, that we do not or cannot simply locate them in their own time. There is a Kant, a Kantian problematic, both before and after Derrida, and both despite of and because of Derrida. And there are resources in Kant with which to formulate a response to Derrida, perhaps (depending on where you stand) points made by Kant or to be drawn from Kant's work essential and necessary to any full response to Derrida's work as a whole. Indeed, one might even want to say that Kant is an exemplary response to Derrida. Or that Derrida would not make sense without Kant.

Responding to a paper on his work by David Carrier (a paper which begins by rehearsing points relevant to those I have just adumbrated, one in which a 'Derridian position' on the history of philosophy is characterised as claiming 'not just that ways of thinking about these issues have changed, but that we cannot even describe the earlier positions in our vocabulary'),[2] Arthur Danto writes (misquoting Carrier):

> "We cannot even describe the earlier problems in our vocabulary." The 'our' is a gesture of unparalleled generosity in bringing Derrida together with 'us' under the same sheltering pronoun, for what vocabulary does he share with Carrier, or with me? No: there are obscurities in Derrida which cannot be dissolved by historicising him, and there is a sense in which Descartes is far more one of us than he.[3]

Leaving aside the way in which Danto assumes a solidarity with Carrier and, as with all expressions of solidarity, operates a concomitant practice of exclusion, despite Carrier at the outset of his paper listing the 'Derridian position' as one of three 'ways that the history of philosophy may be thought of,' presumably by *us*, *today* (the other two are those of Descartes and 'Hegelian historicists'), the interesting question is how a philosopher of another epoch can be thought to be closer to 'us' than one in our own historical time who, in our responding to him, even if it be to reject him, in an important way shapes philosophy today (note that Carrier believes Danto to hold to a 'very basic anti-Derridian assumption', and that an anti-Derridian view is 'implicit everywhere in [Danto's] work'), moreover a contemporary who himself sees the task of philosophy, its very responsibility, to be irreducibly the historical one of 'keeping alive the memory of a tradition,'[4] necessitating before anything else the reading of texts bequeathed us by the history of philosophy - thus one sense of the frame of this paper, 'Kant after Derrida'.

Kant of course is 'the tradition', no less for Derrida than for Danto, and Kant's system an important moment in the movement in that tradition, one which, if we are to believe Danto, bifurcates into a Derridian way of doing philosophy and a Danto-type philosophy. Yet Kant frames the two, and one of the ways we might read the difference between them is in their construal of what in the tradition constitutes its frame; in other words, how they construe what is central to that tradition. You would not find Danto pursuing a text by Kant for 'two or three possibly fortuitous examples from a secondary subchapter' of it,[5] but this is precisely what Derrida sets out to do, not because he sees *parerga* (for that is what he is after) as weaknesses - he *does* see them as weaknesses but that is not why he pursues them (the strengths and weaknesses of a tradition indicate in advance possible approaches to the tradition, and in so doing sketch out the impossibility of beginning philosophy again, there is never a pure origin to what comes 'after') - but because, insofar as he is able, he does not want to presuppose in what consists the 'inside' of Kant's texts, and thus finds it incumbent to look at what is ostensibly on the margins of Kant's texts and perhaps ancillary to them. And nor does he want to presuppose the inside-outside distinction itself. But this is a delicate operation, for of course Derrida *does* have to presuppose what he puts into question, namely in what consists the inside, what the outside, in this case that *parerga* are marginal, but he takes the initial warrant for doing so, Kant's saying that they are. And Derrida will seek to show that it is precisely from their position on the margin that *parerga* will have their greatest deconstructive effect on Kant's texts, for they open up those texts to what is outside of them - and, I will argue, at the same time they open what is outside the text, human beings, to what is inside the text, such that texts become constitutive of the self in the subject's judgment of them.

Heidegger remarks that Kant 'knew more than he was capable of presenting through [the] architectonic of his works', precisely because of Kant having to presuppose a point of view without the architectonic from which it can be viewed as a whole. Kant's system is a whole insofar as it takes itself to be leaving no space for any further metaphysical questions. Heidegger's suggestion is that what unifies the whole is less visible when the whole is given an external form, that is in being framed as a whole.[6] But the whole of Kant's architectonic is not the architectonic by itself (what would that mean?), but in context - but what is its context? Well, what it separates itself off from. For Kant, the centre would not appear were it not for the margin. Which is why Derrida insists that we cannot simply jettison criteria for judging what frames a system, for deciding between what belongs to a system and what does not. But it is precisely this project of Kant's, the delimitation of his system as a whole, which is put into question by the *parergon* - because Kant insists that the *parergon* belongs to the system without being constitutive of it.[7] But questions as to what belongs, or better still what makes belonging possible, are Kant's questions no less than Derrida's - questions of what belongs to reason, what are the limits of reason. Perhaps Kant would not have composed the third *Critique* were it not for the perceived lack of clearness of the separation between the first two, between the critique of pure speculative reason and the critique of practical reason, between the theoretical and the practical, between which Kant thus inserts a third, to make what separates the first two clearer or to make the connection between them clearer, in any case to have the one belong to the other.

Now, Derrida's paper 'Parergon' begins by making great play of its attention to history, specifically the history of philosophical texts on art, to the problem of reading history, and the presuppositions which may or may not go acknowledged by certain ways of reading history, and it begins by making an over-general characterisation of the history of art. For Derrida, the very questions with which the great discourses on art (Kant, Hegel, Heidegger) begin - 'What is art?', 'What is the origin of art or of works of art?', 'What is the meaning of art?', and so on - imply that we already know what we are talking about by 'art' when we ask them, not just that 'there are' works of art ('The chosen point of departure, in everyday representation: there are works of art, we have them in front of us...'),[8] but that what count as objects of the history of art is in an important way agreed in advance (though we might note here, by way of a hesitation, that for Kant, aesthetics cannot be a canon, precisely *because* there are no rules of taste),[9] and that 'art' has a unity of object and concept, and that it is sufficient to unveil this unity *'through history'*, even if that history is at an end (Hegel, Heidegger). And Derrida sees his task, the work of the seminar on which the essay 'Parergon' is based, to transform the concept of history he believes governs these discourses, in particular Kant's:

> ..if the philosophy of art always has the greatest difficulty dominating the history of art, a certain concept of the historicity of art, this is, paradoxically, because it too easily thinks of art as historical. What I am putting forward here obviously assumes the transformation of the concept of history, from one statement to the other. That will be the work of this seminar.[10]

But it is not just, or even importantly, that Derrida will ask questions differing from those with which the great philosophies of art begin (since questions such as 'When and how do we know we are speaking about art?' and 'When does art occur?' are themselves responses to art), it is that if he is to ask the beginning questions, the ones that have always been asked, he will do so in such a way as to transform them, perhaps even destroy them, *as* questions. He does not rule out a repetition of the questions which traditionally have organised philosophical aesthetics and philosophies of the history of art, rather it is that in their repetition will be found the conditions of their transformation.

> When a philosopher repeats this question ["What is art?", "What is the origin of art or of works of art?", "What is the meaning of art?"] without transforming it, without destroying it in its form, its question-form, its onto-interrogative structure, he has already subjected the whole of *space*

to the discursive arts, to voice and the logos.[11]

Derrida is not claiming for himself a position 'outside' the historical trajectory he wishes to transform in his questioning (we shall come to why, then, he should think of 'destroying' the question as question). Indeed he cannot, for his protocol is Heidegger's, for whom *any* philosophical project involves a transformation of what is the same about the tradition.[12] Nor does Derrida exclude the possibility that philosophy's great discourses on art might not themselves be repetitions of this sort, that Heidegger could be the repetition of Hegel's repetition of Kant; on the other hand, they may in their repeating what they inherit simply make explicit what is implicit in the texts bequeathed them, and thereby reinforce the hold those texts have over history. But this 'risk' is not one that can be avoided, and it would be a mistake to think that 'at all costs' it should be.[13] Furthermore, no 'transformation' will once and for all rescue the questioner from 'the interior of the closure' of that which is to be transformed.[14] All transformations are at once and as much a restoration.

What is being promised, then, is a repetition of the traditional questions framing histories and philosophies of art, but in such a way that in their questioning they hold open that tradition just long enough to draw from it a meaning or meanings of history hitherto denied us. Very traditional. No question of going outside history, the history of the meaning of art; just a question of not deciding in advance in what the inside of it consists. 'Just long enough', for we will see too that in an important way, such an approach (if one can use such a term when speaking of coming from within as much as from without) 'changes nothing', 'leaves everything as it is', and, significantly, cannot not change anything, cannot *not* leave everything as it is. There is a necessary complicity, if you will, between a text and its deconstruction. (It is on this point that Derrida distinguishes deconstruction from 'critique', in that deconstruction does not seek to destroy or erase or negate or remove the object in the way that critique might want to). What we have in this complicity is an economy, an oscillation between the two, between the text in question (or, say, the opposition it embodies, for example inside-outside, subject-object), and its being questioned deconstructively.[15] Deconstruction is not something outside the text in question, something to be brought to bear on a text from without or that supervenes on the text, for an essential part of that which enables a text's deconstruction is there 'in the text' already, 'always already'. We can say of Kant's being 'succeeded' by Derrida, deconstruction comes after having come first.[16] There is, strictly speaking, no Kant after Derrida, since 'the deconstruction of Kant' only makes sense if it is understood that that which enables the deconstruction of Kant is already there, in Kant, always.[17] What enables Kant's *Critique of Judgment* to be deconstructed? In one sense its public nature, simply the fact that it can be read. And it can be read because it is framed as a whole, even if it be by the other two *Critiques*, and those *Critiques* in turn framed by the third. But a text's public nature, that which enables its deconstruction, always already, does not wholly belong to it - if the text were to keep itself to itself it could not change (and would not be a text). On the other hand, if a text can change, then it was *already* that (changed) text. Which is the same thing as saying that there is no pre-existent or original text outside of its interpretation, at least not in any interesting sense for Derrida (here, then, things are not as simple for Derrida as Carrier suggests). On the other hand, there is something about it that will, however, return (the opposition inside-outside for example).[18] Just as, for Adorno, art 'is the world all over again', where everything remains the same, but with the smallest of changes,[19] so too deconstruction.

But, and as he is all too aware, and as we shall see, the problem of history is not as monolithic as is suggested by Derrida in his beginning remarks, for it is deepened by the fact that questions of what is 'inside' or 'outside' are themselves not just 'external' to the text, perhaps not external at all, but, more significantly, 'internal' to the texts in question. Internal not just in terms of how texts construe the history of art and the history of its historicising texts - and here, in their response to this question, contemporary 'essentialist' theories of art (such as Danto's for instance) are no different in their concern than are those who, in opposition to them, see history to be culturally real and artworks as culturally emergent (Joseph Margolis, for example)[20] - but regarding too the ways in which we can identify a work of art *as* a work of art. But what Derrida does, in a way which far exceeds the intent of the writers cited here, is to show not just how works of art bring with them this question of what is internal or external to them, but the extent to which, in doing so, works of art perhaps do nothing but lead the viewer outside and beyond the object, such that any and every work of art might be seen to be a *parergon*, but a *parergon* without an *ergon* to be *para*. Then in *that* light consider Derrida's suggestion that Kant's third *Critique* might itself be a work of art, even according to the terms of Kant's own 'intentions'.

II

Now, part of a deconstructive strategy is to put into question the binary oppositions governing and structuring a text, such that the opposition is brought to the point of its 'dissolution'. The opposition central to Derrida's reading of Kant in 'Parergon' is that of inside-outside - by focusing on the place and function of *parerga* in Kant's third *Critique*, Derrida hopes to show how that which is ostensibly outside Kant's text plays a determinant role on the inside of it, contrary to the Kantian certainty that the inside can be rigorously distinguished from the outside. *Parerga* act as what Derrida calls 'clauses of non-closure', allowing what is claimed to be 'outside' to 'penetrate' the inside and *determine* it.[21] However, it will be the contention of this paper that if we heed not so much the oppositionality of the opposition inside-outside, but the oscillation inherent to it, and especially if we do so in the context of his concern for what belongs to reason, the limits of reason, we can see that Kant *was* aware of the movement to and fro at the limits or edges of his system, a *reciprocal* movement, one which is temporal. Indeed, *parerga* are the site of this oscillation between inside and outside, subject and object, which oscillation is also the need for *parerga*. *Parerga*, frames to the object of the judgment of taste, are devices limiting the oscillatory movement of reflective judgment, and are themselves temporal. *Parerga* are not 'beyond the text', they are not outside the text, they function from within texts in order to contain them, they are dispersive of the effect of what is central to the texts, limiting them, containing them, we might say making them present by giving them form. But, and here Derrida is surely right, there is no final frame with which to stop the reciprocal movement between subject and object. That there is no fixed point at which frames begin and end calls for acts of judgment. Hence part of what I shall also want to argue is that judgments about works of art say something about ourselves as human beings, our capabilities of becoming the apt subjects of the agency revealed by the invitation of art objects and works.

Apart from the discussion of them in the 'Third moment of judgments of taste' in the third *Critique*, *parerga* are to be found only at the edges of Kant's texts, be it in the form of 'general remarks' appended to the ends of sub-sections in the revised edition of *Religion Within the Limits of Reason Alone*, or as an appendix at the very end of the 'Doctrine of the Elements of Ethics' in *The Metaphysics of Morals*. And until the publication of a handful of texts in the mid-1970s by Derrida, culminating in 'Parergon', the role and function of *parerga* in Kant went largely unnoticed. Admittedly, mention of them is sparse in Kant's corpus, but that is the point. It is the precise moment of their introduction into Kant's argumentation and the limited and limiting place they occupy at the edges of his system which is significant, and which Derrida exploits.

If we look at what Kant has to say about *parerga*, emphasising his concern with the limits of *reason*, a concern central to all of Kant's work, the third *Critique* no less than the first two, something which we find is *not* a primary theme in Derrida's reading of Kant on *parerga*, we are better enabled to grasp Kant's awareness of the oscillatory movement between inside and outside. Perhaps the difference the third *Critique* bears to the first two is that in this, the last critique, reason really is brought to its limit, the limits of theoretical and practical reason being more fully revealed by the advent of something outside of the critique of them, the third *Critique*. The third *Critique* treats of the power of the faculty of judgment, primarily the aesthetic judgment of taste. Now, judgments of taste for Kant cognise not the object but the subject, but what worries Kant about aesthetic judgments (or more properly, aesthetic sensations) is that they tend to lead attention away from the object to the subject in a manner which accentuates the *subjective* in the subject rather than the objective, whereby one's reason is extended beyond its proper purpose and object in favour of an undue interest in the self's pleasure. Generally speaking, Kant wishes to confer on reason a humility, such that it does not extend into areas where it has no propriety, areas both outwith the subject and within, and this leads him to identify those sorts of sensations which encourage reason to stray beyond its limits, aberrant uses of reason which detract from a proper comprehension of the subject. At the limits of reason, for Kant, we gain a sense of what belongs to reason and what does not, a sense of what is gained on the inside, as it were, when what is insignificant or superfluous is separated off. It is not simply that his critical project strives to adduce the limits of the use and applicability of reason, it is that the value of what is *internal to* those limits is given only when what is outside (or just outside) the reach of reason is properly identified. Thus at the limits of reason emerges the real worth and significance of what is internal to (or pure or law-like about) it. It is only in admitting of the limits beyond which reason cannot go that philosophy becomes concrete. When Kant comes up against limits he lets them stand, his very method is constrained by a feeling for the humility of reason, and it is this which is at the bottom of the systematicity of his work. Man's nature is finite, which determines the finitude of his reason, a finitude which is not merely a factual limitation but which resides in the essential structure of knowledge itself.

For Kant we only have knowledge because we are disposed to receive. Receptivity, for Kant, is not an abstract idea, we have to be able to receive, and have actively to develop the *capacity* to receive. This can be seen in the briefest of glances at the relation of receptivity to our active faculties. Thus, the pure spontaneity of freedom occurs *in reciprocity with* the finitude of reason learnt in the realm of appearances; the spontaneity of the understanding as a faculty for representing things as they are may be 'higher' than the receptivity of sensibility as a capacity to be affected by objects, but it is *no more necessary*. And in presupposing receptivity (the ability to *receive* the communication of the feeling of pleasure of another's taste, and my ability to *feel* my freedom in the play of images in judgments about the external object, which freedom is the presupposition of the sociality in which my pleasure makes sense, is able to be shared and made communicable), taste, nothing if not social, a satisfaction shared and shareable with others, functions to aid in the promotion of morality externally.[22] That Kant repeatedly steps back from the sort of certainty afforded us by *what* we receive does nothing to alter this basic trait of his thinking, a concerted effort to grasp the reciprocal movement between the inner and the outer, and the limits reason sets to that movement. It is the play between the two, the oscillation between receptivity and spontaneity, the *simultaneity* of attraction and repulsion, and reason's legitimacy in limiting the play, and thereby limiting itself, with which Kant is so concerned. And it is at precisely the moment of their play, at the limits of reason, that we find Kant appealing to the notion of a *parergon*.

Kant does not really offer us a definition of *parerga*, perhaps because they are not properly or fully part of the system. Rather, examples of *parerga* are given, and in their general use is discerned their form. It seems we can have only examples at the edges of the system, at the limits of reason, not definitions. But we can at least say that a *parergon*, for Kant, acts is a limiting device at the very edges of those objects of judgment, not just aesthetic judgments but theoretical and practical judgments too, liable to distract reason away from the object towards an unauthorised interest in what is external about the subject and not objective about the object (in the case of the aesthetic judgment), what is not internal and active about the self (in the case of ideas of religion), or to what contributes indirectly to what is best for the world (in the case of moral virtues). There is a definite hierarchy to these types of *parerga*, with the aesthetic being the most deleterious, the religious being the more understandable (Kant does not contest the *reality* of its aberrant ideas, but rather deems them beyond the proper reach of reason), and the moral being 'beautiful illusions' [*schönen Schein*]. In the first case of *parerga*, sensation, aesthetic sensation, lures the subject away from the form of the object towards the pleasures of its materiality, into an illicit interest in what is 'external' about the self. In the second it is reason's 'consciousness of its impotence' in satisfying its own moral needs that leads it to extend itself to extravagant ideas which might make up for this lack. Lastly, and most benignly, the 'moral perfections' which resemble virtue can be put to use in the social realm to promote reciprocity. The examples Kant gives of *parerga* are colonnades around magnificent buildings, drapery on statues and picture frames (aesthetic), effects of grace, miracles, mysteries, and means of grace (religious), and agreeableness, tolerance, mutual love and respect (virtuous).

Discussion of religious and moral *parerga* in this paper will be limited to understanding the aesthetic *parergon*.

The fullest description of aesthetic *parerga* is to be found in §14 of the third *Critique*, in a section entitled 'Elucidation by Examples', it is worth quoting in full:

> the view that the beauty we attribute to an object on account of its form is actually capable of being heightened by charm is a vulgar error that is very prejudicial to genuine, uncorrupted, solid taste. It is true that charms may be added to beauty as a supplement: they may offer the mind more than that dry liking, by also making the presentation of the object interesting to it, and hence they may commend to us taste and its cultivation, above all if our taste is still crude and unpracticed. But charms do actually impair the judgment of taste if they draw attention to themselves as [if they were] bases for judging beauty... all they do is to make the form more intuitable more precisely, determinately and completely, while they also enliven the presentation by means of their charm, by arousing and sustaining the attention we direct toward the object itself. Even what we call ornaments [*Zieraten*] (*parerga*), ie what does not belong to the whole presentation of the object as an intrinsic constituent, but [is] only an extrinsic addition, does indeed increase our taste's liking and yet it too does so only by its form, as in the case of picture frames or drapery on statues, or colonnades around magnificent buildings.[23]

It is precisely because they assist the subject in focussing on the object that aesthetic *parerga* can detract from comprehension of the subject. To be deemed pure, an aesthetic sensation has to be *uninterrupted*; by their 'effects' adornments to the object interfere not with our grasp of the object (on the contrary, they concentrate our attention on it), but of the subject, and in that sense are as much an over-prolonging of the time of a judgment of taste as they are the prompting of the moment for it. Compare how, in the Introduction to the first *Critique*, Kant stresses how the 'effects' of examples, their dazzlingly 'bright colouring' and the pleasure they afford, interfere with the *rapidity* of our perception of the structure of the understanding, and as such are self-defeating and apt to be disqualified from the whole of speculative knowledge. The aesthetic judgment *keeps* (a term Kant, as here, emphasises often), that is it *limits* the subject in the state of having the presentation itself, and keeps the subject's cognitive powers engaged in their occupation without any further aim.[24] It does not provide a cognition of the object, but it does contain a basis for determining the subject's *activity* regarding the quickening of its cognitive powers; and although lingering over something charming repeatedly arouses the attention, that sort of attention is *passive*, where there is no inner causality concerning cognition in general, but rather an interest in the pleasure felt by the self in its being charmed, in such a way that the subject is somewhat detached from the object, *and* from what is essential internally about itself. The aesthetic judgment refers the presentation of the object to the subject in such a way that the presentational powers of the subject are determined in their engagement with the object.

There is a 'basis in truth', which is not a justification, for including charm in the beautiful contributing to universal aesthetic liking, for an artist might clothe or adorn his work to make beautiful what might otherwise be wild and coarse and therefore *repulsive*. Remember, it is not the pleasure or displeasure that Kant is worried about, it is the way in which the subject may be discouraged or disenabled to attend to the object in such a way as to cognise the self, thus the 'truth' of charm is its attracting the subject to the object such that the subject might *then* have a relation to itself; a temporally limited attraction preferably to be given 'all at once'. Displeasure is that presentation which 'contains the basis that determines [the subject to change] the state of presentations into their own opposite (i.e., to keep them away or remove them),'[25] and conversely we might say that the pleasure of the object's adornment is that which keeps the subject's attention. Especially so in the case of the sublime object, without the adornment of which we might not heed its summons, and not experience the awakening of the feeling within ourselves of the greatness and strength of reason in being able to overcome the object. But at the same time that which might attract attention is liable to distract from the self's cognising power if it can be seen to be detached from the form of the object, in other words if it has its own time.[26]

The summons of the sublime object is a dual one, involving the *simultaneous* summons to ourselves to approach the subject's greatness in being equal to the object - we are being asked, then, both to approach the object, but not such as to lose ourselves in it (its size and intensity), and to approach ourselves, but not such as to exceed ourselves in the greatness of our powers of overcoming the object (since overcoming it would negate the first part of the summons), and again it is a matter of the limits of reason, with reason deciding the play of the two, reason compelled to judge its own limits in the face of the object. Attention to the internality of the subject given in the aesthetic judgment is never detached from the presentation of the object, and it is the immediacy or suddenness of this presentation, the 'all-at-onceness' of the object, that charm or adornment tends to interrupt. The stakes are high, for it must be remembered that it is precisely because it is in agreement with the object that the aesthetic judgment is suited to communication universally.

Here it is not unimportant to note, regarding the atemporality of the 'dry liking' mentioned in the citation above, the way in which Kant recommends (in a footnote to §17) that 'models of taste in the art of speech' be composed in a language both dead and scholarly - dead so that it will not have to undergo *changes*, scholarly so that its rules of grammar remain *unalterable*. One everywhere finds in Kant a worry over the temporal effects of history on the articulation of the form of the presentation of the object to the aesthetic judgment.[27] A language 'dead and scholarly' would strive to minimise the effects history might make *after* the fact of our judgments, and would try to lessen the effect of our own history, *before* the fact of our judgment as it were. On the other hand, as early as his *Vienna Logic* Kant acknowledges that history as such, the experience of it (rather than of any particular thing), is essential in the development of taste. Judgments of taste are historical in that, 'in order to choose ... one must have collected a multitude of cognitions. Our cognition has need of a certain means, and this is language. This means, however, is subject to many alterations. Hence one must write in a dead language.'[28]

And there is one last consideration relevant to our discussion of the aesthetic *parergon*. In a number of places, Kant appeals to the same pictorial metaphor to illustrate the relation of feelings to what is essential in a judgment of taste, namely the metaphor of the 'golden frame' [*der goldene Rahmen*]: 'if the ornament itself does not consist in beautiful form but is merely attached, as a gold frame is to a painting so that its charm may commend the painting for our approval, then it impairs genuine beauty and is called *finery*.'[29] 'Stimulation and feelings belong to the essentially beautiful, approximately as a golden frame belongs to a beautiful picture.'[30] 'Not *principale* and *accessorium* (where they are the same kind of object), but rather *primarium* et *secundarium* (*adhaerens*), where they are different kinds [*verschiedener Art*]. - - *Parerga*. E.g., Golden Frames, Arabesque.'[31] The feeling of pleasure, then, is in itself parergonal to the presentation of the beautiful, in the way that a frame is parergonal, 'merely attached', to the painting. In other words, there is a *clearly visible*, indeed all too visible, dividing line between what is essential and what is not, one which draws attention to itself in focusing our attention on that which it frames, as if the frame too could form the basis of judgments of taste. If the frame as matter is given form it is temporalised, it is made present as a constitutive element of the form of the object. But it is in *making itself visible* in this way, as a constitutive part of the object proper, that the inessential detracts from that which it frames and distracts the subject from a comprehension of what is proper to itself. Better, then, that that which divides the inside from the outside be less visible, but not such that it entirely subsume itself beneath the form of the object, for then it would disappear: the framing of the object is a matter of judgment.

To further our understanding of the temporal features of aesthetic *parerga* it is worth mentioning briefly here the way in which *parerga* to religion and virtue function in relevantly similar ways. The same concern with the time, as it were, of that which assists in framing a judgment can be found in four 'general remarks' added to the second edition of Kant's essay 'Religion Within the Boundaries of Mere Reason' in 1794. Here *parerga* are kinds of 'delusory' or 'fictitious' faith, delusory because they 'overstep the boundaries of our reason with respect to the supernatural.'[32] They do not 'belong' within pure reason, yet they border on it.[33] But Kant's point is that to spend too much time worrying over the difficulties or impairments that bear on questions such as whether god exists would itself be parergonal - if, that is, the question they 'touch on' can be shown to be answerable practically. Why remove them when we can understand why they might be held to, and that that which they are held up to can withstand them on their own account? Kant prefers that we judge the proper time to leave aside these ideas. At the same time Kant outlines the disadvantages that result from these ideas of religion, together with their effects, which he describes as 'sheer aberrations of a reason that has strayed beyond its limits,' which limits are temporal. It seems reasonable for reason to extend itself, conscious as it is of its moral need, but to do so brings with it a certain threat, and from this threat Kant works backwards to establish that these ideas are not 'needed', but that on the other hand they have a limited justification, and it would not be at the business end of things to get rid of them. The suggestion is that, because it is impossible to make them theoretically cognisable, precisely of their incomprehensibility, their sublimity, they provoke a feeling such as to awaken our moral disposition. For Kant, the human being has been created for the good, and must *make himself antecedently w*orthy of receiving it by incorporating this positive increase of force into his maxim. The 'original predisposition to the good' is incomprehensible, indeed sublime, and it is this incomprehensibility, 'proclaiming as it does a divine origin,' which *must* have an effect on our reason, to strengthen it in readiness for the sacrifices that respect for the moral law will require of it. But one of the disadvantageous effects of this, enthusiasm, a pretence pertaining merely to feeling,[34] would allege merely passive, supposedly inner illumination, thereby keeping us away from the good based on self-activity.[35] On the other hand, supernatural moral influences, whilst not cognisable, need not be removed, for they awaken our predisposition to the good - so long as we do not construe their influence as a feeling or experience them *passively*.

In much the same way, miracles too are viewed sympathetically, as aids to introducing a new religion, Kant views miracles as an historical need, giving the new religion time before it can hold its own on rational grounds, when there will be no need to contest the earlier narratives and interpretations, or 'historical reports' as Kant calls them. Indeed, we can even venerate the external cover that has served to bring into the public domain 'a doctrine whose authentication rests on a document indelibly retained in every soul and in need of no miracle.' But beware miracles overstaying the time of their utility, the belief that we have cognition of something through experience which we cannot accept as happening according to objective laws of experience, the fear being that 'historical' miracles become, over time, superstitions and be allowed to play a role in our practical affairs. Likewise, the 'letter' of prayer, *clothing* the 'inner spirit' of prayer, should eventually 'fall away'. Children especially are in need of the letter, but it is important to stress to them that speech 'here has no value in itself' and 'serves only as an instrument of the imagination.'[36] Again, then, there is a time to *parerga*, and a time to judge one's departure from them.

The last kind of *parerga*, *parerga* to virtue, are to be found in the very last, and brief, section, §48, of (and as an appendix to) the 'Doctrine of the Elements of Ethics' in *The Metaphysics of Morals*. Here the end is the cultivation of a disposition of reciprocity, 'the *reciprocal* communication and surrender' of friendship grounded on a confederate respect for limiting rules [*einschränkende Regeln*]. Love pulls the subject to the limits of the object (this being the *idea* of friendship); whereas respect returns the subject back from the object to itself (this the *unattainability* of the idea of friendship in practice).[37] We are in need of rules then, the secondary rules of 'sociability', to 'prevent excessive familiarity' and to 'limit mutual love by requirements of respect'. The limit of the other is the limit and possibility of self-disclosure. Friendship has a tendency towards exceeding its limit, an impulse towards dissolution into an unbounded feeling, and the *parerga* of sociability serve to displace this subjective feeling. However, these *parerga*, the ethical duties of virtue, can only be 'appended to the system', but in such a way that their application 'belongs to the complete presentation of the system.'[38]

It is clear that for Kant, *parerga* in the realms of virtue and religion can play a useful function, so long as they do not introduce impurities into reason by becoming the basis of practical action. The latter is a problem of time. *Parerga* become aberrant if we let them go on by themselves, without us, without need of our judgment about them. The aberrant ideas which might arise from the useful and understandable *parerga* to religion can be kept in their place, whilst the parergonal aids to virtue are almost indispensable on a social level. And though the no less necessary *parerga* to the beautiful tend to impair the proper comprehension not so much of what is internal to the frame but of what is internal to the subject, and must therefore be almost invisible, they can be allowed to remain as adornment so long as they do not aggregate to themselves the function of the form of the object and act as if they could themselves form the basis of a pure judgment of taste. But in all cases *parerga* bring with them a moment when we must decide against them, refuse a passive stance towards them in favour of self-activity; they bring with them guidelines, but leave open the possibility that we derive reason to act internally: in other words, their opening is the occasion and possibility of autonomy, but an autonomy which takes the form of a *response*, to that which is departed from.

If there are *parerga* – and both Kant and Derrida seem to think there are – then there are no things in themselves that they adorn. Or rather, it is not that *parerga* are not constitutive or a necessary component of the object they adorn, it is that that which they adorn are not simply objects understood as autonomous things. When Kant speaks of promoting moral virtue or awakening an original disposition to the good he does so on the understanding that the *parerga* are limited, that they must be departed from. But also that the subject too is limited, that it too must withdraw from the example of the *parergon* to the self. The example dictates *that* there be a moment of withdrawal, not *when* that moment should occur: that is for me to decide, else the *parergon would* be the basis on which to form my judgment. The *parergon cannot* ordain the moment of our departure from it, and *that* is precisely its positivity.[39] This is why for Kant the *parergon* is but a moment in the reciprocal movement between subject and object, one which is to be halted by the subject's judgment. *Parerga* do work, but precisely because they are not *part* of the work. Rather, the claim is that they assist in delimiting what is the proper boundary of the work. They 'cross' the boundary inasmuch as they are the occasion for reason's movement in discovering its limits. Reason has to be allowed safe passage back from its aberrations and from its excursions into the realm of sensible pleasure; we might say it has to be allowed the time for interpretation. Then the boundary itself could be said to be comprised of a temporal thickness, with an internal as well as external border.

It is not that *parerga* form the limit, it is that they are situated on the limit. The real limit, in the case of artworks, the limiting frame, is that which is framed - *that* is what is interpreted. And in one sense it is easy to ignore them: one can not look at the frame of a picture. But in wanting to be *para* the *ergon*, part of the *ergon* yet not part of it, the *parergon* is not so easily crossed philosophically. It cannot simply be passed over, as if it were a mere object, nor can it simply be related to from without, as if it were a mere object. The limit is not one thing; as a limit, both to the work of art, ideas of religion, and the social realm, and to the subject's reach, it marks both an enabling condition and a limitation, and as an enabling limitation it is neither one of these simply.

And nor is the limit static, fixed; rather, it is the site of an oscillation, thought coming up against its limit in the form of a judgment's having to decide not just on the object (in terms of what makes it an object of my taste, my relation to god, my friend), but on itself, in the form of the limit of its reach. Judging what is essential to an artwork is a judgment no less about oneself than a judgment regarding what is proper regarding one's friendships.

III

Through an examination of some of the examples he provides, we have seen how *parerga* function in Kant. From these same examples Derrida derives the claim that the *parergon* is formal and general:

> The *parergon*, this supplement outside the work, must, if it is to have the status of a philosophical quasi-concept, designate a formal and general predicative structure, which one can transport intact or deformed and reformed according to certain rules, into other fields, to submit new contents to it.[40]

This is important, for it suggests that these appendages to Kant's texts have no need of a particular content, that they function in the same way each time, and that they need have no particular context to function in that way. If they can function in the same way each time then it is because they are not subject to that which they limit nor that which limits them.

If, for Kant, *parerga* do not belong to the whole but are an extrinsic addition to it, then for Derrida they do belong, but in an extrinsic way, and they are added in this way, for Derrida, because they cover over what would otherwise appear as a lack inherent to that which they are added, they are called for from within by the lack they cover over:

> added on by an internal lack in the system to which [they are] added,[41] such that 'without them, without their quasi-detachment, the lack on the inside of the work would appear; or (which amounts to the same thing for a lack) would not appear'.

Thus they are not simply extrinsic, they are 'riveted' to the 'internal lack in the interior of the *ergon*' by an 'internal structural link'.[42] The lack itself is 'constitutive of the very unity of the *ergon*', and without it 'the *ergon* would have no need of a *parergon*. The *ergon's* lack is the lack of a *parergon*.'[43] In other words, there would be no *ergon* without its *parergon*, no *ergon* without a lack internal to it which necessitates the addition of a *parergon*. Without the *parergon* supplementing a lack in the *ergon* there would be no *ergon*.

But if the *ergon* itself calls for the *parergon*, because it lacks in some way, then this lack is not really a lack. If the lack itself calls for the *parergon*, accepts itself in its lack and thereby necessitates the *parergon*, it cannot really be called a lack in the conventional sense. Might it not be thought of as a moment, one which calls for another moment outside of itself, but not detached from it, that is the moment of its work, the work called for by the artwork, our judgment about it? This need not imply a temporal priority, where the *ergon* comes first; rather, the *ergon* is not the work that it is until it has been met by a judgment about it - the two being in a reciprocal relation one to the other, where the real lack would be the lack of a *parergon* – for then the work's work would not be limited. And if the work were not limited, the object would not be available for judgment. Without the lack internal to it the *ergon* would lack lack, and thereby lack itself as form, and not be able to count as an object of taste. The two, then, *ergon* and *parergon*, arise at the same time (this is their 'internal', 'structural' link). And if the two do arise at the same time, it cannot be the case that 'before deciding what is parergonal in a text which poses the question of the *parergon*, one has to know what a *parergon* is – at least, if there is any such thing.'[44] It would be more accurate to say that what a *parergon* is, for Derrida, is decided in his reading of Kant. Or in other words, it is decided by the work of Kant's text, even if that work is in main part 'rigorously' to delimit itself (as the limit of reason) from what is parergonal to it. What a *parergon* is, then, is each time decided by the work, in that it marks the end of what, for the work, is the end of *its* work. And thus the *ergon*, the work, arises only at that moment what is *para* to it can be grasped.

As we have noted, Derrida asserts that 'the whole analytic of aesthetic judgment forever assumes that one can distinguish rigorously between the intrinsic and the extrinsic.'[45] But does not the very fact of *parerga* in Kant's texts testify to the contrary? Does Kant not admit that reason has a tendency to overstep the bounds of the object? Does this imply that the 'bounds' of the object are identifiable? Or is it rather that experience tells us when reason, with its tendency to exceed (that is, it is natural for reason to exceed), has exceeded them? Then it is a matter of *discovering* the limit of what is inside, what outside. It is a question of judgment, never detached from the object, deciding when to step back as it were. What Kant fears is the loss of the subject in the object, the subject being drawn so far out of himself that the distance with respect to himself exceeds the critical distance of judgment. Moreover, because the gap has to be maintained (that the subject not be subsumed), the self cannot simply be given up unto the present moment, for that might entail reduction to the time of the object; the *reflexivity* of the aesthetic judgment gives time. Art objects have a 'counterthrow', as it were, to their positioning by the subject, to their being placed as objects of judgment before the disinterested view of the subject's aesthetic contemplation. And this movement, between the subject and the object, if we can still utilize these terms, is not unidirectional, and nor does it cease. The reflexivity of judgment takes place in experience of the object, subject to the counterthrow of the object, and must not culminate in detachment. And it is the time of this reflexivity that decides the 'intrinsic' from the 'extrinsic'; they are not decided in advance. At the same time there would not be an object to judge were there no 'frame' to the experience of it. Importantly, such experience does not provide motivation for practical judgment, for no rules can be derived from it, and no rules can be derived precisely because one can *not* distinguish rigorously between the intrinsic and the extrinsic.

Thus the question of what is internal to the work of art is a question posed to us, the subject, by the object, and is itself internal to the work of art - indeed, these are essential features of its being an art work - regardless of whether (*pace* the Greenbergian medium-specific argument, and Danto's post-*Brillo Boxes* problem of indiscernibles) that question is posed explicitly or not. Then what delimits the internality of a work of art, the frame, delimits it such that the question of internality is *itself* split in two, 'half-work and half-outside-the-work.'[46] *Every* judgment abridges aspects and elements given by the object - to the extent that our judgments about the object are sanctioned by the object in its material superabundancy or severity, its narrative concision or discontinuity, its resistance to interpretation or its openness. But what is of interest is not just the extent to which are judgments are warranted by the object, but how we ourselves respond to our disclosive (or concealing) aptitude revealed by our judgments about it.

Much of this is relevant to the relationship deconstruction has to its objects. That which enables a text's deconstruction is internal to it, but does not belong to it. Deconstruction is parergonal to the texts it deconstructs, neither something in itself, nor belonging to the text it borders. Deconstruction is itself split in two, between the text and its deconstruction - it situates and insinuates itself on the borders of texts, neither in nor out, and thereby divides itself in two, issuing from that place where object is divided from context by a double injunction: to keep and to destroy the text it borders. In this way does deconstruction not know whether to keep *itself* or to destroy *itself*, and that is why it does not know when to stop.[47] For Derrida there is no *outer* limit (which can only mean totalising limit; for example, the one Kant sought with his architectonic) to determining contexts, there are just more or less relevant ones, more or less effective ones. There is no final frame - any and every interpretation situates itself in an historical process which no one historical moment can frame. Or rather, *if* there is such a limit, then that limit will, as frame, be parergonal, and lead out (and in) to yet another determining context. Knowing what belongs to the inside is not impossible, rather it is not *completable*.[48]

Would it be too far-fetched to suggest that Kant too, in his own way, saw this, in his attending to the limits of *reason*? It is the sovereignty of reason being able to come to a final *decision* on this that is contested by Derrida. The difference is that whilst Derrida wishes to celebrate it, to take pleasure in the text, to 'multiply the differences' as it were, Kant seeks to constrain it, sees it as a problem to be overcome - a theory of culture might explain the divergence, but it would not account for the necessity of understanding both to be necessary sides to the same problem. Derrida asserts that the question of pleasure, the possibility of it, 'is *the* question' of Kant's book, because in calling anything beautiful at all, 'I do not consult the relation of the representation to the *object*... but its relation to the subject and to its affect (pleasure or unpleasure).'[49] And this observation seems to legitimate Derrida's letting himself be guided by pleasure in reading the book, to the extent that he will treat the third *Critique* as a work of art or as a beautiful object (which 'it was not simply designed to be'![50]). But, as we have seen, Kant does not deny the pleasure to be had from an aesthetic judgment (on the contrary), it is that he wishes to be *able* to withdraw from it to get clear about a cognitive relation to self. There is nothing, in principle, forbidding Derrida from following Kant's injunction not to attend to the pleasure of the text. The enigma of pleasure may well 'put the whole book in movement', but the suspicion is that Derrida stops short that movement in refusing to follow Kant's disinterestedness back to the subject, leaving its reflective force at the edges of the book. It might look as though there could be something illicit here about Derrida's reading, and the pleasure he so obviously takes in 'following' the book, not in seducing it or in allowing himself to be seduced by it, but in acting as if he had been seduced by it. For isn't Derrida's decision here a *judgment*, one which reveals as much about his, Derrida's, view of what philosophy is (even if the object is a work of art) as it does about Kant's work? The whole of Derrida's text can, in one sense, be taken to be a revelling in the pleasure afforded by Kant's; what is at question is not whether Derrida should or should not do so, but whether Derrida is right to say that he was led to do so by the text itself, through an opening in its frame given the reader by the text itself. But is not Derrida's stance absolutely reasonable, in that it follows the way in which the logic of Kant's text leads out of the text? But then again, might not such be reason gone mad: unreasonable in not acknowledging the limits of reason? Derrida's 'Parergon' shows us how reason can follow the content of the picture to a place outside of the frame where no-one has ever been before; but are not such judgments unreasonable if they ask others to follow? Even if it is not incommunicable it is unsociable, hence Derrida's being not one of Danto's 'us', the price of showing us that there is no outer limit, no final frame of interpretation. But if Derrida *is* to show that there is no outer limit then Derrida *has* to wander out into the desert - it is absurd to hold the one who shows us the lack of an outer limit to account for not 'knowing when to stop'. There is no *knowing* when to stop, but this is not the same thing as not being able to stop. That *Derrida* goes as far as he does, does not at all entitle the next man to do so.

I said earlier that there is no Kant after Derrida, there never was, just as little as there is, now, a Kant before Derrida - there is only a Kant before and after Derrida, a Kant at the same time as Derrida, where the before and after are seen to be a completion of each other. If 'at the same time' then we cannot say which comes first. Which is the same thing as saying that there only ever was a Kant neither before nor after Derrida. And the difficulty and the chance for us is in deciding where we think the one begins and the other ends, where the before and after ends, and the neither before nor after begins. Not in the sense of having to worry about Kant's relation to Derrida in these terms, but in seeing how decisions we do reach, as to the historical relation one proper name has to another with which it is in dialogue, *can* be seen in such terms – but not such that those judgments bear a motive force to our practical dealings with the names of those who do not 'belong' with us, for it is only in such judgments that we gain a sense of who 'we' are. Questions as to what is internal to the text of ourselves (cognitively) are 'internal' to the objects of our judgment (reflectively). 'We divide', says Kant, and Kant's question is what is presupposed in our doing so, what would need to be the case for us to do so.[51] In this way are texts, objects, works of art, friends, even god, the occasion for questions about ourselves. It is not, as Derrida argues, that we are led 'back inside ourselves' *because* of the purposelessness of the beautiful art object, that 'we seek purpose within' *because* of the purposelessness of the beautiful object, but that we are returned 'within' because it, the object, offers itself as an object of our judgment.[52]

Deconstruction 'leaves everything as it is'. The slight alteration, if there is one, is not to the content, nor to the context, but to our relation to the content and to the context, it is a slight shift to both the inside and the outside, as if for the first time we have a relation to (what is in fact the same) context - such that, and this is the odd affect arising from the displacement (if we can call it that); the context is no longer specific in the same way, not if deconstruction is not specific to any particular content or context (nothing is immune from deconstruction, everything can be deconstructed).[53] All contexts are 'the same' in this regard. In other words, by insisting on the context, context loses its context-specific specificity and instead becomes something which itself can be contextualised. That there is no outer limit is precisely what calls for the frame.⁵⁴ Frame is the arresting of (the infiniteness of) the deferral of judgment - without the frame there would not be objects to judge. That Derrida shows that there is no *outer* limit reinforces the need for limits (witness the discourse on responsibility that has ensued as a consequence of Derrida's work, most forcibly within Derrida's work itself); even 'demonstrating' its impossibility will do nothing to alter the presupposition - a gap between the theoretical and the practical, *and* the connection between them, which one might say is precisely what is given us to judge by Kant's third *Critique*.

Notes:

1 'If I think of myself and add something further - and were it the map of Greece - then I see into myself as if through a window.' Hugo von Hofmannsthal, *Buch der Freunde* (Frankfurt/Main: Insel Verlag, 1965), pp.44-5.
2 David Carrier, 'Danto as systematic philosopher or *comme on lit Danto en français*', in Mark Rollins ed., *Danto and his Critics* (Oxford: Blackwell, 1993), p.13. Carrier allows that this might not be Derrida's position at all, that it might be an invention on his, Carrier's, part, but that it is nonetheless an 'interesting' position.
3 Arthur C. Danto, 'Responses and Replies', Ibid, p.193. Danto's view of philosophy he himself describes as 'largely ahistorical... always the same and always totally present to itself... Philosophy has no history, one might say, any more than human nature does... What does have a history is the effort to fit a picture of the human mind to... perennialised issues.'
4 Jacques Derrida, 'The principle of reason: the university in the eyes of its pupils', trans. Catherine Porter & Edward P Morris, in *diacritics*, Vol 13 (3), 1983, p.16.
5 Jacques Derrida, 'Parergon', in *The Truth in Painting*, trans. Geoff Bennington & Ian McLeod (Chicago: University of Chicago Press, 1987), p.63.
6 See Martin Heidegger, *The Principle of Reason*, trans. Reginald Lilly (Bloomington and Indianapolis: Indiana University Press, 1996), p.73. The whole passage runs: 'Seen externally, these three works lie next to each other unconnected, like three boulders. Kant himself tried over and again to make the inner unity, which he certainly saw, visible through a rather external architectonic. Yet Kant knew more than he was capable of presenting through this architectonic of his works.'
7 'The very project of such a delimitation itself already belongs to an ensemble set of conditions that remains to be thought. In turn, even the concept of belonging is open to elaboration, that is dislocation, by the structure of the *parergon*.' Jacques Derrida,

'Economimesis', trans. Richard Klein, in *diacritics*, Vol. 11 (2), 1981, p.3 [translation modified].

8 Derrida, 'Parergon', p.28.

9 'The attempts of the fine arts always precede, and then the rules follow, which serve, however, only for criticizing art. One must acquaint oneself with models of beauty, in order to acquire taste thereby.' Immanuel Kant, 'The Vienna Logic', in *Lectures on Logic*, trans. J. Michael Young (Cambridge: Cambridge University Press, 1992), p.271/Ak 24.812. In all references to texts by Kant, the pagination of the *Akademie* edition is given second. *Kants gesammelte Schriften. Herausgegeben von der Königlich Preußischen Akademie der Wissenschaften (von der Deutschen Akademie der Wissenschaften zu Berlin)*, Reimer, 1908. Hereafter Ak.

10 Derrida, 'Parergon', p.21.

11 Ibid. p.22.

12 See, amongst many other texts by Heidegger taking this as their point of departure, the Introduction to *Kant & the Problem of Metaphysics* (1929), rev. edn., trans. Richard Taft, (Bloomington and Indianapolis: Indiana University Press, 1990).

13 Derrida, 'Parergon', p.30.

14 Jacques Derrida, 'Implications: interview with Henri Ronse' in *Positions*, trans. Alan Bass, 1981, pp.12-13.

15 Derrida, 'Parergon', p.50.

16 On the 'possibility and impossibility' of being a disciple of Kant (the reference in this case is to Buber), which perhaps translates to 'we could but we shouldn't' be, or 'shouldn't have' been Kant's disciple, see Jacques Derrida, 'Interpretations at war: Kant, the Jew, the German', in *New Literary History*, Vol. 22 (1), 1991, p.75. Compare 'Derrida cannot be Hegel's Kant... if all his thought is concerned to show the incoherence of any absolutised cut or separation...'. Geoffrey Bennington, 'Mosaic Fragment', in David Wood, ed., *Derrida: A Critical Reader*, (Oxford: Blackwell, 1992), p.103.

17 Compare the following: '..it is clear at least that the performance of parergonality itself exceeds the status of a mere example, replaceable, repeatable, imitable, or capable of identity, and thereby installs itself, necessarily, albeit clandestinely, within Kant's text (via Derrida).' Irene Harvey, 'Derrida, Kant, & the Performance of Parergonality', in Hugh J. Silverman, ed., *Derrida & Deconstruction* (London: Routledge, 1989), p.76. 'Yet the resumption of the arguments, and the continuation of the genre, by, for example, Derrida, in *Truth in Painting*, may make it possible for the first time to recognize and to comprehend Coleridge's art criticism, in his and our terms, and to 'place' more precisely our own cultural condition.' Elinor S Shaffer, 'Illusion & Imagination: Derrida's Parergon & Coleridge's Aid to Reflection: revisionary readings of Kantian formalist aesthetics', in Frederick Burwick & Walter Pape, eds., *Aesthetic Illusion: Theoretical & Historical Approaches* (Walter de Gruyter, 1990), p.157.

18 No matter how much he might wish otherwise (he remarks in 'Passe-Partout', the 'introduction' to his *Truth in Painting*), Derrida wagers that 'at the end the initial residue would return.' Derrida, 'Parergon', p.2.

19 Theodor Adorno, *Aesthetic Theory*, trans. C. Lenhardt (London: Routledge & Kegan Paul, 1984), p.200.

20 See the following exchanges: Joseph Margolis, 'The Endless Future of Art', and

Danto's reply, 'Narrative & Never-endingness: a Reply to Margolis', in Haapala, Levinson & Rantala eds., *The End of Art & Beyond* (Humanities Press, 1996); and, in the *British Journal of Aesthetics*: Joseph Margolis, 'Farewell to Danto & Goodman', Vol 38 (4), 1998; Arthur C Danto, 'Indiscernibility & Perception: A Reply to Joseph Margolis', Vol 39 (4), 1999; Joseph Margolis, 'A Closer Look at Danto's Account of Art & Perception', Vol 40 (3), 2000.

21 Jacques Derrida, 'Afterword: Toward an Ethic of Discussion', trans. Samuel Weber, in *Limited Inc* (US: Northwestern University Press, 1988), pp.152-3.

22 Immanuel Kant, *Anthropology from a Pragmatic Point of View*, trans. Mary J. Gregor (The Hague: Martinus Nijhoff, 1974), p.111/Ak 15.244.

23 Immanuel Kant, *The Critique of Judgment*, trans. Werner Pluhar (Indianapolis: Hackett Publishing Company, 1987), pp.71-2/Ak 5.225-6.

24 Ibid. p.68/Ak 222.

25 Ibid. p.65/Ak 220.

26 Kant, *Anthropology from a Pragmatic Point of View*, p.111/Ak 243.

27 Compare the following: 'We can divide the logical horizon into: 1. the historical horizon, and it can be a) objective (e.g., natural history, history), b) subjective. 2. the rational horizon (objectively rational, insofar as one can have insight into it *a priori*). The historical horizon is incomparably more extensive than the rational... In mathematics the latter is the most extensive, in philosophy the former.' Immanuel Kant, 'The Dohna-Wundlacken logic', in *Lectures on Logic*, p.448-9/Ak 711.

28 Kant, 'The Vienna Logic', in *Lectures on Logic*, p.271/Ak 812. Note also the way in which Kant, in his *Reflexionen*, deems 'subjective' the impressions attending a recollection of past events for example, calling them ornamental emotional interest adhering to what is, in fact, a primary cognition of an objective states of affairs. Immanuel Kant, *Reflexionen* (late 1770s), Ak 15.1.73. I am indebted for this reference to Martin Gammon, '*Parerga & pulchritudo adhaerens*: a Reading of the Third Moment of the "Analytic of the Sublime"', in *Kant-Studien*, Vol. 90, 1999, p.153 (doubt about the date of Kant's remarks is discussed by Gammon in a footnote on page 151). Gammon argues that *parerga* in Kant refer to a relation of 'adherence' between primary and secondary representations, and offer 'an *independent* subjective promotion of an objective state of affairs, which Kant employs in order to articulate how reflection on the beautiful approaches the moral ideal without transgressing the transcendental restrictions of finite cognition' [p.149, my emphasis]. However, *pace* Gammon, whose argument is a strong one, and well made, I do not believe this alters substantively Derrida's central contention that the *parergon* is linked internally to a lack in the *ergon* (which we will come to, below), or indeed the characterisation of the *parergon* being offered here. Gammon's paper deserves a fuller treatment than I can give it here, and I hope to respond to it in more detail in a subsequent paper on beauty.

29 Kant, *The Critique of Judgment*, p.71-2/Ak 225-6.

30 Kant, 'The Vienna Logic', p.270/Ak 811.

31 Kant, *Reflexionen*, Ak 15.I.11. See note 6.

32 Immanuel Kant, 'Religion Within the Boundaries of Mere Reason', in *Religion & Rational Theology*, trans. Allen W Wood and George Di Giovanni (Cambridge: Cambridge University Press, 1996), p.209/Ak 6.194.

33 Ibid. p.122/Ak 83.

34 Ibid. p.210/Ak 194.

35 Ibid. p.122/Ak 83.
36 Ibid. p.210-12/Ak 95-8. Here again there is reference to the sublime in the form of the moral exaltation of representing the way in which the wish of each human being is united to the wishes of all towards the same end (the kingdom of god). Thereby do public addresses of this sort have a stronger rational basis than private prayer.
37 Compare how, in the 'Dohna-Wundlacken Logic', Kant characterises the reciprocal relation of the imagination to understanding as that of 'two friends who cannot do without one another but cannot stand one another either, for one always harms the other.' Kant, *Lectures on Logic*, p.447/Ak 710.
38 Immanuel Kant, *The Metaphysics of Morals*, §45
39 See Olivia Custer, 'Ornament's work: the efficacy of Kant's "Parerga"', in *Tijdschrift voor Filosofie*, Vol 60 (3), 1998, for whom the *problem* is the difficulty of knowing when the 'role playing' stops, and the claim that '.."beyond" is always just another modality of the production dictated by the laws of the *parerga.*' (pp.565-6). Custer takes there to be an analogy between the virtuous act and the work of genius, where the example of the genius 'acts as a catalyst for similar production' (p.563). But the analogy does not work. The original production of art is new, different each time, whereas that produced morally is the same: but there are different senses of 'ownness' at work here, the 'own' work of a genius can be anything, the 'own' work of the virtuous man is an identifiably virtuous act. *If* the virtuous man and the genius are 'analogous', then it is because each invents the time of his own act.
40 Kant, 'Parergon', p.55.
41 Ibid. p.57.
42 Ibid. p.59.
43 Ibid. p.59-60.
44 Ibid. p.63.
45 Ibid.
46 Ibid. p.122.
47 Compare Pierre Bourdieu, for whom Derrida 'knows how to suspend "deconstruction" just in time to prevent it tipping over into a sociological analysis bound to be perceived as a vulgar "sociologistic reduction", and thus avoids deconstructing himself qua "philosopher".' *Homo Academicus* (1984), trans. P. Collier, (Cambridge: Polity Press, 1988), p.xxiv. Bourdieu believes himself to have shown this in the 'postscript' to his book *Distinction*, where it is argued that Derrida's 'Parergon' keeps to the principles of a 'pure reading', never withdrawing from 'the philosophical game', 'whose conventions [Derrida] respects, even in the ritual transgressions at which only traditionalists could be shocked'. 'Postscript: Towards a 'Vulgar' Critique of 'Pure' Critiques", in *Distinction. A Social Critique of the Judgment of Taste* (1979), trans. R. Nice, (Harvard: Harvard University Press, 1984), p.495.
48 Thus Jay Bernstein is only partially right to say, 'Once the logic of the parergon is acknowledged, the task of knowing what belongs to the inside of a work and what belongs to the outside becomes incompletable, *epistemically impossible*' [my emphasis]. Epistemically impossible? No. It is that knowing what belongs completely to the inside becomes epistemically impossible, that completeness becomes, epistemically, an untenable claim. Which is not the same thing as saying that knowing what is inside is an epistemic impossibility: if that were the case we would not be able to tell that it is incomplete. J. M. Bernstein, *The Fate of Art: Aesthetic Alienation from Kant to*

Derrida & Adorno, (Cambridge: Polity Press, 1993), p.169.
49 Kant, 'Parergon', p.44.
50 Ibid. p.43.
51 'We divide: things that are beyond, outside, and beneath our horizon - outside it, what we do not need to know; beneath it, what we ought not to know. This is concerned with the end, the practical.' Kant, The 'Dohna-Wundlacken Logic', in *Lectures on Logic*, p.448.
52 Derrida, 'Economimesis', p.14.
53 Apart from 'justice' perhaps - see Jacques Derrida, 'Force of Law: the "Mystical Foundation of Authority"', trans. Mary Quaintance, in Drucilla Cornell, Michael Rosenfeld, David Gray Carlson, eds., *Deconstruction & the Possibility of Justice* (New York, London: Routledge, 1992), pp.3-67.
54 Which is in part why Derrida insists that deconstruction 'must not dream of the pure and simple absence of frame.' Derrida, 'Parergon', p.73. Whether it can adhere to the other side of the imperative, 'must not reframe', is obviously what is in question here.

6
Reflecting the Form of Understanding: The Philosophical Significance of Art

Andrea Kern
translated by Jack Ben-Levi

Aesthetic experience, according to Kant, is a kind of experience that is distinct from both theoretical and practical experience not only in terms of its content but in terms of its form as well. Whenever we experience an object (a text, a piece of music, or a painting) as beautiful, we enter into a relationship with it such that our primary aim is neither to pass a theoretical judgment nor to pass a practical judgment on it. Aesthetic experience, Kant claims, has a form that is particular to it alone. Yet in what does the distinctive form of aesthetic experience, a form that cannot be reduced to those of other kinds of experience, consist?

To this question Kant provides an answer which subsequent philosophical aesthetics has sought to comprehend by means of a variety of interpretations. Aesthetic experience is irreducible to the ordinary mode of experience because it has an essentially self-reflexive character. When confronted with art we are not experiencing the world, but rather our mode of experiencing the world. This self-reflexivity of aesthetic experience, which distinguishes it from ordinary experience, also establishes its connection to philosophy. Instead of relating to *the world*, as we do in our ordinary experiences, in aesthetic experience as in philosophy we reflect our *relation* to the world. Thus, aesthetic experience does not simply represent one object *among others* for philosophical inquiry; rather, it is itself already philosophical in character.[1]

In what follows I shall defend this Kantian thought by suggesting an understanding of the self-reflexive character of aesthetic experience according to which the experience of art is a kind of experience in which a feature of our relation to the world is revealed that philosophy can never show us by itself. To display this feature of our relation to the world, philosophy has no choice but to describe the experience of art.

I shall proceed, firstly, by showing how Kant himself conceives of the essentially self-reflexive character of aesthetic experience (section I). Then I shall show why we need to comprehend the self-reflexive character of aesthetic experience in another way than Kant himself does, namely, not as a reflection upon our faculty for judging in general but upon a particular exercise of this faculty in interpretive understanding (sections II through IV). Accordingly, as I shall then suggest, aesthetic experience is philosophical not on account of its thematising of particular philosophical views, but on account of what it does: namely on account of its making explicit the form of our ordinary interpretive understanding (section V). From this it follows that the distinction between philosophy and art cannot be thought of as representing a difference in content but, as I will argue, in perspective (section VI).

Aesthetic experience as self-reflection

According to Kant ordinary experience ought to be thought of as an exercise of our faculty for judging which consists in a cooperation of two of our faculties: the faculty of imagination (*das Vermögen der Einbildungskraft*), which provides us with intuitions, and the faculty of understanding (*das Vermögen des Verstandes*), which gives us concepts. Only when these two faculties cooperate such that our faculty of understanding gives us the concept in virtue of which we can relate an intuition provided to us by imagination to some object, will we be in a position to cognise that object. In the *Critique of Pure Reason* Kant writes:

> Our cognition arises from two fundamental sources in the mind, the first of which is the reception of representations (the receptivity of impressions), the second the faculty for cognising an object by means of these representations (spontaneity of concepts); through the former an object is *given* to us, through the latter it is *thought* in relation to that representation (as a mere determination of the mind). Intuition and concepts therefore constitute the elements of all our cognition, so that neither concepts without intuition corresponding to them in some way nor intuitions without concepts can yield a cognition.[2]

Hence, *every* cognition *as such*, not as this or that particular cognition with some specific content but as 'cognition in general', is characterised by the cooperation within it of two faculties; imagination and the understanding.[3] Only under the condition that these two faculties are cooperating with one another is cognition possible. So when we experience an object in the ordinary way, what we are doing is relating an intuition, with the help of a concept (or a combination of concepts), to the object and then cognising it by virtue of this conceptual determination. Thus every ordinary experience can be formally characterised as follows: our cognitive faculties relate, by means of an empirical concept, a representation given in intuition to an object and thereby determine it. If the object of our intuition is a white tea cup, for instance, then, assuming that we are engaged in the ordinary mode of experience, our cognitive faculties relate our sensory intuition to the object, the white tea cup, by linking the concepts 'white' and 'tea cup' together as predicate and subject, thereby judging that the object given to us in intuition is a white tea cup. According to Kant, the cooperation of these two faculties of ours is the *common form of all cognition*.[4]

On the basis of this understanding of ordinary experience in the *Critique of the Power of Judgment*, Kant now argues that that the logic particular to aesthetic experience, in distinction from ordinary experience, consists in the peculiarity that, here, our faculty for judging, rather than determining an object with the help of concepts, takes the object as an occasion for focusing on itself. An aesthetic experience, according to Kant, is an experience in which our faculty for judging, rather than being directed to an object given in intuition in order to determine it conceptually as is usually the case, instead takes an object to be an occasion for turning back upon itself so as to make itself into its own 'object', as Kant says.[5] In aesthetic experience our faculty for judging is involved in a quite particular operation: rather than relating the representation of the object given in intuition to an empirical concept and thereby determining the object conceptually, as is the case in ordinary experience, in aesthetic experience one compares a representation given in intuition 'with one's faculty of cognition.'[6] Instead of relating the representation given in intuition to an object by means of a concept, it relates the representation to itself and compares the former 'with its faculty of relating intuitions to concepts.'[7]

The key to clarifying the particular logic of aesthetic experience, according to Kant, is the notion of a distinct form of *reflection*, namely, that in which our faculty for judging reflects upon itself. Only if our faculty for judging undertakes this kind of self-reflection, he insists, can the resulting experience be aesthetic in kind, that is, experience in which the object appears beautiful to us. This self-reflexive activity is the necessary condition for an individual subject's ability to experience an object in an aesthetic manner. Yet it is only a necessary condition, not a sufficient one, for not all objects that lead our faculty for judging to turn back upon itself are shown to be beautiful in the course of this self-reflection. Only certain objects are called beautiful. Kant goes on to insist that we call objects beautiful only when something extraordinary happens during this self-reflexive activity: we call them beautiful only when in our self-reflection a specific relationship is established between the two faculties of imagination and understanding - namely, the relationship that represents the 'subjective formal condition' of all judgments, as

Kant argues in §35 of the third *Critique*.[8] And this 'subjective formal condition of all judgments', as we have seen above, consists in nothing other than 'the faculty for judging itself, or the power of judgment. This, employed with regard to a representation by means of which an object is given, requires the agreement of two powers of representation: namely, the imagination (for the intuition and the composition of the manifold of intuition), and the understanding (for the concept as representation of the unity of this composition).'[9]

In other words, we have aesthetic experience of some object only when the reflection upon our faculty for judging yields precisely the relationship between its two faculties that exists in *every* ordinary experience *as such*, regardless of its specific content. Hence Kant's main idea is that we gain aesthetic experience of an object whenever the cooperation between our faculties that makes cognition possible becomes available to us in the *medium of experience* itself. In aesthetic experience we are shown that objects become cognisable by us precisely because these two faculties of ours, that of providing the object in intuition and that of determining it conceptually, cooperate with one another. This is Kant's point when he says that in aesthetic experience these two faculties of ours cooperate in 'free play' with each other.[10] That our faculties cooperate in free play with one another means that they are not compelled to cognise the object by means of a particular concept but that they refrain from all cognitive effort - they relate to each other free from the 'constraint of determinate concepts.'[11] We can call this free cooperation of our faculties their performing an *aesthetic play* since whenever in our self-reflection our faculties get involved in such a play we experience the object as beautiful. And it is precisely because our faculties, in aesthetic experience, cooperate with one another free from the constraint of particular concepts, that in aesthetic experience this cooperation *as such* can be brought to the fore and thus become the content of this kind of experience. In aesthetic experience we do not experience an *object* by means of a cooperation of our faculties that is directed by a particular concept (as happens in ordinary experience); rather, when confronted with an object we experience the *form* taken by all our experiences of objects: that of a cooperation of our faculties.

Thus, according to Kant, aesthetic experience has a form of its own that is not reducible to that of ordinary experience precisely because the former consists in experiencing the form of the latter kind of experience. The particular logic of aesthetic experience with respect to ordinary experience consequently consists in aesthetic experience being characterised by a kind of reflection having the very same content as that of philosophical reflection, namely, the form of our cognition in general. Hence the point of Kant's definition of aesthetic experience is to distinguish it from all ordinary experience by placing it on the same plane as philosophical reflection. Philosophy and aesthetic experience are at one insofar as in both we are concerned not with the world but rather with the form of our ordinary experience of it. Nonetheless, according to Kant there is a crucial difference between aesthetic experience and philosophy. In distinction to aesthetic reflection, in which in aesthetic play we *experience* the form of our cognition, in philosophy the form of our cognition does not become the content of an experience *of* a given object; rather, it becomes the content of a conceptual analysis of the conditions for the *givenness* of objects. Accordingly, in philosophical reflection upon our cognition it is shown that the mediation between given intuitions and concepts is a transcendental condition of possibility for any object of experience's being given to us at all. From the point of view of philosophical reflection, the cooperation of these two faculties of ours possesses the status of a transcendental condition, that is, the status of something one cannot 'experience' in the same sense as one experiences objects, for it is the condition of possibility for the givenness of objects of experience in general. Therefore, according to Kant, aesthetic experience is the paradoxical experience of something that, from the perspective of philosophical reflection upon our experience, cannot be *experienced* at all.

Aesthetic undecidability

The history of philosophical aesthetics is to a great extent a history of the interpretation of this Kantian thought according to which aesthetic experience on account of its structure stands on the same plane as philosophy. In one important respect, however, the history of post-Kantian aesthetics is more than merely the history of the various interpretations of this Kantian thought. At the same time post-Kantian aesthetics formulates an important criticism - and on this point the critics, from Hegel through Heidegger and Adorno up until Derrida, are in full agreement - in objecting to Kant's theory that it does not comprehend the whole truth about aesthetic experience: it is concerned with establishing the truth about the *subject's* aesthetic experience, but not the truth about the privileged *objects* of this kind of experience, the objects we call works of art.[12] Why precisely it should be works of art that are privileged to afford us the possibility of aesthetic experience, remains for Kant's aesthetics a systematic enigma.[13] Kant's theory of aesthetic experience is conceptualised in such a way as to prevent the subjects of this experience from understanding why it is precisely this object and not some other that they experience in an aesthetic manner. The relationship between, on the one hand, the involvement in an aesthetic experience and, on the other, those qualities of the object of this experience by means of which the subject is able to experience it in this manner, is not left conceptually under-developed by Kant's theory - rather, this relationship is simply not developed conceptually at all. Kant's aesthetic theory does not clarify which characteristics of an object make it possible for us to experience this object aesthetically.

Aesthetics after Kant, therefore, does not only represent a continuation of his definition of aesthetic experience as essentially self-reflexive, it also criticises this blind spot in his conception. The so-called *Werkästhetik*, taking its lead from Hegel, aims to overcome this difficulty in Kant's aesthetics. In its view, the self-reflexivity of aesthetic experience must be understood in such a way as to clarify which specific features of a particular object - most especially a work of art - make this object one we experience aesthetically.

Against Kant's position therefore, one has to say that it cannot be by mere chance that our aesthetic experience is prompted first and foremost by works of art. It is essential, in order to describe and define aesthetic experience, that we acknowledge it to be an experience whose privileged locus is constituted by works of art. In Kant's text works of art are defined most generally as being essentially 'representations' of something.[14] Consequently, they are objects of a quite particular kind, namely those that are meaningful. They are objects to which we relate in an essentially *interpretive* way, in contrast to non-intentional, purely material objects to which we ordinarily relate in passing theoretical judgments on them, for example the judgment that the object in front of me is a stone, or a white tea cup.

What does this sort of ordinary interpretive understanding look like? What do we do when we try to understand the meaning of some meaningful object, for instance that of a sentence or a text, that of a drawing or a picture? Drawing on Gadamer, we can say that when we understand a meaningful object in the ordinary way, we are necessarily involved in doing two things *at once*: we are determining which elements are the supports of the object's meaning, and we are linking these elements to one another so as to yield a meaningful unity. Each of these determinations depends on the other. We could not identify those elements that are the supports of the object's meaning separately before having determined that they together constitute a meaningful unity.[15] Interpreting a meaningful object is not an act that can be divided into two steps: we cannot first determine which elements support the meaning and then produce a meaningful unity by linking them together. On the contrary, the elements that are the meaning's supports can be identified as such only by relating them to a meaningful unity. Yet a meaningful unity, for its part, can only be defined by determining the individual meaning-supporting elements of which it consists. Thus, every interpretive act is carried out in the form of a circle between the determination of such elements, for which a fore-conception (as Gadamer says) of their combination into a meaningful unity is required, and the definition of this meaningful unity itself, which requires that its elements be identified.[16]

Our reflection upon works of art is therefore necessarily characterised, to begin with, by a circularity of interpretive understanding. We determine the meaningful elements of works of art by linking them together in a certain way, in accordance with our fore-conception. In what follows I would like to suggest, reformulating and correcting Kant's idea that aesthetic experience is an essentially self-reflexive process, that we are able to experience a meaningful object aesthetically only when, in addition to determining it *interpretively*, we also turn back upon this initial interpretation and *reflect upon* the process by which we reached it.[17] Hence, Kant is right when he says that it is essential for aesthetic experience to contain a special form of reflection. However, we have to think of this kind of reflection differently than Kant himself did. That upon which we reflect whenever we are experiencing something aesthetically is not, as Kant thought it was, those *faculties* by means of which we experience objects in general; rather, in aesthetic experience we reflect upon a particular exercise of these faculties, namely that of *interpretively understanding* an object. We need to think of the self-reflexivity of aesthetic experience as being a self-reflection upon our ordinary mode of interpretive understanding of meaningful objects. When we experience an object aesthetically, what we are reflecting upon in this aesthetic experience is nothing other than precisely our ordinary interpretive understanding of that object's meaning.

Yet this sort of reflection upon our initial interpretation only represents a necessary, not a sufficient, condition for an aesthetic experience because an aesthetic experience, as we saw earlier in the discussion of Kant's conception, does not consist simply in reflecting upon ourselves. Rather, according to him, it necessarily requires that we be involved in aesthetic play. Consequently, as he suggests, an aesthetic experience results only when our initial interpretation of a particular meaningful object is, in the course of such reflection, transformed into aesthetic play. And not every reflection upon our initial interpretation of a meaningful object brings about the transformation of our interpretation into aesthetic play. Were this so, it would follow that all objects upon which we happen to reflect would be beautiful by virtue of that very fact. But this is not the case. Whereas it seems true to say that we can reflect upon the interpretation of any object it does not seem true to say that we can experience any object as beautiful. If that were the case the concept of beauty would lose its discriminative character since it would follow that simply all objects given to us are such that we can experience them as being beautiful. According to Kant, at least, this seems nonsensical. In calling objects beautiful we distinguish them from objects that we do not call beautiful. The transcendental task is to understand how such judgments about an object's beauty are possible. We have to ask, therefore, how some particular meaningful object must be constituted for us to be able to experience it as beautiful and thus for our interpretation of it to be transformed into aesthetic play.

Following up on some ideas formulated most strongly by Derrida in what follows, I will argue that the operations of our interpretative understanding will be transformed into aesthetic play whenever we see, in the course of aesthetic reflection upon the determination of the object's meaning we undertook in a first 'reading',[18] that with respect to at least one meaningful element there is an alternative interpretation, one that stands in a quite particular relation to our first interpretation of the element in question: such that to decide between them is *unavoidable* and *impossible* for us in equal measure. The situation that arises whenever such an alternative interpretation occurs to us and we are placed in the bind of making a decision that is both unavoidable and impossible, I shall in the following call 'aesthetic undecidability' - I have chosen this designation because this kind of undecidability indicates that our interpretive effort to determine the meaning is necessarily being transformed into play. The state of aesthetic play corresponds to the experience of a quite specific kind of undecidability, one that can be encountered in aesthetic play alone.

Aesthetic undecidability, I have suggested, arises whenever two different interpretations of a meaningful element are related to one another in such a way as to make deciding between them both unavoidable and impossible. Such a relationship between them exists whenever, in the course of aesthetic reflection upon a particular meaningful unity, we notice that (at least) one of its elements partakes of an irreducible ambiguity on account not of its 'lexical richness', but of its syntactic role.[19] An irreducible ambiguity of this kind is at issue whenever our redefining of the syntactical role of the element in question brings about a new arrangement of all the other meaningful elements as well, such that both the initial arrangement and this rearrangement are *equally* meaningful. In such circumstances, a decision between the two interpretations of the element whose syntactical role is ambiguous is *unavoidable* because the process whereby such an object becomes a meaningful unity for us in the first place, namely, our syntactical structuring of the various elements in accordance with our fore-conception of a unity of meaning, is at the same time the process that *prevents* us from bringing the other (or indeed, any other) interpretation to bear on the element in question. At the same time, however, making a justified decision between the two interpretations of this element is *impossible* for us, because they both make the object into a meaningful unity in equal measure.

In a situation of aesthetic undecidability we are in a situation in which we, in order to comprehend some object as a meaningful unity at all, have no choice but to decide for one of the two interpretations of a particular element, though this is precisely what we are unable to do. In the case of linguistic objects, the most basic level at which we construct meaningful unities, our dilemma is the combination of letters into the unity of a word; at a higher level words are brought together into the unity of a sentence or a poem; these in turn we combine into the unity of a story, of a novel, and so on. And in the case of visual objects too, this undecidability comes into play on a great variety of levels, for instance at the level of joining lines and colors into the unity of a depicted object, or at that of gathering a number of pictorial elements into the unity of a scene, a picture, a series. This enumeration of possible ways of constructing unities is more or less arbitrary, for here my point is only to suggest that the idea of syntactic ambiguity is relevant at all levels at which unities are formed, or more precisely, at all the levels at which we combine *ordinary* elements into meaningful unities.

We should clearly understand why, in the case of our experience of aesthetic undecidability, it is impossible to make a justified decision between two interpretations: it is impossible not because we could not possibly find a reason for the one and against the other interpretation *within* the terms of a single combination of elements into a meaningful unity, but because *between* two different ways of combining these elements into a meaningful unity there is no justification for choosing one over the other. Any reason for the appropriateness of a particular interpretation has its locus solely within the bounds of a specific meaningful unity. Reasons for the appropriateness of a particular interpretation only make sense *inside* the hermeneutic circle we establish between our determinations of the various elements and our determination of the meaningful unity into which they are combined, not however *between* two of these circles. Thus, in a situation of aesthetic undecidability it is not the case that we lack the reasons with which we would be able to decide on the appropriateness of a particular interpretation within a given context. Rather, in a situation of this kind we are confronted with an alternative between two ways of giving any meaning at all to the very idea of such reasons.

An example

Let us illustrate this understanding of aesthetic experience by means of an example that Derrida unfolds in his reading of Maurice Blanchot's 'The Madness of the Day'. In this *récit* what is at issue is the chronological and topological ambiguity of a certain passage, an ambiguity that causes two different meaningful unities to be formed at the level of the narrative.[20] At issue is an undecidability deriving from the laws of chronology and topology, in accordance with which we combine individual sentences into the unity of a narrative.

In a first reading of Blanchot's *récit* we read his text - which begins: 'I am not learned; I am not ignorant. I have known joys' - as a narrative in which a first-person narrator, after introducing himself with a few brief remarks, tells us of an event in which he was caught up at an unspecified point in the past and that represented a significant caesura in his life.[21] He recounts how one day he was the victim of a curious robbery which, though he says no more about it, led him to be admitted to a public hospital on account of his injuries at the hands of the robbers, by which he had nearly been blinded; there he was placed under the supervision of medical specialists and so-called representatives of the law. He tells us how one day they required - it would seem primarily in his own interest - him to recount to them as fully as possible the course of the events in which he had become involved, to testify to them, in order that, with his true recounting of how he was injured, justice might be served.

Accordingly, on a first reading 'The Madness of the Day' appears to be a narrative in the sense of a literary genre, to whose themes, topics, and occurrences there also belongs, as one among others, the event of the narrator's recounting of the incident, which, he says, the doctors asked him to provide for the sake of the justice to be obtained for him. Thus his report of this incident seems to be, on our first reading, one of the events the frame-narrative, the *récit* bearing the title 'The Madness of the Day', is concerned to relate. And so it is one of the topics, themes, and events that this other narrative, as gradually becomes clear, is about. That Blanchot's text represents a meaningful unity for us depends, most fundamentally, upon our having brought its elements, its sentences, into an order that is both chronological and topological. It is a chronological order, insofar as we have established that the beginning of this *récit* occurs when the narrator starts to tell his story, on the first page, by announcing 'I am not learned; I am not ignorant. I have known joys.' And it is a topological order, to the extent that we established the particular elements making up the text, such as the topics, themes, and occurrences with which it is concerned, among which is included the event of the narrator's recounting the incident in which he had been caught up, as the doctors had requested him to do.

Now, Blanchot's readers become enmeshed in a situation of aesthetic undecidability for the reason that the two sentences taken, in a first reading of 'The Madness of the Day', to be those with which the *récit* as a whole begins - namely, 'I am not learned; I am not ignorant. I have known joys' - also mark the beginning of the narrator's report to the doctors which opens up the possibility of a second reading of the text that is incompatible with the first. Let me cite the third to last paragraph of Blanchot's text:

> I had been asked: Tell us *'just* exactly' what happened. A story? I began: I am not learned; I am not ignorant. I have known joys. That is saying too little. I told them the whole story and they listened, it seems to me, with interest, at least in the beginning. But the end was a surprise to all of us. 'That was the beginning,' they said. 'Now get down to the facts.' How so? The story was over!²²

Thus the story within the story begins with exactly the same sentences, in the same order, as the *récit* of which it had seemed to be a part, without these sentences having been quoted, strictly speaking. Without quotation marks, as Derrida suggests, 'these words commence or recommence a quasi-*récit* that will engender anew the entire sequence including this new point of departure.'²³ This means that the very narrative that begins, as it is claimed, upon the request of the authorities, at the end, is none other than the one begun at the outset of 'The Madness of the Day', in which the first-person narrator will finally say that he is just beginning to tell the story. The chronological and topological order of this *récit* is for us, on account of the repeated use of the two opening sentences within it, where they also mark the beginning of the narrator's telling of his own story, irreducibly ambiguous: because we could not possibly decide, firstly, with respect to the chronology, which of the two instances of these sentences represents the beginning of the narrative and which only a citation of the other, doing no more than to pick it up again; and secondly, with respect to the topological order, which narrative has the other for its object and thus encompasses it as a part of itself. It is impossible to determine, according to Derrida, 'which one quotes the other, and above all which one forms the border of the other. Each includes the other, comprehends the other, which is to say that neither comprehends the other. Each "story" (and each occurrence of the word "story," each "story" in the story) is part of the other, makes the other a part (of itself).'²⁴

This is a case of aesthetic undecidability for the reason that on account of the chronological and topological ambiguity of a particular element of the *récit*, namely, the pair of sentences in question, there are two possibilities for combining the individual sentences of the text together into the unity of a narrative. The syntactical alternative that becomes evident in the course of aesthetic reflection upon our initial determination of the meaningful unity of this object, is an alternative on the level of topology and chronology, in accord with which we join the sentences into the unity of a narrative. Thus the undecidable ambiguity of this passage of the text is a function not of the wealth of meaning of its sentences, but rather of a syntactical activity that links these sentences into the meaningful unity of a narrative. It is not the meaning of some few sentences within the narrative that is undecidable but rather the syntactical praxis itself, by which the individual sentences were combined together into the unity of a narrative in the first place. It is a situation of aesthetic undecidability because, while we cannot avoid putting the sentences of this *récit* into the chronological and topological order without which it would be no narrative at all, it is also impossible for us to decide one way or the other about the shape of that order - impossible to the extent that we cannot decide with which pair of sentences the *récit* actually begins, nor which of the narratives represents the frame of the other and thus contains it as a part of itself.

Playing with meaning

To experience aesthetic undecidability means to experience, in the course of one's aesthetic reflection upon a particular understanding of a meaningful unity, that there is a double entrance to this unity, an entrance in the dizzying shape of a revolving door.[25] Yet what does it mean, exactly, to be in a situation where we stand incapable of decision before two syntactical alternatives? What does it mean when such alternatives become clear to us during our aesthetic reflection upon a particular understanding of a meaningful unity? When this occurs, it annuls the validity of our initial determination of the object's meaning. We have lost the possibility of continuing to claim this initial determination to be valid, that is, sufficiently justified.

Let us clarify the precise way in which this cancelling of the validity of our first determination of the object's meaning takes place. When the possibility of our continuing to assert its validity is destroyed, this does not happen because aesthetic reflection has shown that the reasons for that first determination are insufficient. Rather, aesthetic reflection upon our initial way of meaningfully ordering the material annuls its validity only by showing us that an alternative way of doing so is *equally possible*.[26] The annulment in our aesthetic reflection of the validity of a determination is brought about by the emergence of another equally possible determination. That our initial determination's validity is annulled, therefore, does not mean that we have recognised our *inability* to justify it *sufficiently*, but that we have seen that maintaining it presupposes a decision we are *entirely unable* to justify.

But how can we respond properly to such a situation? The only way, when a meaningful element we are seeking to interpret is neither the one nor the other element we had thought it was and yet it is, in an undecidable manner, both simultaneously, is to suspend every effort to determine its meaning. This we do precisely by holding both of its possible meanings in play, in an 'indefinite fluctuation' between them.[27] Such a movement characterises the activity of aesthetic play. In aesthetic play we are not involved in the effort of interpretation in the strict sense; what we do is to take a 'series of leaps' between two possible interpretations.[28] Every advance into the depths of a particular meaningful unity, in aesthetic play, we undertake only by advancing simultaneously into the depths of the unity opposed to it. Instead of deepening, as we ordinarily do, the meaning of the object by entering into a hermeneutic circle between the determination of the elements and the unity that they comprise, in our aesthetic play we make no attempt to settle the object's meaning at all. In aesthetic play we are not entering ever more deeply *into* a single hermeneutic circle. Rather, we move *back and forth* between two of them. Aesthetic experience consists in just such play with meaning. Consequently, in aesthetic experience, the slow and ever more precise consideration of an object takes the form not of a steady interpretive effort to establish the meaning of a particular meaningful unity, but of a frequently interrupted movement between (at least) two such unities.

The groundlessness of interpretive understanding

At the beginning, I raised with Kant the question of what the distinctive and irreducible form of aesthetic experience consists in. The irreducible logic proper to aesthetic experience, according to the explanation I have proposed, consists in the fact that this kind of experience does not represent an interpretive operation, but is, rather, play with two possibilities of interpretation between which we cannot decide. This explanation now permits us to understand something that Kant's theory fails to clarify: namely which characteristics of the object of aesthetic experience make such experience possible for us. The answer given so far is that a meaningful object can become an object for aesthetic experience in virtue of its possessing a syntactical multiplicity of meaning.

The history of post-Kantian aesthetics, I claimed earlier, is the history of giving content to Kant's thought according to which the irreducible logic proper to aesthetic experience can be understood only if we conceive this experience to be one whose distinctiveness with respect to the ordinary kind of experience is based on the fact that it represents - just as does philosophical reflection - a reflection upon the form of the latter. In distinction to ordinary kinds of experience, aesthetic experience has a logic that is irreducibly particular to it alone, for it is typified by a self-reflexivity that lends it its philosophical character.

In what follows I shall argue that Derrida's claim that aesthetic experience consists in playing with interpretations among which one cannot decide, in fact represents a way of giving this Kantian insight a specific shape. Aesthetic play with two such possibilities of combining the elements of an object into a meaningful unity, is play of a kind in which we, confronted with a specific meaningful object, obtain experience of the *form of our interpretive understanding*. Aesthetic experience, consequently, is structurally distinct from the ordinary operations of interpretation precisely because in it we are not concerned with interpreting a particular *meaning* but rather with reflecting upon our ordinary interpretive *relationship* to the world of meaning.

At this point let us recall once more the form of ordinary interpretive understanding, as it was earlier discussed. Drawing on Gadamer, I characterised it as a procedure in which we are able to identify individual elements of meaning *only insofar as* we relate them to some meaningful unity. This means that identifying these elements is not a step we take *before* determining the meaningful unity that they comprise; rather, we identify them precisely *by* relating them to that meaningful unity. Consequently, it is characteristic of the mode of being of such meaningful elements that they as such are first identified by our interpretive effort. This entails, however, that there can be no such thing as a meaning existing apart from the activity of our interpretive understanding, for that would presuppose that it makes sense to seek out this meaning even before - or without - involving our interpretive understanding in the search: it would presuppose, to put the point somewhat differently, that a meaningful element has *come into focus* before we turned our interpretive attention upon it. The meaning to which we refer while interpreting and that constitutes the standard in accordance with which our interpretation is right or wrong, does not *logically precede* our interpretive effort but rather stands in need, as Derrida writes, of an ever renewed 'reinstitution'.[29] In Gadamer's words, the circle of interpretative understanding 'is not a "methodological" circle, but describes an element of the ontological structure' of such understanding.[30] However it may be performed, the hermeneutic circle is not something we could assess, with respect to the meaning of an object, as being right or wrong, appropriate or inappropriate.[31] Thus the insight that interpretation consists in performing this kind of circle is the insight that nothing outside our own interpretive understanding can guarantee the correctness of our answer to the question of how a sentence, an expression, a text or a picture is to be understood.[32] Interpretive understanding is without grounds, we might say, because it has no ground outside of itself. The meaning we refer to in interpretation is *given* to us by such interpretation alone.

It is precisely this *groundlessness* of our interpretive understanding that is shown whenever, confronted with a beautiful object, we realise that justifying a decision between two possibilities of combining the object's meaningful elements into a unity is impossible. Realising that we cannot decide between two circles of interpretation is the realisation that our interpretive understanding has no ground outside of itself. *In aesthetic play between two such circles, the inescapable circularity of all our interpretation is revealed.* Moving interminably back and forth between two of these circles without finding any resting place where we could decide which of them is the more appropriate with regard to the meaning in question, we become aware that the meanings we refer to in interpretation are *given* only when we are involved in such a circle. The insight that between two ways of combining an object's elements into a meaningful unity there is no room for grounds enabling us to decide between them, is the insight that our interpretive understanding has no ground outside of itself.

Let us imagine this were not the case. Suppose that our interpretive understanding was not without an external ground and that we could base the hermeneutic circle on a meaning that logically preceded it. In other words, let us suppose our interpretive understanding had its ground in a meaning that did not require an ever renewed 'reinstitution' but was logically independent of our being involved in a hermeneutic circle. Were this the form taken by our interpretive understanding, were the meaning of an object something that logically preceded our involvement in a hermeneutic circle, the experience of aesthetic undecidability would be a *conceptual impossibility*, because then the choice between two hermeneutic circles could never be undecidable: in principle it would be possible to justify the decision for one or the other of them.

Yet the experience of standing undecided between two hermeneutic circles is nonetheless a *real* one for us. We experience it in reading Blanchot's 'Madness of the Day', as I showed earlier. And we cannot conceptualise it if we do not insist that meanings are only ever given while we are involved in an interpretive circle. But then we also must insist that the experience of an undecidable choice between two such circles is one which makes the *form* of our ordinary interpretation *explicit*. To experience that it is impossible to justify entering into a hermeneutic circle, means experiencing that the meanings we ordinarily try to interpret are only ever given *while* we are involved in such a circle. In discovering that Blanchot's text offers us no exterior standpoint from which the appropriateness of either circle could be justified with respect to his text itself, and that we must instead already have entered into one of them for us to be able to relate to this text as a meaningful unity at all, we see that there simply *is* no meaning whatsoever outside of any such circle.

Thus, in aesthetic experience we do not actually interpret. Rather, by refraining from doing so when prompted by a particular meaningful object, we turn our attention upon the form of our interpretive understanding in general. In aesthetic experience the form of our interpretation, which is an inescapably circular procedure, becomes the explicit content of an experience.

Philosophy and art

So it turns out that aesthetic experience has a fundamentally philosophical character. It has this character not because, as is sometimes claimed especially with respect to literature, the content of aesthetic objects may be composed of philosophical lines of thought. Aesthetic experience is philosophical not on account of its thematising of particular philosophical views, but by its having the very same content as philosophy. If we experience something aesthetically we are doing precisely what we do when philosophising: we turn back upon our ordinary interpretive understanding in such a way that its form is displayed *explicitly* to us in this self-reflection.

At this point we have to ask where the difference lies between reflecting philosophically upon the form of ordinary interpretive understanding on the one hand, and experiencing it aesthetically on the other. For even if, as I have been suggesting, aesthetic experience has a philosophical character by virtue of its reflexive relationship to ordinary interpretive understanding, nonetheless it is not simply identical with philosophical reflection. Philosophy seems to be one thing, aesthetic experience another. So in what does the difference consist?

In order to comprehend the difference it will be helpful, first of all, to briefly review Kant's position and his own definition of the difference between aesthetic experience and philosophy. They are distinguished, Kant claims, according to the medium in which reflection upon our ordinary experience takes place. If we reflect philosophically upon the form of our ordinary experience, we are attempting to gain access to it in the medium of a conceptual analysis. Aesthetic experience, by contrast, makes this form of our ordinary experience accessible to us in a different medium, namely, that of *experience* itself. In aesthetic experience we are shown the form of our experience not as a result of reflection operating with concepts, but in the free play of our faculties occasioned by a particular object. I believe that this insight of Kant's into the relationship between aesthetic experience and philosophy is profound. He saw rightly that this relationship cannot be defined in terms of a difference in their respective contents. If both aesthetic experience and philosophy are characterised by their involving reflection upon the form of our ordinary experience, the difference between them cannot be in content. Rather, they are at one as to content: it is this which distinguishes them both from ordinary experience.

The insight that the difference between aesthetic experience and philosophical reflection cannot be understood as a difference in content has sometimes engendered the suspicion that the aesthetics of deconstruction would deny that there is any difference at all between philosophy and art. Yet this objection pertains to the aesthetics of deconstruction as little as it would to Kant. When Derrida denies that the difference between philosophy and art is one of content, he is proceeding entirely in Kant's footsteps - whom no one has ever suspected of 'levelling' the distinction between them.[33] To claim that the difference is not one of content, does not mean claiming that there is no difference between them. On the contrary, the claim is that the distinction will be understood only if we comprehend what difference it makes for the content they share to be made available to us at one point in the medium of a conceptual analysis and at another in the medium of the experience of aesthetic play. Following Kant, we might say that in philosophy we try to illuminate the conditions for the givenness of meaning by means of conceptual analysis. By uncovering, in the medium of conceptual thought, the conditions under which meanings can be *given* to us at all, we reveal how it is possible that our ordinary interpretive understanding can be what it claims to be: namely an interpretive understanding of meaning. Philosophy gains insight into the groundlessness of our ordinary interpretive understanding by looking at our interpretive understanding in a particular way, namely by thematising it from the *point of view of its successful performance*. In other words, in asking which condition must be fulfilled for meanings to be given to us at all, philosophy claims that there is a necessary connection between the givenness of meaning and operations of our understanding such that it is impossible that there can be any meaning given to us that exceeds our interpretive understanding in principle. The idea of such meanings is not intelligible, philosophy argues, because our activity of interpretation is constitutive of the meanings given to us.

It is precisely this connection between the givenness of meaning and the operations of our understanding that aesthetic experience also reveals. In playing with two possibilities of interpretation that we cannot decide between, it becomes clear to us that there can be no meaning that exceeds our interpretive understanding in principle because the latter is itself already constitutive of the givenness of the former. 'Beautiful things,' as Kant puts the point, 'indicate that the human being is suited to the world.'[34] Beautiful things, just as does philosophy, show us that there is an internal connection between the world of meaning and our capacities of interpretive understanding.

Yet aesthetic experience displays this connection between the world of meaning and the operations of our interpretive understanding in a quite special way: not in the medium of a conceptual analysis, as does philosophy, but rather in the medium of a concrete *experience* in which the operations of our interpretive understanding are *interrupted* entirely. For in aesthetic experience the groundlessness of our interpretive understanding is revealed to us precisely by the fact that we are faced with two hermeneutic circles between which we cannot decide, and this makes it impossible for us to interpret and comprehend the meaningful object in question. Aesthetic experience is experience of the groundlessness of our interpretive understanding, seen from the point of view of the thoroughgoing interruption of the latter. Thus, aesthetic experience looks at our interpretive understanding with different eyes than philosophy does - not examining it from within, from the perspective of its successful performance, but considering it in light of a *radical failure*. Thus, aesthetic experience renders visible the horizon within which our interpretive understanding is inescapably located precisely *on account of* its groundlessness: the horizon of the possibility of an undecidable choice between two hermeneutic circles, where, without grounds for deciding, there is no longer any route that leads to a justified interpretation. The groundlessness of our interpretive understanding places the latter within the horizon of a possibilty where an undecidable choice blocks the path of interpretation.

The difference between philosophy and art, consequently, pertains to their different viewpoints on our interpretive understanding.[35] While philosophy thematises our interpretive understanding from the point of view of its successful performance, art thematises it from the vantage point of its radical failure. The particularity of art with respect to philosophy, therefore, does not consist in saying something else about our interpretive understanding than philosophy does, but in illuminating from a quite different angle the insight into the workings of the interpretive understanding that philosophy, viewing interpretation from the vantage point of its successful performance, makes explicit. As conceptual analysis, taking its bearings from the successful performance of the operations of our interpretative understanding, philosophy is unable to show us our interpretive understanding from this other angle. Philosophy cannot come to terms conceptually with that which art, from its point of view, reveals about our interpretive understanding, because what is shown to us about our ordinary interpretive understanding in aesthetic experience is nothing other than the possibility of aesthetic experience itself: the possibility of a radical failure of our ordinary interpretive understanding. That the latter, on account of its groundlessness, is confronted with the possibility of an undecidability that brings it to a full standstill, is something only aesthetic experience can display to us precisely on account of the experience that it itself *is*. Thus, as conceptual analysis of the form of our ordinary interpretive understanding, taken from the vantage point of its successful performance, philosophy has a blind spot that it can only overcome by describing the experience of art. In order to see that every success of our ordinary interpretive understanding is inseparable from the possibility of radical failure, philosophy has no choice but to turn to art.

Notes:

1 When concerned with aesthetic experience, consequently, philosophy does not only reflect upon yet another form of experience: it also reflects upon itself. For the twofold nature of the relation between aesthetic experience and philosophy, compare, with reference to romanticism, the essay by Brigitte Hilmer, 'Kunst als Spiegel der Philosophie', and with reference to Kant, my own essay, 'Ästhetischer und philosophischer Gemeinsinn,' both included in Andrea Kern and Ruth Sonderegger, eds., *Falsche Gegensätze: Zeitgenössische Positionen zur philosophischen Ästhetik* (Frankfurt am Main: Suhrkamp Verlag, 2002).
2 Immanuel Kant, *Critique of Pure Reason*, ed. and trans. Paul Guyer and Allen W. Wood (Cambridge: Cambridge University Press, 1998), A 50/B 74, p.193.
3 Immanuel Kant, *Critique of the Power of Judgment*, ed. Paul Guyer, trans. Guyer and Eric Matthews (Cambridge: Cambridge University Press, 2000), § 9, p.103.
4 Kant, *Critique of Pure Reason*, B 146, p.254. See also B 75, p.193 f., and B 125, p.224.
5 Kant, *Critique of the Power of Judgment*, § 36, p.168.
6 Ibid. First Version of the Introduction, V, p.15.
7 Ibid. Introduction, VII, p.76.
8 Ibid. § 35, p. 167; see also § 9, p.109.
9 Ibid.
10 Ibid. § 9, p.102.
11 Ibid. § 40, p.175.
12 The objection to Kant's aesthetics made by the post-Kantians finds an exemplary expression in Gadamer's verdict that Kant subjectivised aesthetics. See Hans-Georg Gadamer, *Truth and Method*, second revised edition, translation revised by Joel Weinsheimer and Donald G. Marshall (New York: Continuum, 1998), pp.42-81.
13 Of course one finds discussions of art in Kant. Yet they cannot be squared with the definitions with which he characterises aesthetic experience in the 'Analytic of the Beautiful'. Hence, for Kant, aesthetic experience falls asunder into the act of judging beauty and the entirely different act of interpreting beautiful objects, and it is this second act that is investigated in his theory of art. That in Kant's case the theory of art and the theory of the beautiful cannot be made to agree has been shown at length in my

book *Schöne Lust: Eine Theorie der ästhetischen Erfahrung nach Kant* (Frankfurt am Main: Suhrkamp Verlag, 2000), Chs. I and II: for a summary, see pp.117-27.

14 See Kant, *Critique of the Power of Judgment*, § 49, p.191 ff.

15 Concerning this point, see Gadamer, *Truth and Method*, p.280 f.

16 Ibid. p.292 ff.

17 For this reformulation of the self-reflexive character of aesthetic experience see also Christoph Menke, *Die Souveränität der Kunst. Ästhetische Erfahrung nach Adorno und Derrida* (Frankfurt am Main: Suhrkamp Verlag, 1991), pp.19-91, who develops this understanding on the basis of Adorno's aesthetics.

18 For the concept of reading I am making use of here, see above all Paul De Man, *Allegories of Reading: Figural Language in Rousseau, Nietzsche, Rilke, and Proust* (New Haven and London: Yale University Press, 1979), ch. 1, 'Semiology and Rhetoric'.

19 Jacques Derrida, 'The Double Session', in *Dissemination*, trans. Barbara Johnson (London: The Athlone Press, 1981), p.220.

20 Concerning this example, see my more extended presentation in *Schöne Lust*, pp.201-27, where it is discussed along with two other examples (one of them a painting).

21 Maurice Blanchot, 'The Madness of the Day', trans. Lydia Davis, in *The Station Hill Blanchot Reader: Fiction and Literary Essays*, ed. George Quasha (Barrytown, NY: Station Hill Press and Barrytown, Ltd., 1999), p.191.

22 Ibid. p.199.

23 Jacques Derrida, 'The Law of Genre', trans. Avital Ronell, in *Acts of Literature*, ed. Derek Attridge (New York and London: Routledge, 1992), p.236.

24 Jacques Derrida, 'Living On: Borderlines', trans. James Hulbert, in Harold Bloom et al, *Deconstruction and Criticism* (New York: Continuum, 1984), p.99.

25 On this point, compare de Man, ch. 1. See also Derrida, 'The Double Session', p.280.

26 Derrida, 'The Double Session', p.231; see also p.221, where he speaks of an 'irreducible excess of the syntactic over the semantic.'

27 Ibid. p.225.

28 Derrida, 'Living On', p.155.

29 Jacques Derrida, 'Force of Law: The "Mystical Foundation of Authority"', trans. Mary Quaintance, in Drucilla Cornell, Michel Rosenfeld, and David Gray Carlson, eds., *Deconstruction and the Possibility of Justice* (New York and London: Routledge, 1992), p.26.

30 Gadamer, *Truth and Method*, p.293. On this point, see also Martin Heidegger, *Being and Time*, trans. John Macquarrie and Edward Robinson (New York: Harper and Row, 1962), § 32, pp.191-95.

31 See also Heidegger, *Being and Time*, § 32, p.195.

32 Cf. ibid. p.24.

33 For this sort of objection to Derrida, see in particular Jürgen Habermas, *The Philosophical Discourse of Modernity: Twelve Lectures*, trans. Frederick G. Lawrence (Cambridge, Mass.: The MIT Press, 1987), ch. VII, 'Beyond a Temporalized Philosophy of Origins: Jacques Derrida's Critique of Phonocentrism.'

34 Immanuel Kant, *Kant's gesammelte Schriften*, vol. XVI: *Kant's handschriftlicher Nachlaß, Logik*, ed. Königlich Preußische Akademie der Wissenschaften (reprint;

Berlin and Leipzig: Walter de Gruyter & Co., 1924), nr. 1820a, p.127. For a commentary on this passage from Kant's papers, see also Rüdiger Bubner, *Ästhetische Erfahrung* (Frankfurt am Main: Suhrkamp Verlag, 1989), p.121 ff.

35 For further elaboration on this point see *Schöne Lust*, esp. pp.296-310.

7
System of (Kantian) Pleasure (With a Freudian Postscript)

Jean-Luc Nancy
translated by Céline Surprenant

We are here proposing nothing else than a programmatic remark on the systematic place of 'pleasure' in the organization of the Kantian edifice as a whole. This remark emerges out of the commentary of the first sections - but mainly the third - of the First Introduction to the *Critique of Judgment*.[1]

As might be expected, the Kantian example and perspective here allows us to draw attention to the place of pleasure in philosophical thought in general: not to what philosophy thinks of pleasure, but to the extent to which a pleasure, some pleasure or 'pleasure' provokes thinking. Or else, to the extent to which thinking enjoys - and suffers. To the way in which thinking is systematically related to enjoying-and-suffering. To put it in still other words, it here allows us to draw attention to the extent to which thinking has no other object than a pleasure and/or a suffering: perhaps the tension towards what is precisely not an object, but the thing itself and the cause of all thought. In this matter, Kant is obviously not just any witness. The one, whose name no doubt evokes the least pleasure and the most ascetic rigour, will provide the best example.

*

It is under the heading of the 'system', the system of 'philosophy', 'of the powers of the mind' and 'of experience' that the whole of the First Introduction to the *Critique of Judgment* begins and concludes. The 'system of powers' is the system that must allow one to conceive of 'experience as a system,' that is, to endow this experience with the purposive organization that is lacking to the cognition of the object alone, as the *Critique of Pure Reason* defined it. It will thus be possible to establish a systematic correlation between '*theoretical* philosophy', which posits objects without purpose, and '*practical* philosophy', which posits the unconditioned purposiveness without object.[2] By tying purpose in general with experience, the systematic articulation must therefore ensure the purpose of philosophy itself, that is, 'the *system* of rational cognition through concepts.'[3] The critique has only prepared the conditions of such a system, by drawing out the two major concepts of 'nature' and 'freedom', and by demarcating them from each other. 'Purpose' or 'purposiveness' is what must ensure their connection without overstepping in any way their strict reciprocal delimitation.

From the point of view of the 'powers of the mind,' this delimitation is that of the understanding and reason. It is here that the determination of powers, and their distribution on each side of the strict boundaries of the critique take their full importance. The transcendental process requires the elementary considerations of powers as such, that is to say, both the consideration of their might and of their orders of legitimacy, therefore of their circumscriptions, their reciprocal division, and thus precisely, the consideration of powers in the plural. This plurality forms the unity of pure reason, and the condition of its systematicity.

The system of powers must thus be maintained not by a type of immediate unity such as the *intuitus originarius* (which would in fact not be strictly speaking a 'power,' but an *act executing* at once all its power, suppressing in itself all potentiality), but rather by another power. A third power is therefore introduced, which means at once the possibility of the connection of the two others, *and* the maintenance of their reciprocal delimitation through what could be called a supplementary delimitation. Neither cognitive nor imperative, and thus standing apart from these two modalities of imposition of a law in general, the *power of judgment* must simply make up for the absence of a legislation of the purpose, which would give *a priori* the content of such a legislation. It will thus have the task of conceiving of 'an *experience as a system in terms of empirical laws*,'[4] that is, an experience that should not be solely that of the object, but that of the 'necessity' of the whole of nature in its 'infinitely diverse' and its 'so very heterogenous' formations.[5] The 'necessity' of the whole is nothing else than the connection of nature, which is given, and of freedom, which is ordered, and this connection must present itself as purposiveness.

This is however only a question of the 'higher cognitive powers,' which are themselves 'at the basis of philosophy.'[6] As such, they designate and circumscribe the diverse registers of cognition of the object (understanding), of freedom (reason), and of the purpose (reflective faculty of judgment). The registers of philosophical knowledge are however not yet the modes of apprehension of presentations. A mode of the 'mind' corresponds to each register: that of 'cognition' *stricto sensu*, that of 'desire', and that of the 'feeling of pleasure and displeasure'.[7] Hence, philosophical knowledge, in its systematic unity, is called 'cognition' only in the broad, and above all, disjointed sense of the term [*qu'en un sens large et surtout inégal à lui-même*]. It is either a matter of the ('theoretical') cognition of the object (which, in knowing, knows itself to be limited to experience), or of the ('practical') cognition of the will (which, in knowing itself recognizes itself as freedom). Or else, it is a matter of a third kind of relation to presentations, which is the 'feeling of pleasure and displeasure.'

Only the first two 'powers' are here called 'powers' [*Vermögen*], and the third one is called 'feeling' - which, through its very name and the dissymmetry of the appellation, confers it at once the distinct tonality of what could be called, in a nutshell, 'passive power'. Without further ado, Kant thus treats the tripartition that Section III of the First Introduction brings in as a bipartition. On the one hand, there are the presentations that are 'referred merely to the object and to the unity of consciousness,' as well as presentations that are considered 'as cause of the actuality of the object,' and thus according to this other 'unity of consciousness,' which is the will (or desire). Generally speaking, this is the side of the object which is referred to the subject. On the other hand, there are presentations that 'are referred merely to the subject,' and this is the feeling of pleasure and displeasure. Here, presentations are not only 'mine,' while being presentations of an object and applying only to that object (nature or freedom), but they only ever apply to the object as mine, which amounts to applying only to themselves, since this 'mineness' does not send us back to any substantial subject of appropriation. Here, the 'presentations themselves are bases merely for preserving their own existence.'[8] The feeling of pleasure is the preservation of presentation for itself, without any other relation either to the object (of cognition or of action), or to the subject (of cognition or of action).

(As feeling of displeasure, let us add, it must be the refusal or the rejection of this very upholding, and, here again, without consideration for cognition or action. It is no doubt significant that Kant only gives a characterisation through pleasure, suddenly forgetting or cutting off the symmetrical 'and displeasure.' We cannot, however, here pursue the examination that would here be required. Besides, for the convenience of the present note, we will henceforth sometimes simply speak of 'feeling,' since in Kant in general it is to the *Gefühl der Lust und Unlust* that the *Gefühl* in general is brought back, and sometimes of 'pleasure', since Kant himself limits itself to it. The examination that we are now setting out to do will also show how delicate this simple matter of denomination could ultimately be: in fact, what exactly are we talking about?)

*

In conformity with the entire system that has just been briefly recalled, feeling should be carefully kept apart from the two other powers. Hence, as we already said, it is all the more distinct and separate since it is not even entitled to be called a 'power', and 'neither is nor provides any cognition at all.'[9] It is the non-cognitive mode of connection of presentations, and consequently the mode without legislation (without a given legality, either of the understanding or reason).

In fact, Kant notes, if it is easy to recognize 'empirically' a link between cognition or will and feeling, we cannot recognize anything there that is *a priori*. It is only in a contingent manner that a cognition or a volition can please or displease me, and therefore the beginnings of an 'organization' that we find here, by not being 'based on any *a priori* principle,' only gives an 'aggregate' and not a 'system' of faculties.[10]

At this point, Kant feels obliged to clarify that 'it is true that we can show [the following] *a priori* connection between the feeling of pleasure and the other two powers.'[11] What is at issue, he explains, is the connection of the *a priori* cognition of freedom with the will as the principle of freedom, a connection, which is nothing other than the link that is given in the form of the categorical imperative. So in this 'objective determination' (for it has an object of cognition and it involves at once the realisation of this object in experience), we 'can then find [*es gelingt . . . auszutreffen*] . . . [something] subjective as well: a feeling of pleasure.'[12] However, Kant immediately adds that this pleasure does not precede the will: it follows it, or 'perhaps is nothing other than our sensation of this very ability of the will to be determined by reason.'[13] Consequently, there is here, strictly speaking, no new *a priori* principle, which is yet what one is looking for in order to establish the autonomy of the 'higher power'.

Many things are worth noticing here. First, the exceptional 'case',[14] which Kant feigns to discover and which he immediately challenges, is constituted in a singular manner, since, on the side of the first power, it calls upon an '*a priori* cognition' that is not the cognition of an object, but that of freedom. However, this cognition, as we know very well, is knowledge [*wissen*] without perception or without comprehension [*einsehen*].[15] It is not of the same order as the cognition of the object (even though it is also the cognition of a fact of experience, and as such scibile).[16] Kant therefore cannot state that the first power is at issue here without a certain degree of distortion. If it is at issue, it is as the power of a paradoxical 'cognition', for being devoid of object, or having an object only in the having-to-be-object of its very object (a nature under the law of freedom). The first power is here, at best, present only in an amputated form, limited to the cognition of concepts without intuition - or else, whose intuition has a very particular character that would not appear to correspond to space-time conditions ... In any case, in this cognition, nothing else is cognised (nothing is theoretical) but the practical determination of reason.

If there is, however, something like intuition for there to be some knowledge, if there is something that should be grasped, perceived or felt [*eingesehen*], it could be in the order of feeling, which Kant introduces here. But he specifies that this feeling does not intervene in the *a priori* constitution of the practical determination of reason, which would be contrary to the autonomy of that determination. The 'connection' of the two first powers therefore remains at least incomplete, or seemingly unilateral, and it is therefore itself far from being 'connected' with the third power (it is remarkable that in both cases, Kant should use *Verknüpfung*, while the translation uses 'connection' and then 'to link' [*lier*]).

The feeling that can only ensue from the moral law is well known; it is respect. What Kant here says of its secondariness conforms to what he was saying about it in the *Critique of Practical Reason* ('On the Incentives of Pure Practical Reason'). He was then, however, also saying that this feeling 'of reason', 'is the only one that we can cognize completely *a priori* and the necessity of which we can have insight into [*einsehen*].'[17] The *einsehen* here appears to fade or to become somehow blurred in Kant's hesitation as to the nature of the said feeling ('or perhaps is ... '). Besides, respect is not mentioned, and the allusive periphrasis that can yet only point to it leaves us dissatisfied. For what is at issue is a 'feeling of pleasure', a quality that the *Critique of Practical Reason* energetically denies to respect: '*So little* is respect a feeling of *pleasure* that we give way to it only reluctantly with regard to a human being'.[18] But also '*so little displeasure* is there in it' that, in front of the moral law 'one can in turn never get enough of contemplating the majesty of this law.'[19] Whatever the case may be, respect is well and truly the pure *incentive* of pure practical reason. Here, the anonymous sentiment that redoubles it or that supplements it is nothing but the appreciation and the approbation of a 'talent,'[20] and does not amount to a 'special kind of feeling'.[21] From the one to the other, there is a displacement, indeed discordance. On the other hand, even though respect as an incentive has nothing to do either with pleasure or with displeasure, it nevertheless produces 'an *interest* ... which we call *moral* interest.'[22] The pure interest proceeds immediately from the fact that this feeling 'depends on the representation of a law only as to its form and not on account of any object of the law.' Respect therefore acts (or is structured) like a pleasure, that is, like the relation to itself of a presentation, which finds in itself a reason to remain . . .

In the main part of the *Critique of Judgment*, in §37, Kant presents the same argument in a slightly discrepant way, which is destined to exclude feeling from all determining apriority: 'I cannot connect *a priori* a definite feeling (of pleasure or displeasure) with any presentation, except in the case where an underlying *a priori* principle in reason determines the will; but in that case the pleasure (in moral feeling) is the consequence of that principle, and that is precisely why it is not at all comparable to the pleasure in taste . . .'.[23] The incomparable character of two pleasures does not deprive them of an identity of denomination that implies at least a close community of nature. In §12, Kant proposes another confused variation, by speaking of respect as 'a special and peculiar modification of the feeling of pleasure and displeasure which does not seem to differ somehow from both the pleasure and the displeasure we get from empirical objects:'[24] the 'modification' surely also implies some community of substance.

Now, this community is that of a rather particular apriority, which §12 expounds. The *a priori* that is impossible in the connection of feeling and of presentation is that of causality. It 'can never be cognised otherwise than *a posteriori*' that a feeling be the effect of a presentation (and this corresponds, either to agreeableness in the 'pathological order', or, in the moral order, to an 'intellectual presentation of the good', of which we know that it can only be the matter of a *'postulat'*.[25] On the other hand, there is a pleasure, which, without being the effect of a presentation, is nothing but this presentation itself relating to itself through an 'inner causality (which is purposive).'[26] Such is 'the state of mind of a will determined by something or other,'[27] and thus the state par excellence of the categorical imperative. This state is more 'in itself already a feeling of pleasure,' rather than being the cause of some affection or other. Pleasure is always the self-enjoyment of a presentation, that is to say, of a 'state of mind', in accordance with its pure form. This pleasure, however, can be either 'merely contemplative' or 'practical': that is, the form of the presentation can be either that of 'a merely formal purposiveness in the play of the subject's cognitive powers,' or that of the will. Nothing else distinguishes the two *'a priori* pleasures' but two forms or two states of mind, which are in themselves nothing but two ways of relating to itself: presentation as purpose for itself, or presentation as cause of its own reality. At this point, the two pleasures indeed are systematically related in the strongest sense of the term: the system of the cause and purpose of reason for itself.

But it is precisely here that we should once again summon up the rigorous distinction to which Kant ceaselessly comes back, as if in order to ward off the possible contamination of one pleasure by the other, or rather, and in spite of everything, the contamination of a pure will by a pure affection.

The distinction obliges us to affirm that the apriority of respect is not comparable to what it most resembles. What is incomparable is ultimately that with respect everything happens as with pleasure (*and* with displeasure) but nothing in it must please or displease. In respect, there is the form or the structure of pleasure, but not its taste or its flavour.

*

In order to cut short analyses that would otherwise need to be indefinitely refined,[28] let us say that pleasure is certainly not linked *a priori* with the power of desire, but rather that it is *a priori* included - which is at once less and more - as a refused or a forbidden pleasure, or as the singular pleasure that arises (in reason) from the *a priori* banishment of pleasure itself.

Kant's complicated and awkward discussion of the eventuality that is immediately rejected of an '*a priori* connection' thus plays a quite ambiguous role. It proposes fleetingly on the one hand, what it otherwise takes away on the other: something of pleasure, or, if one dares say so, of a 'pleasure principle', which has something to do with the power of desire of pure reason. There is a trace of the third power in the second.

We also saw, however, that in this connection, the power to cognise was present only in a restricted and doubtful fashion. In any case, it pertained only to the knowledge of freedom, which is knowledge without objective content (and the only one of its genre). It turns out however that if we consider the first power, we can also find an indication, in Kant himself, that there is another kind of trace of pleasure.

In the Second Introduction to the *Critique of Judgment*, we read that 'the concurrence of our perceptions with the laws governed by universal concepts (the categories) has not the slightest effect upon our feeling of pleasure; nor can there ever be any such effect, because the understanding proceeds with these [laws] unintentionally [*unabsichtlich*], by the necessity of its own nature.'[29] Moreover, this 'concurrence with the laws' is also a *Zusammentreffen*: in short, a meeting, and not a *Zusammenhang*, an internal organisation (which actually constitutes the *leitmotiv* of the First Introduction). Thus, 'it is a fact that when we discover that two or more heterogeneous empirical laws of nature can be unified under one principle that comprises them both, the discovery does give rise to a quite noticeable pleasure, frequently even admiration, even an admiration that does not cease when we have become fairly familiar with its object.'[30] The motif of a supreme pleasure of purposiveness is thus announced under the heading of 'admiration'. It runs through the last moments of the *Critique of Judgment*, both as a support and as a supplement to the thought of purposes which, if it does not make of this admiration 'the final purpose', yet attribute to it 'something about [it] similar to a *religious* feeling,' and, on this account, which 'seem[s] to affect the moral feeling . . . because we [then] judge [nature] in a way analogous to the moral way.'[31] Cognition could thus be promising itself a specific pleasure, no doubt contained within the limits of the conditions of reflective *judgment*, through which purposes are posited. A specific pleasure that would pass by itself beyond the theoretical in order to effect a kind of strengthening of the 'moral feeling' - once again, in a merely analogous fashion - and consequently, a strengthening of the pure motive of practical reason: *as if* something of the final purpose made itself known for determining the will. This something can certainly not be the unknowable freedom - but it cannot either be opposed to it, and should thus be the knowledge of freedom as knowledge enjoying itself.

The simple presentation of the purpose and of a pleasure under this analogical (or 'symbolic') condition, however, could not even be presented as an enjoyment of cognition if the former did not, from the outset, somehow contain its germ. In any case, this is what the rest of the passage in the Introduction states:

> It is true that we no longer feel any noticeable pleasure resulting from our being able to grasp nature and the unity in its division into genera and species that alone makes possible the empirical concepts by means of which we cognise nature in terms of its particular laws. But this pleasure was no doubt there at one time, and it is only because even the commonest experience would be impossible without it that we have gradually come to mix it in with mere cognition and no longer take any special notice of it.[32]

There has thus been, there must necessarily have been, a primitive pleasure of cognition. Kant no doubt is here only speaking of cognition through 'empirical concepts' and of the 'particular laws', and not of cognition through 'universal concepts' that he was recalling a few moments ago. The one is, however, not purely and simply separable from the other. Besides, Kant's text remains visibly hesitant. For it coordinates a 'comprehensibility of nature', which presumably corresponds to a general cognition of the type of the understanding, with a 'unity in [the] division into genera and species,' which is no longer a matter for the understanding alone, and which, on the contrary, creates the opportunity for, at least, the *Critique of Judgment*. At this point, physico-mathematical knowledge cannot be separated from biologico-chemical, or from that of culture and of taste, and the analogy moves on to determination . . .

If, from the point of view of the object, cognition produced by determinative judgment has nothing to do with cognition that proceeds from reflective *judgments* - no more than mechanism has to do with finality - the final unity of a nature nevertheless presupposes, as its minimal condition, the unity of nature in general, 'for without this *a priori* unity no unity of experience, and hence also no determination of objects of experience, would be possible.'[33]

Thus, 'the commonest experience' of which Kant speaks here is not in itself, in its generality and in its principle, divisible into *a priori* and *a posteriori* experience (in 'possible experience' and in empirical). On the contrary, what is at issue here is what, in the *a priori*, pertains from the outset to the *a posteriori* as such: the donation of the sensible material manifold, of its heterogeneousness and of the problematic character of its unity as a final unity. This a priority, which is neither that of the forms of intuition, nor that of concepts - nor even that of schematism - is the supplementary apriority of a feeling: of the self-enjoyment of a presentation of unity in general. Without this, we would not have even begun to be the subjects of any experience. If the most general condition for cognition through the understanding was the synopsis of intuition conjoined with the categorical synthesis,[34] it is still necessary to presuppose - what the *Critique of Pure Reason* did not have to worry about - something like a motive for the activity of cognition.

This motive can certainly only be found in the cognitive activity itself, and in short, in the relation of cognition to itself, that is to say, in the self-relation of the presentation as a connection, or in the self-relation of the connection of presentations. However, there must be a motive, which is to say that it is not sufficient that experience be possible; the mind still has to get going in order to carry out this possibility. This swaying can only take place through - or as - a feeling, and not only as the exposition of the principles of the possibility of experience.

It looks as though the *Critique of Judgment* discreetly also provided the mobilising transcendental, if one dare say so, of that which the *Critique of Pure Reason* had established only the *a priori* conditions of possibility with the bounds of their legitimacy. On the one hand, it is moreover as though the critical worry about demarcations of cognition had left the mobile or the spring of the act of cognition in the shadow. But on the other hand, it is simultaneously as though the question of such a motive had arisen here, on this side and beyond a simple critique of possible cognition - a question that is rarely raised for itself everywhere where the theory, and not freedom, is 'the *keystone* of the whole structure of a system of pure reason.'[35] If there is indeed trace of pleasure in the first of the powers of the mind, this trace is not simply a residue, it is an index of the destination of a reason whose *Trieb* effectively pushes towards an enjoyment that goes well beyond cognition: self-enjoyment.

On this account, it is surprising that when Kant states that 'the understanding, by proceeding according to its nature and without intention,' can experience no 'feeling of pleasure,' he appears to be oblivious to the fact that this process of the understanding, in so far as it involves the simple conformity of its activity with itself, offers exactly the conditions of the self-harmony that make pleasure . . . It may be precisely, however, what he detects when he speaks of a forgotten, lost or cooled off pleasure.

(We should still wonder whether we could find, on the side of theoretical pleasure, the element symmetrical to what practical pleasure presented to us as a connection with theoretical presentation, of which we noted that it then appeared as a first power limited to the concept without intuition. And no doubt this symmetrical counterpart is found in the universal communicability of aesthetic pleasure: this universal, which is a sensible and, if not strictly practical, a pragmatic universal is like a universal of the understanding now severed of its own legislation.)[36]

*

Once both the active and the thwarted presence of pleasure in the two powers of reason is acknowledged, it is possible to understand fully the 'transcendental definition' that Kant gives of it (after having established aesthetic judgment as the 'relation between the presentation and the feeling [of pleasure or displeasure]': [37]

> A definition of this feeling in general [terms], *without considering the distinction as to whether it accompanies sensation proper [Sinnesempfindung], or accompanies reflection, or the determination of the will*, must be transcendental. It may read: *Pleasure* is a mental *state* in which a presentation is in harmony with itself [and] which is the basis [*Grund*] either for merely preserving this state itself . . . or for producing the object of this presentation. On the first alternative the judgment about the given presentation is an aesthetic judgment of reflection; on the second, a pathological aesthetic judgment or a practical aesthetic judgment.[38]

This tripartition of aesthetic judgment is later abandoned in the *Critique of Judgment*, at least as far as its third term is concerned. This demonstrates once again the difficulty Kant has in attempting simultaneously to grasp a strict critical distribution of the 'powers' *and* what is nothing other than the unique motive of reason, its *Trieb* itself as *Triebfeder* (spring) of its supreme destination and, finally, as *Grund* of its very *rational* being. Pleasure is therefore less a third power than, as it appears in the *Critique of*

Judgment, the exhibition for itself of an active principle (indeed of the sole principle that is really active and mobilizing) within the theoretical and practical powers. Pleasure taken in isolation only manifests the form - self-harmony, self-preservation and self-enjoyment - of the intimate and ultimate motive of reason in its double authority. This form is active in theoretical reason - but it appears only as erased, or lost in habit - just as it is active in practical reason - but it appears only as restrained or sublimated in obedience.

Or rather, pleasure is active *as* theoretical and *as* practical reason, but this very activity requires that it be here impugned, there forgotten: in short, it requires that it be repressed on either sides, on two different but parallel modes. This repression of pleasure is necessary if the major critical precaution ought to be to ensure that reason does not find enjoyment immediately in itself, in the metaphysical *Schwärmerei* and in the pretension to give itself the Good of the Realm of Final Purposes. But this double repression is the condition that makes possible and necessary the exhibition of pure pleasure as the pure principle of a third faculty, which is both in charge of upholding the critical gap between the two others (this is the whole stake of the 'only reflective judgment') *and*, if one dare say so, of mobilising the unique motive of reason, in the form of a pleasure irresistibly one and diverse, identical to itself in the strangeness to itself [*identique à soi dans l'étrangeté à lui-même*].

Or else, if the concept of a repression runs the risk of too external an importation, and uselessly raises the question of a repressing agency, let us speak of a relinquishment: Kantian reason relinquishes, or is made to relinquish self-enjoyment - it does this as if to manifest that its destination is there, in this act of enjoyment that Spinoza called 'beatitude', 'joy', and that is announced here as a division of the self, a division within the self.

Pleasure is thus at the very heart of the system, and organises it. More exactly, what joins the heart of the system up and brings it into play, what gives it self-harmony and the internal purposiveness that makes genuine systematicity, is the feeling of pleasure and of displeasure. That is to say that if 'pleasure' is still the value of the ultimate destination, the deep structure is first of all that of self-relation, and of self-relation in so far as it is not given (but rather that it somehow mobilises itself only for itself), comprises essentially the ambivalence of the permanent possibility of disharmony. To please or to displease oneself: Kantian reason finds itself falling prey to this worry. This is why its stake is condensed in the final formula of the *Critique of Practical Reason*: '*the starry heavens above me and the moral law within me*' are the double object and the double spring of an 'ever new and increasing admiration' which at once 'annihilates, as it were, my importance as an *animal creature*, which after it has been for a short time provided with vital force . . . must give back to the planet (a mere speck in the universe) the matter from which it came' *and* 'infinitely raises my worth as an *intelligence* by my personality, in which the moral law reveals to me a life independent of animality.'[39]

This worry may appear to be narcissistic, and no doubt, it is. It is so, however, neither in the sense of a vain complacency or of an auto-eroticism, but in the sense in which narcissistic identification is necessary, and is the absence of identification (the very one of an *intuitus originarius*) that dramatically *founds* Kantian reason, in a double relinquishment - a forgetting and a prohibition - of self-enjoyment, of its principle and of its purpose.

*

'Pleasure identical to itself in the strangeness to itself': is this not the formula of pleasure itself and in general? More particularly, is this not the nature or the structure of difference to oneself that might be developed in Freud? I will here only indicate the principle of a possible analysis.[40]

First, there should be a short pause over the word *Lust*, that is always translated as 'pleasure,' whereas it can also have the meaning of 'desire', at any rate, of 'envy' - however what has been traditionally translated as 'desire' in Freud is called *Wunsch*, which in fact means 'wish', and which has less of an erotic connotation. *Lust* comprises, with the satisfaction that is found in pleasure (but that would rather be *Wollust*, 'sensual or voluptuous pleasure,' and *Befriedigung*, 'satisfaction' or, more literally, 'appeasement' - a very important term in Freud), the element or the moment of tension, of attraction and of excitation.

However, the moment of excitation presents Freud with a problem, the general form of which is the following: how can one find pleasure in what, in itself, is tension, and thus partly displeasure? Freud calls this particular pleasure *Vorlust* - preliminary pleasure - and distinguishes it from the *Endlust* - terminal pleasure, the pleasure of release, of discharge. The enigma of the *Vorlust* (raised in the *Three Essays on the Theory of Sexuality*) is repeated as the enigma of the aesthetic form (in *Jokes and their Relation to the Unconscious*): indeed, the form (as a case in point, that of the joke) does not properly give the pleasure that is sought, which must consist in an instinctual discharge. The form only gives access to this discharge, it makes it admissible and thus accessible. In this case, Freud calls it *Lustprämie* - 'yield of pleasure' - since here, the 'yield' allows a satisfaction, which is in principle forbidden, to pass through. The analogies between the aesthetic and the sexual registers are manifest: a passage through preliminary attraction for acceding to a satisfaction that is at first not acceptable to the ego and/or the super-ego, the 'formal' and 'partial' character of this attraction (it pertains 'only' to the aspect, only to an exteriority with respect to what must be enjoyed: the ingenious form of the joke, which Freud generalises as an aesthetic quality, or the pleasant form of a body for sight, the sense of smell, touch, as well as the drawing out of 'erogenous zones' on this body). Under the heading of *Vorlust*, there is thus an aesthetic of the sexed body and the eroticisation of the artistic form.

This chiasmus could help us resolve the enigma of the pleasure-of-tension. That is not it at all. In each of the two books (written during the same period on twin desks, as we know thanks to Freud himself), Freud refers us back to the other in order to clarify the analysis of this thorny issue. Pleasure that is not terminal bothers Freud: he cannot entirely fit it within a schema that is ultimately regulated by the lowering of tensions. (We should still add to this that terminal pleasure communicates almost immediately, for Freud, with impregnation: a purposive sexuality that sustains this pleasure.)

We should therefore deduce from this that *Lust* as such - the pleasure which does not consist in the entropy of desire, but on the contrary, in its upholding and in its intensification - does not exactly find its place here. However, it is equally in this way that *Lust* is most properly inscribed as pleasure: that is to say, not as satisfaction, as repletion, saturation, and/or lowering of tensions, but as the intensification and renewal of the *conatus*. The satisfaction or the discharge is on the side of equalisation, of neutralisation and of the identical. The tension is on the side of difference that does not become equal to itself. (Besides, it is this incomparable difference that I would be tempted to detect in Lacan's too famous formula: 'enjoyment is impossible', by turning it over: 'the impossible is enjoyment' - 'impossible' meaning here the infinitely incomparable difference. And it is also in this way that I would understand the sexual figures or roles, in so far as 'the woman' is the one who knows about enjoyment.)

There would thus be in Freud two logics of pleasure, and that of the *Vorlust* could well disturb the other, the one that leads to the 'beyond the principle of pleasure': for the *Vorlust*, or difference as pleasure (and not a pleasure taken in difference) might constitute by itself an entirely other 'beyond', this time internal to pleasure itself. Pleasure might be exactly what cannot be brought back to itself or in itself, and what can be 'identified' only as its difference from itself and in itself, or even as its *différance*.

But this difference as pleasure might therefore come close to what sets Kantian reason into motion: the impossibility of self-enjoyment in the order of a given self-identity, and the necessity to enjoy in the order and the tension of difference. Self-enjoyment and enjoying the other, being enjoyed - seduced, excited - by the other and making him/her enjoy are one and the same thing, which ceaselessly precedes and exceeds itself. There is no auto-eroticism. Pleasure is a structure of self-excess, like suffering. In pleasure, self-excess proceeds by attraction, in suffering, by repulsion.

Notes:

1 Immanuel Kant, *Critique of Judgment*, trans. W. S. Pluhar (Indianapolis and Cambridge: Hackett Publishing Company, 1987).
2 Ibid. Ak. 195, p.385.
3 Ibid.
4 Ibid. Ak. 204, p.392.
5 The passage to which I refer reads: 'For although experience forms a system in terms of *transcendental* laws, which comprise the condition under which experience as such is possible, yet empirical laws might be so *infinitely diverse*, and the *forms* of nature which pertain to particular *so very heterogenous*, that the concept [*Begriff*] of a system in terms of these (empirical) laws must be quite alien to the understanding, and that the possibility - let alone the necessity - of such a whole is beyond [our] grasp [*begriffen*]' (*Critique of Judgment*, Ak. 203, p.392).
6 Kant, *Critique of Judgment*, Ak. 201, p.391.
7 Ibid. Ak. 207, p.396.
8 Ibid. Ak. 206, p.395.
9 Ibid.
10 Ibid.
11 Ibid.
12 Ibid Ak. 207, p.395.
13 Ibid.
14 Concerning the 'case' in general in Kant (and even though the word 'case' - *Fall* - does not appear expressly at this point in the text), see Simon Zavadil's important thesis *Situation et modes de présentation du 'cas' dans la philosophie kantienne*, Strasbourg, Université Marc-Bloch, 1998.
15 See Preface of the *Critique of Practical Reason*.
16 See Kant, *Critique of Judgment*, in particular the 'General Comment on Teleology'
17 Immanuel Kant, *Critique of Practical Reason*, trans. and ed. M. Gregor (Cambridge: Cambridge University Press, 1997), 5:73, p.64.
18 Ibid. 5:77, p.66.
19 Ibid. 5:77, p.67.
20 Ibid. 5:78, p.67.
21 Ibid. 5:92, p.77.
22 Ibid. 5:80, p.68.
23 Kant, *Critique of Judgment*, Ak. 289, p.154.
24 Ibid. Ak. 222, p.67.
25 The passage reads: This pleasure is also not practical in any way, neither like the one arising from the pathological basis, agreeableness, nor like the one arising from the intellectual basis, the conceived good'; Kant, *Critique of Judgment*,

Ak. 222, p.68.
26 Kant, *Critique of Judgment,* Ak. 222, p.68.
27 Ibid. Ak. 222, p.67.
28 By passing through other texts of the *Critique of Judgment* and through the texts on pleasure in the Introduction to the *Metaphysics of Morals* and in the *Anthropology* (§64 sq.).
29 *Critique of Judgment*, Ak. 187, p.27.
30 Ibid.
31 Ibid. Ak. 482, p.377.
32 Ibid. Ak. 187, p.27.
33 Kant, *Critique of Pure Reason*, Trans. by W. S. Pluhar (Indianapolis and Cambridge: Hackett Publishing, 1996), A 216/B 263, p.281.
34 See Kant, *Critique of Pure Reason*, 'On the Deduction of the Pure Concepts of Understanding', Section II.
35 Kant, *Critique of Practical Reason*, 5:3, p.3.
36 Cf. in particular *Critique of Judgment*, §60 and §83, where one indeed reads: 'the fine art[s] and *the sciences* [my emphasis] . . . involve a universally communicable pleasure as well as elegance and refinement, and through these they make man, not indeed morally [*sittlich*] better for [life] in society, but still civilised for it'. (Ak. 433, p.321)
37 Kant, *Critique of Judgment,* Ak. 229', p.418.
38 Ibid. Ak 230-32, pp.419-20.
39 Kant, *Critique of Practical Reason*, 5:162, pp.132-3.
40 For a fuller analysis of this problem, see J.-L. Nancy, 'In Statu Nascendi' in *The Birth to Presence*, trans. B. Holmes (Stanford, California: Stanford University Press, 1993), pp.211-33.

8
Kingdoms of God

Kevin Hart

I

What are we being invited to imagine when presented with the picture of Kant after Derrida? First of all, I presume we are asked to see how the critical philosophy has very subtly changed because Derrida has written on it. It is a characteristic modern gesture, one that T. S. Eliot and J. L. Borges have made familiar to us.[1] After Derrida, Kant can never be quite the same again; and so our man would join Schelling, Hegel, Schopenhauer and Heidegger as figures who adjust how we construe the great philosopher of Königsberg. This latest understanding of Kant would enable us to view him from a new angle - from 'parergon', 'tone' or 'hyperjuridicalism', perhaps - and could well unsettle the German's sense of having laid incontestably solid grounds for science.[2] We might come to see Kant in the heaven of philosophers as saddened by a terrible loss, for his firm foundation for 'any future metaphysics' might seem rather less secure after we have read Derrida, all of him and not just what he has said about Kant.[3]

Or we might even come to see, if we squinted a little, that in some respects Kant himself is a severe critic of foundationalism. After all, the critical philosophy mounts a sustained attack on Christian Wolff's claim that logical and ontological grounds form a unity. Kant separated practical from both real and logical grounds, and thereby guaranteed the individual's freedom of action. The very same move, though, might also have set in train a historical reflection on the relation of ground and non-ground, one that has been extended and ramified by Derrida. If so, historians of philosophy might begin to find quite unexpected facets of Kantian brilliance.[4] As it happens, Kant thought that squinting was unhealthy.[5] Yet if one risks his disapproval and squints hard while reading him perhaps the philosopher concerned to establish incorrigible limits for reason, to judge the judges, and to determine universal laws will go out of focus and leave us with another Kant, a writer who anticipates Rimbaud's 'Je est un autre', someone 'who means Big Trouble for settled ways of thinking.'[6]

Were that to happen we might be tempted to regard Kant as 'after Derrida' in a way that Harold Bloom has taught us to appreciate, for the long dead German could seem to be imitating the French Algerian who lives in Ris Orangis.[7] Perhaps he would even, for febrile partisans of deconstruction, be seen as 'after Derrida', less important than him in the history of philosophy: a position that Derrida would be the first to dismiss.[8] Inevitably, given the nature of philosophy in the academy, this lopsided judgment, or anything approaching it, would quickly generate a new, feisty Kant who would be 'after Derrida', pursuing his arguments in the name of reason and not resting until justice has been done. In the future a new generation of Kantians would then be able to say that Kant is 'after Derrida': he has turned out to dominate, in ways no one could have foreseen, the decades that have followed people's wayward interest in the philosophy of difference. We are invited to picture all this and more in being offered the image of 'Kant after Derrida', and some people might reasonably complain they have already seen a good deal of that sort of thing, maybe far too much of it.[9]

We know very well that Derrida sometimes condenses complicated arguments about citationality, translation, and the relations of text and context in the titles of his works. Sitting alone above an essay, the title *Survivre* can mean 'living on', 'reprieve' or 'afterlife', as the text itself shows. Similarly, without a context *Pas* can mean 'stop' or 'not', and the dialogue beneath that title explores the effects of this undecidable word in the writings of Maurice Blanchot.[10] The general point has often been made that no text can be completely determined by context, yet perhaps it needs to be repeated with respect to particular cases. Does it need to be underlined, for example, that the proper names 'Kant' and 'Derrida' signify more than two individuals and two bodies of work? To ponder 'Kant after Derrida' could well be to glimpse new possibilities for rethinking the Enlightenment, humanism, the subject and rationalism. 'Derrida', here, would stand for post-modernism or post-structuralism, and a distinguished group would be gathered under the shelter of his name: Philippe Lacoue-Labarthe, Jean-François Lyotard, Paul de Man, Jean-Luc Nancy, Richard Rorty, and surely many others. Yet that too has become overly familiar, both the gesture and what tends to be uncovered.

Or perhaps that same vision, 'Kant after Derrida', might jolt us so that we begin to take more seriously doubts about the critical philosophy that were raised by Kant's contemporaries, worries that now come into focus because we have read Derrida. In this way J. G. Hamann's metacritique of 'the purism of reason' would come to be seen as anticipating deconstruction, albeit in a direction that does not converge with Derrida's own work.[11] Once we are thinking along these lines, we would not be out of order to contemplate someone before Kant who, from this or that perspective, can seem uncannily like Derrida, someone who has become more visible for us now only because we have studied *De la grammatologie* and all the rest. People have sometimes spoken of Gorgias, Meister Eckhart, John Duns Scotus and even David Hume in these terms;[12] and the invitation on offer is to read Kant as overcoming an earlier form of sophistry, scepticism or nihilism, or succumbing to one or more of these in ways that we simply have not realised.

It is also possible, and perhaps more interesting in the long run, to recognise that 'Kant' is a signature as well as a name, and that it may be found as a countersignature that neither Plato nor Aristotle, Leibniz nor Wolff, could have foreseen when they signed their texts. Kant does not receive a single tradition and pass it on. He acquires different legacies from the past and situates them in a singular manner, and one cannot begin to read him without determining the plurality of his inheritance. Certainly Derrida has encouraged us to approach major writers in just this way, and long before he spoke of improbable countersignatures he had meditated on the difficulties of textual transmission through history.[13] It was Edmund Husserl in *The Origin of Geometry* who maintained that the contingency and materiality of writing, *Verkörperung*, can be bracketed, leaving only the pure possibility of embodiment, *Verlieblichung*. And it was Derrida who argued that in language *Verkörperung* and *Verlieblichung* cannot be separated: no text can be protected in advance from being misread or misdelivered.[14] Nor is this the only difficulty associated with textual transmission, for an earlier philosophy cannot maintain a strict self-identity, even if it had it in the first place, once it has been taken into a later philosophy. Derrida makes the point with respect to attempts to uncover Platonic and Aristotelian elements in Kant. The motifs original to the Greeks cannot be detached from the German's works and returned to one or the other. 'Folded into a new system, the long sequences are displaced: their sense and their function change. Once inserted into another network, the "same" philosopheme is no longer the same, and besides it never had an identity external to its functioning.'[15]

On this account of tradition, motifs we associate with *The Critique of Pure Reason* or *Groundwork of the Metaphysic of Morals*, for example, will function differently in the work of those who come after Kant than they do in the writings of the master himself. But who comes after Kant? Who countersigns his treatises and essays? Philosophers of course, but also all kinds of other folk, including theologians. With this in mind, we could see how Kantian themes have been variously folded, unfolded and refolded in nineteenth- and twentieth-century theology. It would be an immense project, for the Kantian scansion of 'faith and reason', along with his demolition of the ontological and cosmological arguments for the existence of God, have massively influenced theology after him, especially in the Protestant churches. More generally, a Kantian stress on freedom and ethics can be found everywhere in modern theology from transcendental Thomism to liberation theology. Even Protestant theologians who eschew philosophy and say with the reformers *sola Scriptura* have found themselves to be beneficiaries of biblical themes with a Kantian inflection. And even those theologians who answer to Schleiermacher and Hegel, and therefore belong to traditions that dispute the Kantian attempt to centre religion in ethics, are nonetheless marked by the different ways in which those two mighty thinkers reacted to the critical philosophy. Schleiermacher insisted, in Kantian fashion, that religion can adduce its own ground in feeling, and influenced the Troeltsch who later argued for the 'religious *a priori*'; while Hegel sought to overcome the distinction between phenomena and *noumena*. Taking only those theologians who make explicit use of Kant, we can identify three main sequences.

The first is the liberal school, centred on Albrecht Ritschl and Wilhelm Herrmann, whose Kant is profoundly anti-metaphysical and ethical.[16] Not all liberals are against metaphysics, however, at least not as Kant understood the word. He followed Christian Wolff in distinguishing 'general metaphysics' or ontology from three areas of 'special metaphysics': psychology, cosmology and theology. It is one thing to deny that theology is a special metaphysics and quite another to say that theology has no interest in ontology. Consider Paul Tillich who developed a comprehensive theology of correlation, with roots reaching back to Kant, in which religious symbols are taken to be implicit answers to questions arising from culture, while also constructing a religious ontology. A second sequence features Joseph Maréchal, Bernard Lonergan and Karl Rahner, for whom Kant is first and foremost the philosopher of transcendental subjectivity who enables us to read Thomas Aquinas afresh. As Rahner put it in 1966, 'dogmatic theology today must be theological anthropology,' and there is to be no going back, he thought, on 'modern philosophy's transcendental anthropological change of direction since Descartes, Kant . . .'[17] Finally, a third sequence passes through neo-orthodoxy, most notably in the work of Karl Barth for whom Kantian epistemology is entitled to announce the grounding questions about God - the relevant section of the *Church Dogmatics* is called 'The Knowability of God' - while that epistemology is forbidden to retain pride of place when faith begins to be properly understood.[18]

One of Kant's notions that theologians, especially those of a liberal stamp, have repeatedly countersigned is his interpretation of the kingdom of God as an ethical commonwealth.[19] I would like to organise a brief reading of Kant around his treatment of the kingdom, and would like to keep my reading sufficiently open so I can be attentive to the legacy that Derrida receives from the Kantian doctrine of the kingdom. Inheritance is itself a theme of the kingdom (Luke 12:32), though it jostles against competing themes. I will not be able to begin at the beginning, whether it be in the Hebrew Bible or *Targumim* or the New Testament, for the expression 'kingdom of God' is neither simple nor singular there; and no one would be surprised to learn that it was folded in quite different ways by the Church Fathers. For Irenaeus, the kingdom will be a divine reign on earth after the general resurrection.[20] Yet, for Origen, Christ himself is the kingdom.[21] Eusebius, perhaps trying to educate the Emperor, declared Constantine to have ushered in the kingdom, thereby allowing it to be bodied forth as μοναρχια, while Augustine maintained that the church and the kingdom form a unity here and now, although they are not yet identical.[22]

The kingdom could never have remained exclusively a theological theme; others were always listening when it was being talked about. Since the Enlightenment philosophers and poets have appealed to the idea in their social thought, especially when it has had a utopian bent. Kant sharply creases the notion although, like others before and after him, he takes himself to be unfolding it rather than folding it anew. There is a tradition that the kingdom is a mystery or a secret. Jesus says to the twelve, 'Unto you it is given to know the mystery [μυστηριον] of the kingdom of God; but unto them that are without, all these things are done in parables' (Mark 4:11). On Kant's understanding, however, the kingdom is not a mystery or a secret: it is not a coded message proclaimed by a messianic cult, or that which is signified by baptism or the eucharist; and his moral philosophy, wholly reasonable and universal, elaborates itself with reference to it. Before turning to that philosophy, however, I take fair warning from Derrida: 'One always inherits from a secret - which says "read me, will you ever be able to do so?"'[23]

II

What was Kant reading about the kingdom? The Gospels of Matthew and Luke, to be sure, since he cites them in old age when writing *Religion within the Limits of Reason Alone*. Earlier he may have dipped into Johannes Cocceius whose *Summa doctrinae de Foedere et Testimento Dei* was well received by the pietists who influenced him so strongly in his youth. Cocceius's doctrine of a covenant of grace that would have the kingdom as its historical horizon certainly brought the kingdom to the attention of Enlightenment thinkers. If Kant did not encounter Cocceius, directly or indirectly, the theme of the kingdom would have arisen for him in hearing the fierce discussion in 1770s about Hermann Reimarus's view that Jesus saw himself as a political messiah.

The kingdom breaks into the *Critique of Pure Reason*, though not until the end is almost in sight, when the questions 'What ought I to do?' and 'What may I hope?' are posed. Answering the first of these, Kant says, 'I entitle the world a *moral world*, in so far as it may be in accordance with all moral laws.'[24] This world is intelligible when considered as a moral structure. It is only an idea - granted; but it is nevertheless a practical idea. It refers to the sensible world 'as an object of pure reason in its practical employment, that is, as a *corpus mysticum* of the rational beings in it.'[25] The Latin expression abbreviates *corpus Christi mysticum*, an adaptation of the Pauline metaphor of the Church as the body of Christ, although the gloss on it - 'the free will of each being is, under moral laws, in complete systematic unity with itself and with the freedom of every other'[26] - quickly removes the faintest hint of an appeal to patristic ecclesiology. Kant soon reveals that he is following Gottfried Leibniz when he distinguishes the 'kingdom of grace' [*Reich der Gnade*] from the 'kingdom of nature' [*Reich der Natur*].[27] In the *Monadology* Leibniz had proclaimed that 'This city of God [*cité de Dieu*], this truly universal monarchy, is a moral world within the natural world' and had spoken of a 'harmony which appears between the physical realm of nature and the moral realm of grace.'[28]

'Kingdom of God' translates βασιλειας του θεου, and like all authoritative translations it both adds to and substracts from the original. When removed from its inaugural context in the gospels, the word βασιλεια loses a good deal of its richness: in the synoptic gospels it signifies the full lordship of God which is here yet to come, and the parables about it are extremely hard to harmonise, even when the strange logic of 'already but not yet' is duly acknowledged. However, when βασιλεια is cast as *regnum*, *Reich*, *royaume* or kingdom, a sense of a fully realised and observable state is quietly added to the Greek. This additional meaning is retained by Leibniz when he writes of the 'city of God', a metaphor that goes back at least as far as Origen who speaks of 'the city of God' [η πολις του θεου] in his homilies on Jeremiah. More than likely, though, Leibniz is alluding to Augustine for whom the βασιλεια is one of two cities formed by two loves, 'the earthly by the love of self, even to the contempt of God; the heavenly by the love of God, even to the contempt of self . . . For the one seeks glory from men; but the greatest glory of the other is God, the witness of conscience.'[29] Kant maintains the image of the βασιλεια as a city, and it is well to keep in mind that he is an heir to Augustine in more than one way.

A hint of the βασιλεια is next found in the *Groundwork*, in the third formulation of the categorical imperative. At first the categorical imperative is framed in order to stress that morality should be in accordance with a universal law: '*Act only on that maxim through which you can at the same time will that it should become a universal law.'*[30] Such is the moral law. Then the imperative is rephrased to underscore the dignity of persons: *'Act in such a way that you always treat humanity, whether in your own person or in the person of any other, never simply as a means, but always at the same time as an end.'*[31] The two formulations converge, for a rational being, considered as an end in himself or herself, must also be a legislator of any universal law to which he or she is subject. Because the law is universal and because one must always treat other persons as ends in themselves, Kant is able to make good the claim about a *corpus mysticum* that he made in the *Critique of Pure Reason*. He heralds 'a world of rational beings (*mundus intelligibilis*)' that is 'possible as a kingdom of ends - possible, that is, through the making of their own laws by all persons as its members.'[32] So the categorical imperative is revised once again, this time as a formula concerning a moral community: 'every rational being must so act as if he were through his maxims always a law-making member in the universal kingdom of ends.'[33] 'What may I hope?' opens to include the question 'What may *we* hope?'

Kant placed the kingdom of ends last in his working out of the categorical imperative, and made comparatively little of it (there is no spacing out for emphasis, for example), mainly because he feared that we might mistake our moral goals as being prior to our affirmation of the moral law itself. Yet the kingdom of ends is the basis for his elaboration of the ethical commonwealth in *Religion within the Limits of Reason Alone*. In the first two *Critiques*, and as late as the essay 'On the Proverb: That May be True in Theory, But Is of No Practical Use', Kant figured the highest good as having no reference to any earthly end at all, including human happiness.[34] Since it is the end of the moral law, the highest good imposes itself upon us as that which we must strive to realise; and since experience gives us no assurance that happiness and virtue will be achieved together in this world, the highest good must exist in a supersensuous world.[35] Only in the *Critique of Judgment* and *Religion* is there a relenting of this formalism and an image given to us 'of a visible kingdom of God on earth [*Reich Gottes auf Erden*].'[36] Not only is the βασιλεια 'being brought ever near' but also it is to be understood as eventually 'arriving'[37]; it will be 'the highest good possible on earth.'[38] Although Kant does change his mind about the realisation of the highest good between the second and third *Critiques*, there is no justification to talk of him passing from a religious to a secular notion of it.[39] Like Irenaeus, Kant comes to understand the βασιλεια as the kingdom of God on earth, and its being on earth does not of itself make the notion 'secular'.

Anyone examining the structure of this ethical commonwealth will note that all individuals must undergo a change of heart in order to belong to it, whereas the commonwealth itself unfolds gradually through history. There is no need to talk of a 'stark contrast' here, for there is no ground against which a difference could be seen: conversion is the *sine qua non* for membership of the commonwealth.[40] It is entirely possible, Kant thinks, for all members of a juridico-civil society [*rechtlichbürger Zustand*] also to belong to the ethico-civil society [*ethischbürgerlicher Zustand*], that is, the ethical commonwealth [*ethischen gemeinen Wesens*]. This is the hope that the βασιλεια inspires in us. Yet of course in the present it is quite feasible to be a good citizen in a juridico-civil society and not belong to the ethical commonwealth. One can be coerced to be a good citizen though not to be a good person. Indeed, on Kant's account, the Jews may be good citizens although they have no sense of an ethical commonwealth: the βασιλεια has no decisive relation to the Hebrew scriptures, he thinks.[41] We need to remember that the Christian faith is never neutral in Kant's philosophy of religion; on the contrary, he thinks it is the only public religion which is moral.[42]

The highest good is a consequence of following the moral law which 'unfurls a banner of virtue as a rallying point for all who love the good.'[43] An ethical-civil society, consisting of those who love the good, must exist within juridico-civil societies if the highest good is to be disseminated over the earth. To be sure, the ethical commonwealth is founded by God; however, we are not to wait for God to act. 'Rather must man proceed as though everything depended on him; only on this condition dare he hope that higher wisdom will grant the completion of his well-intentioned endeavors.' [44] The Christian will therefore live in two societies, hoping for one of them to pass away in the fullness of time. This image might seem to set Kant at variance to Augustine who writes of 'two diverse and conflicting cities.'[45] Yet the *civitas terrena* and the *civitas dei* will be separated only at the Last Judgment; and in truth they are not rival kingdoms, for the *civitas terrena* is at heart a privation of the good.[46] Where Kant differs most from Augustine is in affirming a development of the ethical commonwealth: the *civitas dei* changes only by getting larger (although Augustine's late doctrine of predestination makes even this doubtful).[47] And where Kant is closest to Augustine is in recognising that the commonwealth is an invisible community, what the saint called the 'invisible bond of love' [*invisibilis caritatis compages*].[48] For Kant there is 'a certain analogy' between the two societies, and because of this the ethical commonwealth can be regarded as an 'ethical state' [*ethischer Staat*] or what Kant falls a 'kingdom of virtue' [*Reich der Tugend*][49]. In making this move, Kant folds the *basileia* in a complicated way, and I will consider it in some detail.

To understand the *basileia* as an 'ethical state' is not to regard it merely as a modification of a political state, not even one that seeks to improve itself. It is, however, to conceive it in relation to the church. This conception requires several distinctions, and Kant gathers them together when entertaining the question, 'What period in the entire known history of the church up to now is the best?'

> I have no scruple in answering, *the present*. And this, because, if the seed of the true religious faith, as it is now being publicly sown in Christendom, though only by a few, is allowed more and more to grow unhindered, we may look for a continuous approximation to that church, eternally uniting all men, which constitutes the visible representation (the schema) of an invisible kingdom of God on earth . . . The true (visible) church is that which exhibits the (moral) kingdom of God on earth so far as it can be brought to pass by men. [50]

Here the basileia is required to pass through a distinction between the visible and the invisible church. More than likely, Kant would have come across the distinction, directly or indirectly, by way of Calvin's discussion of it in *Institutes* IV:1,7. Yet the distinction has grown luxuriantly in the west; it was planted by Augustine in soil prepared by Origen and Clement of Alexandria, and it is easy to point to any number of Catholic and Protestant counter-signatures to Augustine here.[51] The 'church invisible' for Kant 'is not an object of possible experience'; it is 'a mere idea of the union of all the righteous under direct and moral divine world-government, an idea serving all as the archetype of what is to be established by men.'[52] Its counterpart, the 'visible church', is 'the actual union of men into a whole which harmonises with that ideal.'[53] The true church - the visible one that continually approaches pure religious faith - will be universal, motivated only by duty, organised with respect to freedom, and unchangeable in its fundamental constitution.

The ethical commonwealth, Kant tells us, is not political. It is 'a mere *representative* of a city of God [*blobe* Repräsentantin *eines Staats Gottes*],'[54] he says, although he uses two of the most highly charged words in the entire vocabulary of politics in making that claim: 'representative' and 'city' (or, more accurately, 'state' or even 'city state'). The commonwealth is not monarchical, aristocratic or democratic; the best model for it is 'a household (family) under a common, though invisible, moral Father, whose holy Son, knowing His will and yet standing in blood relation with all members of the household, takes His place in making His will better known to them; these accordingly honour the Father in him and so enter with one another into a voluntary, universal and enduring union of hearts.'[55] One might well wonder if the notion of family has ever been unpolitical. Certainly a politics can be discovered in a family whose daily activities turn on an invisible father and a son and no mention is made of the mother. More to the point, when Kant goes on to speak of members of the church he does not choose familiar relations but civic ones.

Clinging to the Augustinian metaphor of the city of God, Kant tells us that we are obliged 'to behave not merely as men but also as *citizens* [*Bürger*] in a divine state on earth'[56]. Yet Kant's *Bürger* are not quite the same as Augustine's *cives*. For the German philosopher every member of the kingdom of ends is both legislator and subject: 'though each obeys the (non-statutory) law which he prescribes to himself, he must at the same time regard this law as the will of a World-Ruler revealed to him through reason,'[57] but in effect mortals and God are still co-legislators. How could *God* be king in such a kingdom? How could it be a *king*dom? How could it be harmonised with the parables and sayings of the *basileia* which invoke the absolute lordship of God?

Any answer to these questions would have to be considered with reference to 1 Peter 2:9 ('But ye are a chosen generation, a royal priesthood [βασιλειον ιερατευμα]'), although I doubt that even the most subtle exegesis would allay all anxiety. Rather than follow that path, I pause to note that Kant is bothered by a rather different question: 'How does God wish to be honored in *a church* (as a congregation of God)?'[58] Only revelation can supply an answer, and it is contained in a contingent and publicly experienced historical faith which results in several instances of 'ecclesiastical faith'.[59] When discussing the distinction between the visible and the invisible church, I quoted Kant talking about 'the seed of the true religious faith', and this 'religious faith' is to be distinguished from 'ecclesiastical faith'. It is 'concerned only with what constitutes the essence [*Materie*] of reverence for God, namely, obedience, ensuing from the moral disposition, to all duties as His commands,'[60] and therefore is not a matter of experience. Ecclesiastical faith is not essential to religious faith but is merely its 'vehicle'[61]: not as a developing tradition (as for Catholics) but as the preserver of scripture (as for the Reformers).

That said, Kant does not maintain the metaphor of ecclesiastical faith as a 'vehicle' [*Vehikel*] but begins to speak of a 'transition' [*Übergang*] from ecclesiastical to religious faith, from experience to non-experience. This is by no means a straightforward movement, since religious faith, as a saving faith, has a dimension of atonement as well as a dimension of moral action, and therefore it would seem that there can be no jettisoning of ecclesiastical faith. Since Jesus is the one who has brought about our atonement, there must always be a historical reference to him. Or so it would seem. If we separate 'Jesus' and 'Christ' we can maintain the purity of religious faith by downplaying the historical Jesus and elevating the Christ of faith, 'the archetype, lying in our reason.'[62] It is not the preaching of Jesus that heralds the βασιλεια for Kant. Rather, as he puts it in a chapter title, 'The Gradual Transition of Ecclesiastical Faith to the Exclusive Sovereignty of Pure Religious

Faith is the Coming of the Kingdom of God'.[63] Notice that the passage from ecclesiastical to religious faith, as announced here, brings about not the *basileia* but its coming. The church remains the 'church *militant*'[64] until the transition is entirely complete. Or, if you like, there is no 'church *triumphant*' until there is a triumph of ethics, and this entails the complete extinction of all religious experience. Notice too that Kant distinguishes two kingdoms: the 'Kingdom of God' [*Reichs Gottes*] and the 'Sovereignty of Pure Religious Faith' [*Alleinherrschaft des reinen Religionsglaubens*]. Only when pure religious faith is all powerful will God bring about his kingdom. We remember that only when God founds his kingdom can men and women work towards bringing about the sovereignty of pure religious faith. Although we must acknowledge that God is the supreme power at the beginning and end of time, in history it is moral faith that must come to rule, and in terms of that faith we are co-legislators with God. Kant's *caput mysticum* appears to be just another part of the *corpus mysticum*.

III

'The Teacher of the Gospel revealed to his disciples the kingdom of God on earth only in its glorious, soul-elevating moral aspect, namely, in terms of the value of citizenship in a divine state...'[65] To hear Kant talking about the βασιλεια is to be struck by a tension between an unearthly Christ, no more than 'the personified idea of the good principle',[66] and the insistence that the βασιλεια is to be realised 'on earth'. It is also to be conscious that the reading of Jesus' parables and sayings is highly reductive, paying no attention to the presentation of the βασιλεια as excessive, mysterious and violent, and bypassing the great petition of the Lord's Prayer in which God is asked to act: 'Thy kingdom come [ελθετω η βασιλεια σου]' (Matt. 6:10). It is to be uneasily aware of a tension between the image of 'earth' and 'citizenship'. Like Augustine's City of God, Kant's ethical commonwealth is defined against man in the state of nature, although nature itself is also left out of the picture. Nature is sidelined by Origen and Augustine in representing the βασιλεια as a city, and then occluded by Kant in locating the βασιλεια in a moral realm that is sharply distinguished from the natural realm. The βασιλεια as the consummation of creation, a recreation of the natural and spiritual realms, is not a Kantian theme.

These and other features of the Kantian ethical commonwealth have been folded and refolded in theology for the past two hundred years. One finds them in Ritschl's theology of justification and reconciliation, in the *Kulturprotestantismus* with which it is sometimes too readily linked, in the 'social gospel' of Walter Rauschenbush and the Swiss religious socialists - in fact, in all modern theology whenever the basileia is not interpreted eschatologically.[67] Even when the basileia is interpreted eschatologically, as in neo-orthodoxy, it is placed at a remove from nature. With all this in mind, I would like to recall what Jacques Derrida names the '"Kantian" gesture', namely, 'the circumspect and suspensive attitude, a certain *epoché* that consists - rightly or wrongly, for the issue is serious - in thinking religion or making it appear "within the limits of reason alone."'[68] Derrida said these words on Capri in 1994, in the company of several other philosophers. His remarks are centred on the theme of 'faith and knowledge', although they intersect with another theme, one that he makes apparent when he identifies the political sympathies of his fellow philosophers on the island:

> an unreserved taste, if not an unconditional preference, for what, in politics, is called republican democracy as a universalisable model, binding philosophy to the public "cause", to the *res publica*, to "public-ness", once again to the light of day, once again to the "lights" of the Enlightenment . . .'[69]

Against the general wash of these remarks, Derrida asks, 'what of this "Kantian" gesture today? What would a book be like today which, like Kant's, is entitled, *Religion within the Limits of Reason Alone?*'[70] The *epoché* 'within the limits of reason alone' is not asocial, Derrida reminds us, it:

> gives its chance to a political event . . . It even belongs to the history of democracy, notably when theological discourse was obliged to assume the forms of the *via negativa* and even there, where it seems to have prescribed reclusive communities, initiatic teachings, hierarchy, esoteric insularity or the desert.[71]

Derrida is not updating or rewriting Kant's treatise. His essay is entitled 'Faith and Knowledge: the Two Sources of "Religion" at the Limits of Reason Alone', and it weaves together motifs by Hegel and Bergson as well as Kant.[72] The Kantian *epoché* is reset: Derrida does not speak of religion *within* the limits of reason alone but of 'religion' *at the* limits of reason alone. In titling his essay 'Faith and Knowledge' he draws attention to the doublet inherited by Hegel from Kant. Yet his interest is not so much in 'faith and knowledge' as a traditional topos in the philosophy of religion as in what he makes these stand for: the incalculable and the calculable, social credence and tele-technology. These stand for apparently distinct ways of spreading different 'kingdoms'.

Tele-technology is used to evangelise: for example, to promote the pure scriptural teaching of a kingdom to be inaugurated with the second coming of Christ. Yet there can be no iteration of a faith without the possibility of corrupting the holiness to which it testifies, a possibility that is realised time and again, and that results in what Kant diagnosed as the *parerga* to religion within the limits of reason alone: fanaticism, superstition, illuminatism and thaumaturgy. No appeal to the 'anti-modernist oath', as happened in the Catholic Church under Pius X, or to the letter of the Bible, as still happens among fundamentalists, can eliminate the possibility of debasing the holy. It is a structural trait of the relation between holiness and faith, and indeed oaths of loyalty and affirmations of biblicism sew their own seeds of corruption. Against this iteration of faith and the essential possibility of introducing evil, Derrida urges us to take part in a democracy to come, 'a universalisable culture of singularities'.[73] He does not see this 'democracy to come' as an iteration of the βασιλεια, although it is, but as a way of sidestepping testimonies to the holy, which it also is. To speak of Derrida's βασιλεια might seem inappropriate given that he affirms a democratic republic and that he 'quite rightly passes for an atheist.'[74] Yet the βασιλεια has been delivered or misdelivered to Derrida, as to many others, Marx and Ritschl no less than Kant; it might even be regarded as one of their secret inheritances. In Derrida's case it has come by way of a liberal Christianity made possible by Kant. That is not to say that Derrida merely repeats Kant but that he receives generously from him, including elements that could be criticised before being reinscribed.

Derrida's title indicates two moments when he distances himself from Kant. First, in placing 'religion' within quotation marks, he suggests not only a prudent reserve in dealing with such a fraught and massive concept but also an awareness that, in his treatment, religion is no longer to be simply religion. It is not a matter of rethinking religion as duty and what borders it, as Kant did, but of refiguring faith and holiness in the wake of the sage of Königsberg. In fact it is a wake for God since, for Derrida, Kantian ethics turn in effect on the death of God (11-12). If religion is within the limits of reason alone, and this religion answers to the universal moral law and we are not required to ponder how God supplements our adherence to duty, then God does not count in the exercise of our religion. Second, in recasting 'in the' as 'at the' Derrida suggests that his treatment of religion will differ considerably from Kant's. There will be no attempt to position himself at the very source of law, as Kant does, to enclose all discourse within the gaze of a philosopher-judge. Instead, he will speak 'at the limits of reason alone'. Negatively, this means that he will be focused on the evils of dogmatic abuse, the *parerga*, and positively it means he speaks with an awareness that religion, as he conceives it, will not abide within the limits of the possible, within the generality of the law, but will be excessive and will pass through the incalculable or the impossible.

The ethical kingdom of liberal theology was severely taken to task at the end of the nineteenth century by Johannes Weiss for ignoring the eschatological dimension of the βασιλεια. 'The Kingdom of God as Jesus thought of it is never something subjective, inward, or spiritual, but is always the objective messianic Kingdom, which usually is pictured as a territory into which one enters, or as a land in which one has a share, or as a treasure which comes down from heaven.'[75] The βασιλεια has no essential connection with the ethical progress of a community; it breaks into the world in order to reorient it to God. Now although Derrida identifies and analyses an 'apocalyptic tone', he does not propose a βασιλεια as a realised or realisable eschatology. Not at all: Derrida's βασιλεια, if I can continue to call it that, remains thoroughly ethical, like Kant's, although his ethics differ from the German's in that it incorporates a recoding of eschatology as unrealisable. 'The future is that from which we are provoked to take a responsibility, and to say, beyond a determining knowledge, "come".'[76] Like Kant, Derrida abstracts the kingdom from particular messianisms; and like Kant he affirms a universal structure, which he calls the messianic. Unlike Kant, Derrida does not enforce a sharp distinction between faith and reason: for him, reason works in tandem with a non-religious form of faith: *croyance* rather than *foi*.[77] Also unlike Kant, Derrida does not construe ethics as the evacuation of experience but rather regards the call prior to all others, 'come', as its very opening.[78]

Can one grasp the βασιλεια as both a duty assigned by God to men and women, as Kant suggested, and a gift that transcends the world, as Weiss believed? Adolf von Harnack thought so in his *What Is Christianity?*, one of the most popular works of liberal theology ever: 'He offered them a gift and with it set them a task'.[79] Although Derrida does not write in support of a kingdom of *God*, his βασιλεια also appears to combine the languages of ethics and transcendence. It is worth quoting at length a concluding passage of 'Faith and Knowledge':

> There is no opposition, fundamentally, between 'social bond' and 'social unravelling'. A certain interruptive unravelling is the condition of the 'social bond', the very respiration of all 'community'. This is not even the knot of a reciprocal condition, but rather the possibility that every knot can come undone, be cut or interrupted. This is where the *socius* or the relation to the other would disclose itself to be the secret of testimonial experience - and hence, of a certain faith [*foi*]. If belief [*croyance*] is the ether of the address and relation to the utterly other, it is <to be found> in the experience itself

of non-relationship or of absolute *interruption* (indices: 'Blanchot', 'Levinas' . . .). Here as well, the hypersanctification of this non-relation or of this transcendence would come about by way of desacralisation rather than through secularisation or laicisation, concepts that are too Christian; perhaps even by way of a certain 'atheism', in any case by way of radical experience of the resources of 'negative theology' - and going beyond even this tradition.[80]

'Absolute *interruption*', here, is not the divine rule breaking into the world in order to contradict it. It is a matter of ethics, not religion - or, better, not religion understood by way of positive revelation. We are invited to view a scene with just two people, Self and Other. The Other is not to be approached dialectically or with the aim of effecting a fusion that dissolves both selves. On the contrary, the aim is to loosen whatever leads one to regard Other as a modification of Self, and in so doing to open up ethical relations with him or her.[81] To do this, Derrida implies, is to mark 'an *absolute interruption* in the regime of the possible that nonetheless remains, if this can be said, in place.'[82] To call 'come' to the Other or to the kingdom is to invite the unforeseen into one's life, for one cannot know in advance or even in the present the nature and extent of one's responsibility for the Other. An experience - in the sense of *Erfahrung*, not *Erlebnis* - is opened, and one risks changing one's life. Nothing is overtly added or taken away, but another register is introduced into the realm of the possible.

This other register is signalled in the quotation marks that Derrida places around 'community', a word he distrusts because of its associations with homogeneity and unity. Derrida speaks of a 'democracy to come': not a utopia abiding in a future present, an 'end of history', but rather a promise of justice to which we, as people living in imperfect democracies, must always be true, partly because of our ideals and partly because of the everyday faith, *croyance*, that allows us to function socially. Thus Derrida speaks of 'a trust that "founds" all relations to the other in testimony' and then construes it as 'justice' which 'allows the hope, beyond all "messianisms", of a universalisable culture of singularities.'[83] No democracy that aspires to form a just community can ever be completely at one with itself; there must always be a space in which Other can distinguish itself from Same. One could be forgiven for recalling Kant's distinction between a juridical and an ethical society. A society could be ethical, for Derrida, only if its quest for justice exceeds juridical norms. Yet while we must always strive for justice, there is no suggestion entertained by Derrida that the juridical society will one day yield to an ethical society, let alone a community of good conscience. Democracy is always 'to come' [*à venir*]; it will never be present, not even in the future [*l'avenir*].

There is no question, then, of passing 'democracy' as a project from one generation to another, for a democracy to come is characterised by plural traits rather than a single end. Democracy has no assured horizon; it is always unforeseeable, which means that it must be invented and therefore risked time and again if there is to be a just society. Also there can be no question of abandoning constitutions, bills of rights, laws. Invention proceeds not in the absence of a concept but through exceeding what has already been thought. Constitutions and the rest encode the promise of democracy which we are invited to affirm perpetually, and which we do in being alert to whatever has been 'forgotten, repressed, misunderstood, or unthought in the "old" concept and throughout its history.'[84] The '"old" concept' here is democracy, but it might as well be the βασιλεια which is itself one of the sources of Christian social democracy in those countries that appeal, sometimes in bad faith, to such a notion. Kant conceived the ethical commonwealth being established on earth, while Ritschl argued that the βασιλεια is co-ordinate with justification.[85] Derrida, of course, does not think that his 'democracy to come' is regulative or transcendent, although he might agree with Ernst Bloch, doyen of utopia studies, when he talks of the need to 'transcend without transcendence'.[86]

A democratic republic of justice is not the divine kingdom of justification. Nor is it a secular analogue of the kingdom, since Christians believe that the basileia will indeed come, and Derrida has no such faith, *foi*. What can be said, however, is that Derrida inherits a great deal from the Kantian idea of the ethical commonwealth, its precursors, and its various extensions in the liberal Christian tradition. Ritschl declared that Christianity resembles 'an ellipse which is determined by two *foci*,' redemption and the kingdom, while Derrida argues that faith and the holy 'comprise two distinct sources or foci. "Religion" figures their *ellipse* because it both comprehends the two foci but also sometimes shrouds their irreducible duality in silence, in a manner precisely that is secret and *reticent.*'[87] The common metaphor is surely accidental; it is the broad vision of an ethical society bound by faith and justice that is shared. It comes as no surprise, then, that Derrida's 'democracy to come' has been used to interpret the βασιλεια as already received within liberal Christianity.[88]

IV

Does Derrida inherit too much from Kant with respect to religion? The question cannot be answered easily or directly, since Derrida himself intimates that he could derive his case from Hegel, Kierkegaard or even Heidegger.[89] No doubt there are Kantian theses curled inside each of these philosophers' works, though it would take a fair time to find them, given that they have been reset by such powerful writers. Yet Derrida elects Kant as his main host or guest in 'Faith and Knowledge' rather than Hegel, Kierkegaard or Heidegger, and this choice must be respected. It must also be said that, for all its many flourishes, 'Faith and Knowledge' is at heart a modest essay. Derrida makes no attempt to offer a comprehensive philosophy of religion: he outlines a *Glaubenslehre* in the specific sense of *croyance* rather than *foi*. His concern is with an overlap of the philosophy of religion and political philosophy that can be used to explicate 'religion today'. This means that there are many areas that he leaves untouched or barely sighted, and by way of conclusion I would like to mention one and examine another.

The passage of the βασιλεια into 'city of God' and then into a moral realm rigorously divorced from nature does not enter into Derrida's deliberations, either in 'Faith and Knowledge' or his studies of friendship and hospitality, or in his reflections on Marx, the 'new Europe' and cosmopolitanism. He wishes to investigate the possibility of a universal faith, though one that is not natural: we are saved from a natural theology but little interest is shown in developing a theology of nature. Pondering the '*religion of the living*', however, Derrida draws attention to a double postulation at the heart of the monotheistic religions: 'on the one hand, the absolute respect of *life*' and 'on the other hand . . . the no less universal sacrificial vocation.'[90] Even without demanding human sacrifices, Derrida thinks, a religion of the living has required 'sacrifice of the living, more than ever in large-scale breeding and slaughtering, in the fishing or hunting industries, in animal experimentation.'[91] He then entertains the suggestion that ecologists and vegetarians might come to 'bear responsibility for what could well be the future of a religion.'[92] We see here a point where the Kantian assumption of the distance between the natural and the moral worlds can be rethought with respect to the βασιλεια or a democracy to come. To call 'come' to democracy these days involves a difficult set of questions as to how justice can be distributed on an earth whose ability to sustain life has been badly compromised. And to pray 'come' to the βασιλεια, with any sense that it concerns justice here and now, increasingly requires one to integrate it into both a theology of creation and a theology of sacrifice. Is it possible in religion today to think justice without sacrificing some of the benefits of democracy and possibly rethinking what 'democracy' can mean in the future? The question is attached to one of the many traits in a democracy to come. It already presses hard on us, and it weighs most heavily on those of us who regard democracy as a heritage and a promise to which we are bound.

Even to sketch the outline of this question with respect to Kant and Derrida on sacrifice would be a long essay in itself. So I will conclude by considering a point at which Derrida seems to agree with Kant and restates the Kantian view in a fresh and provocative manner. I should say at the outset that I disagree with Kant's emphasis on this matter, but rather than return to this aspect of *Religion*, I wish to focus on Derrida's attempt to keep this emphasis in play. As is doubtless already apparent, one basis of my unease with Kant's philosophy of religion is his reworking of the βασιλεια by way of the kingdom of ends, in which each subject is also a legislator and in which God does not appear. Derrida understands this rightly and puts the point forcefully when he aligns the Kantian application of the moral law in the field of religion as 'the experience of the death of God'.[93] I say 'forcefully' because the image is sublime in its concentrated simplicity and because it forces the matter a little, perhaps in the sense that one forces a door although also a little more than that.

Thus Kant after Derrida: 'in order to conduct oneself in a moral manner, one must act as though God did not exist or no longer concerned himself with our salvation.'[94] Is this a Kant who comes into focus only when one squints? To be sure, Kant removes God from the stage of salvation but not from the task of building the stage or dismantling it after the performance is over. Kant's God is not dead, although one might well think He is napping while the drama of world history unfolds before Him. Derrida's God might be dead, however. At least that is suggested when he relaunches the 'Kantian' equivalence of the moral law and the death of God by suggesting that 'hypersanctification . . . would come about by way of desacralisation.'[95] This reformulation of Kant passes through the Lévinas who asks 'if holiness . . . can dwell in a world that has not been desacralised [?]'[96] For Derrida, the answer seems to be no, since he takes Levinas to say that 'a certain disenchantment' is 'the condition of authentic holiness'[97], and glosses 'holiness' as hypersanctification, the excess that responsibility bears within itself. Certainly Levinas distinguishes the holy from the sacred. Holiness, for him, is the movement from being to being-for-the-other, and is an ethical rather than a religious value. 'The kingdom of heaven is ethical,' he says in a very Kantian moment.[98] Yet desacralisation for Levinas does not mean stripping mystery or religious ritual from the world.[99] Derrida appears more equivocal than Levinas, for his relating of hypersanctification and desacralisation has a double mark. On the one hand, it is associated with negative theology. An affirmation of the alterity of the Other must precede any attempt to form relations with him or her, and one must be mindful that the Other exceeds being: he or she cannot be reduced to a phenomenon for me. If one thinks, as Derrida does, that the deity exceeds being only by assuming an ineffably higher mode of being, then an ethics that begins by puncturing being would be more radical than any negative theology. On the other hand, this same linking is an appeal to the Enlightenment. The world must be disenchanted by reason, rid of all spiritualism and superstition, before we can begin to live in a true, adult fashion. Indeed, he rejects 'secularisation' and 'laicization' as 'too Christian',[100] and suggests that the path to hypersanctification might pass 'by way of a certain "atheism".' [101] Whether or not it goes in that dark place, it certainly winds its way through a politics of enlightenment.

Anticipating what he and his fellow philosophers will do on Capri, Derrida says,

> we shall doubtless attempt to transpose, here and now, the circumspect and suspensive attitude, a certain *epoché* that consists - rightly or wrongly, for the issue is serious - in thinking religion or making it appear "within the limits of reason alone".[102]

This movement is likely because of the philosophers' presumed taste for 'republican democracy', and we are reminded that the Kantian *epoché* 'belongs to the history of democracy': it affirms the possibility of emancipation 'from all external power (non-lay, non-secular), for example from religious dogmatism, orthodoxy or authority.'[103] Derrida moves quickly here, with only a parenthetical qualification ('rightly or wrongly, for the issue is serious') to slow him down, and one might well wonder why the seriousness of the matter does not make him pause. That religion is a social phenomenon goes without saying, and so politics can offer itself as a judge of religion. From its own viewpoint, though, a religion such as Christianity sees itself as not simply or exclusively social; it is grounded in revelation, and to that extent cannot submit to politics as a judge.

It is at this point that Derrida considers 'two temptations'.[104] The first is Hegelian - to affirm ontotheology as the truth of religion - and there is little chance that Derrida will accede to its charm. 'The other temptation', he says - and adds 'perhaps there are still good reasons for keeping this word' - 'would be "Heideggerian"':

> It would accordingly be necessary that a 'revealability' (*Offenbarkeit*) be allowed to reveal itself, with a light that would manifest (itself) more originarily than all revelation (*Offenbarung*). [105]

And he reflects on this temptation:

> In its most abstract form, then, the aporia within which we are struggling would perhaps be the following: is revealability (*Offenbarkeit*) more originary than revelation (*Offenbarung*), and hence independent of all

religion? Independent in the structures of its experience and in the analytics relating to them? Is this not the place in which "reflecting faith" at least originates, if not this faith itself? Or rather, inversely, would the event of revelation have consisted in revealing revealability itself, and the origin of light, the originary light, the very invisibility of visibility?' [106]

Resisting the temptation, Derrida finds a more originary place than either revealability or revelation which he explores by way of two names: messianism and *chora*. Usually Derrida insists that there is no escape from an *aporia*; one is caught by its contradictory performatives and must suffer their double pull. In passing through the *aporia* one might not be able to overcome it but might be able to discern there another 'structure of experience'.[107] Here, though, the *aporia* is suspended in favour of exploring 'a *third* place that could well have been more than arche-originary, the most anarchic and unarchivable place possible'. [108]

Because Derrida moves quickly here ('Let us step up the pace in order to finish,' he says), an important thread is left hanging: the claim that revelation is prior to revealability is assigned to 'the believer or the theologian'[109] and is not considered. There are various reasons why Derrida does not ponder the possible priority of revelation. First of all, as he said several months after visiting Capri, 'I must confess I oscillate' between prizing revelation or revealability, 'and I think some other scheme has to be constructed to understand the two at the same time.'[110] Second, he construes revelation as gift, and has identified a logic of the gift which 'needs to think the possibility of such an event [in this case revelation] but not the event itself.'[111] This is not a denial of the gift, only a rejection of the view that a gift can appear *as such*: it cannot be disclosed or intuited in the present, and therefore cannot be used in theoretical determinations or judgments. Perhaps the gift can be affirmed outside the economies of philosophy and rational theology - in the sphere of faith, for example - although that is not a possibility for Derrida himself. The third reason is political. If revelation is held to be prior to revealability, then there is a justification for hierarchies and priesthoods: scriptures need to be interpreted by those trained in hermeneutics.[112] One can see here the beginning of a politics from which Derrida wishes to liberate himself and us - 'religious dogmatism, orthodoxy or authority' [113] - although one might wonder if these are any worse than the dogmatism, orthodoxy and authority one finds on both the right and the left of politics, and indeed, whether any society can be said to be free of them. Yet if revealability is prior to revelation, then issues about reason and universalisation come to the fore, and these are coordinate with democracy. And if messianism and *chora* precede even revealability, one can expect them to mesh with a more radical politics, a 'democracy to come'.

Derrida draws the distinction between revelation and revealability from Heidegger, principally from the summary of a dialogue held at the Académie évangélique in December, 1953. There the philosopher told his audience that 'Revelation itself determines its mode of manifestation'.[114] Two years earlier, in a conversation with students at the University of Zurich, he observed that 'the experience of God and his manifestation . . . occurs in the dimension of being.'[115] Where Heidegger grants a privilege to revelation, Derrida prizes revealability:'Is this not the place in which "reflecting faith" at least originates, if not this faith itself?'[116] Yet what he chiefly takes from Heidegger is the hint to displace the distinction of revelation and revealability and find 'totally new distinctions and delimitations'.[117] Perhaps he also takes something else, this time indirectly from Heidegger: the thought that the sacred is always anterior, no matter what.[118] Certainly we can read the messianic and *chora* in both sets of terms. Derrida might not yield to the Heideggerian temptation as he presents it, although he accepts without question the vision of revelation as extrinsic to the world. It is as if his sense of God's self-revelation is tramelled in the *duplex ordo* theory, prominent in late nineteenth- and early twentieth-century Catholicism, in which the orders of nature and grace admitted only few relations, and those external.

The *duplex ordo* theory was combated by Maurice Blondel and prosecuted by Henri de Lubac and Karl Rahner, among others. Men and women have a natural desire for God, de Lubac argued, although our longing for God does not coerce Him into forgiving our sins. Saving grace is always and only freely given.[119] One cannot figure a criticism of the Heideggerian temptation along exactly the same lines, since Derrida is concerned with universalisation, not nature, and he follows Heidegger in detheologising 'human being'.[120] Nonetheless we can find another path that Derrida could have taken had he conceived revelation as a gift that resists being thought as presence, a path that begins with revelation but that does not regard it as extrinsic to the world. For one could argue that revelation, if it occurs, is always and already involved with a process of universalisation that is more than globalatinisation. A revelation will be held by the faithful to be singular, although its singularity will not be able to be protected from iteration. The Christian claim is that God decisively and uniquely reveals Himself in Jesus, in his preaching of the *basileia* and his actions; and this claim is supported, believers say, by the texts of the New Testament and the traditions that these texts generate. The production, interpretation and translation of the New Testament as witness to Jesus creates an open network of religious ideas and practices. It expands in all directions, especially once one considers that the 'original' motifs of the primitive testimony and confession are reset in different cultures; and with that expansion there inevitably comes the possibility of corrupting the primitive testimony as well as the testimonies of all subsequent reformations and counter-reformations. Revelation, on this account, is not a presence. The absolute singularity of the God-man is erased in his incarnation, that is, in his entire mortal life and orientation as a human being; and we are left with the trace of an event that was never fully present to anyone's consciousness and that must now be sought for in holiness and its corruptions, assuming that we can tell them apart.

Only a believer would argue in this way, and that is the major reason why Derrida does not do so himself. Only a believer would insist that revelation is an event, and only a believer who has taken Derrida seriously would come to think of that event as never fully present to anyone's consciousness and therefore never able to be rigorously determined by way of constative statements. No one can prevent that event from being sacralised or indeed demonised, although form and redaction criticism, along with their progeny, can do much to help us sheer away a certain amount of sacralisation. They will help us to see that the revelation of God in Jesus occurs in the preaching of the βασιλεια, and that the resurrection is to be regarded as the confirmation of that preaching, not the final miracle that retrospectively grounds the mission of Jesus. In prizing the βασιλεια, however, one is not thereby affirming it as the imposition of a divine presence that quashes otherness and singularity, nor is one thereby regarding it by way of the assumption of duty as divine command. Not at all: the *basileia* is the name given to the many ways in which the triune God enters into loving relations with His creation; it is the promise that one day we, even we, will be fully converted, turned directly to God, and all our relations with one another and with creation will pass by way of the Trinity. Once again, no moment of presence is presumed: the inexhaustible divine mystery overflows any and all consciousness.

No event falls wholly within a horizon of expectation, Derrida tells us. Thus the preaching of the βασιλεια finds itself strangely reformed by Kant, Marx, Ritschl and even Derrida in his talk of a 'democracy to come'. Deconstruction comes as an event, one that deals a blow, in good Kantian fashion, to 'religious dogmatism, orthodoxy or authority',[121] and that then finds itself taken up in competing liberal and orthodox theologies. It comes to tell us that experience is opened by an encounter with the Other, a meeting made possible by an 'absolute *interruption*'.[122] Meanwhile the faithful look on, note that the one Other whom Derrida, like Kant, bypasses in his philosophy of religion is God, and ask, 'If God were allowed to be God, what experience would be possible?' To know how to answer that question would be to know what Jesus meant by the βασιλεια.

Notes:

1 See T. S. Eliot, 'Tradition and the Individual Talent', in *Selected Essays*, 3rd ed. (London: Faber and Faber, 1951), p.15, and J. L. Borges, 'Kafka and His Precursors', in *Selected Non-Fictions*, ed. Eliot Weinberger, trans. Esther Allen *et al.* (New York: Viking, 1999), p.365.

2 See Jacques Derrida, 'Parergon', *The Truth in Painting*, trans. Geoff Bennington and Ian McLeod (Chicago: University of Chicago Press, 1987), 'On a Newly Arisen Apocalyptic Tone in Philosophy', trans. John Leavey Jr, in *Raising the Tone of Philosophy: Late Essays by Immanuel Kant, Transformative Critique by Jacques Derrida*, ed. Peter Fenves (Baltimore: The Johns Hopkins University Press, 1993), *Du droit à la philosophie* (Paris: Galilée, 1990), p.96. The full extent of Derrida's writing on Kant is not widely acknowledged and will not be until all his seminars — including, above all, 'Kant, le Juif, l'Allemand' (1986-87) - are published.

3 See Immanuel Kant, *Prolegomena to Any Future Metaphysics*, trans. Paul Carus, rev. James W. Ellington (Indianapolis: Hackett, 1977).

4 A history of the concept of 'ground' in modern philosophy would attend to Arthur Schopenhauer's *The Fourfold Root of the Principle of Sufficient Reason*, trans. E. F. J. Payne, introd. Richard Taylor (La Salle, IL: Open Court, 1974), Martin Heidegger's *The Metaphysical Foundations of Logic*, trans. Michael Heim (Bloomington: Indiana University Press, 1984)§§ 8-9, pp.13-14, his *The Principle of Reason*, trans. Reginald Lilly (Bloomington: Indiana University Press, 1991), and more generally the relations of *Abgrund*, *Grund*, *Ungrund* and *Urgrund* in modern German philosophy.

5 Immanuel Kant, *Vorkritische Schriften bis 1768*, II, in *Werkausgabe*, II, ed. W. Weischedel (Frankfurt am Main: Surkamp, 1988), p.997.

6 See Gilles Deleuze, *Kant's Critical Philosophy: The Doctrine of the Faculties*, trans. Hugh Tomlinson and Barbara Habberjam (London: The Athlone Press, 1984), vii, and Diane Morgan, *Kant Trouble: The Obscurities of the Enlightened* (London: Routledge, 2000), p.56.

7 See Harold Bloom, *The Anxiety of Influence: A Theory of Poetry* (New York: Oxford University Press, 1973), Ch. 6.

8 Derrida indicates his admiration for Kant whenever he writes on him, and as he observes 'each time that I read Kant . . . it is always the first time', *Du droit à la philosophie*, p.81.

9 There have been different sorts of attempts to reread Kant in the light of Derrida. Some have directly sought to apply Derrida's insights or characteristic ways of proceeding to major or minor texts by Kant. See, for example, John Sallis, *Spacings - of Reason and Imagination in Texts of Kant, Fichte, Hegel* (Chicago: University of Chicago Press, 1987), Stephen Watson, 'Regulations: Kant and Derrida at the End of Metaphysics', in *Deconstruction and Philosophy: The Texts of Jacques Derrida*, ed. John Sallis (Chicago: University of Chicago Press, 1987), Irene E. Harvey, 'Derrida, Kant, and the Performance of Parergonality', in *Derrida and Deconstruction*, ed. Hugh J. Silverman (London: Routledge, 1989), Geoffrey Bennington, 'X', in *Applying - To Derrida*, ed. John Brannigan, Ruth Robbins and Julian Wolfreys (London:

Macmillan, 1996), and Diane Morgan, *Kant Trouble*. With others, it is very hard if not impossible to imagine them writing on Kant without the example of Derrida before them. See, for example, J. Hillis Miller, 'The Search for Grounds in Literary Study', *Genre* 17: 1 and 2 (1984), Paul de Man's essays on Kant in his *Aesthetic Ideology*, ed. and introd. Andrzej Warminski (Minneapolis: University of Minnesota Press, 1996), and the contributions by Philippe Lacoue-Labarthe and Jean-Luc Nancy to *Of the Sublime: Presence in Question*, Jean-François Courtine *et al.*, trans. and afterword Jeffrey S. Librett (Albany: State University of New York Press, 1993).

10 Both essays may be found in *Parages* (Paris: Galilée, 1986).

11 See John Milbank, 'The Theological Critique of Philosophy in Hamann and Jacobi', *Radical Orthodoxy: A New Theology*, ed. John Milbank, Catherine Pickstock and Graham Ward (London: Routledge, 1999).

12 See, for example, John D. Caputo's discussion in 'Mysticism and Transgression: Derrida and Meister Eckhart', *Continental Philosophy*, 2 (1989), pp. 24-39 and Michael Allen Gillespie's discussion of Duns Scotus and William of Ockham in his *Nihilism before Nietzsche* (Chicago: University of Chicago Press, 1995). E. D. Hirsch Jr portays Hume as a deconstructionist in his 'Derrida's Axioms', *London Review of Books*, 21 July-3 August 1983, p.18.

13 For Derrida's comments on tradition, see Jacques Derrida, *Specters of Marx: The State of the Debt, the Work of Mourning, and the New International*, trans. Peggy Kamuf, introd. Bernd Magnus and Stephen Cullenberg (London: Routledge, 1994), p.16.

14 Jacques Derrida, *Edmund Husserl's* Origin of Geometry*: An Introduction*, trans. and pref. John P. Leavey, ed. David Allison (Stony Brook, NY: Nicolas Hays, 1978), p.92.

15 Jacques Derrida, 'Economimesis', trans. R. Klein, *Diacritics*, 11 (1981), p.3.

16 This is not to say that Ritschl was uncritical of Kant's philosophy of religion. See his *A Critical History of the Christian Doctrine of Justification and Reconciliation*, trans. John S. Black (Edinburgh: Edmonston and Douglas, 1872), pp.404-18. Nor is it to say that his younger contemporary liberal theologians accepted his view. Ernst Troeltsch, for one, argued that 'a complete rejection of metaphysics is itself a metaphysic, a metaphysic which is, moreover, contrary to faith', *The Christian Faith*, foreword Marta Troeltsch, ed. Gertrud von le Fort, trans. Garrett E. Paul (Minneapolis: Fortress Press, 1991), p.54.

17 Karl Rahner, 'Theology and Anthropology', *Theological Investigations*, 9, trans. Graham Harrison (London: Darton, Longman and Todd, 1972), p.28.

18 See Karl Barth, *Church Dogmatics*, II.i, ed. G. W. Bromiley and T. F. Torrance, trans. T. H. L. Parker *et al.* (Edinburgh: T. and T. Clark, 1957), § 26. Directly relevant is Barth's *Anselm: Fides Quærens Intellectum*, trans. Ian W. Robertson (London: SCM Press, 1960).

19 Ernst Staehelin considers Kant in his monumental *Die Verkündigung des Reiches Gottes in der Kirche Jesu Christi* (Basil: Friedrich Reinhardt, 1951-65), vol. 6, §31. The influence of Kant can be traced through that volume and the one that follows it and concludes the work, although Kant's influence is undoubtedly more pervasive than Staehelin suggests: Ritschl, for instance, is not examined in his study. Ritschl reminds us that 'Kant was the first to perceive the supreme importance for ethics of the "Kingdom of God" as an association of men bound together by laws of virtue', *The*

Christian Doctrine of Justification and Reconciliation: The Positive Development of the Doctrine, trans. H. R. Mackintosch and A. B. Macaulay (Edinburgh: T. and T. Clark, 1900), p.11.
20 Irenaeus, *Against Heresies*, 5.33.3.
21 Origen, *Comment. in Matthaeum*, Tomus XIV, 622 (Migne, 13-G).
22 See H. A. Drake, ed., *In Praise of Constantine: A Historical Study and New Translation of Eusebius' Tricennial Orations*, University of California Publications: Classical Studies, Vol. 15 (Los Angeles: University of California Press, 1976), III, 5. Also see Augustine, *City of God*, trans. Marcus Dods, introd. Thomas Merton (New York: The Modern Library, 1950), 20, 9; 18, 29.
23 Derrida, *Specters of Marx*, p.16.
24 Immanuel Kant, *Critique of Pure Reason*, trans. Norman Kemp Smith (London: Macmillan, 1933), A 808/B 836.
25 Ibid.
26 Ibid.
27 Ibid. A812/B840.
28 Gottfried Leibniz, 'Monadology' in *Discourse on Metaphysics, Correspondence with Arnauld, Monadology*, trans. Montgomery, rev. Albert R. Chandler, introd. Paul Janet (La Salle: Open Court Publishing, 1973), §§ 86, 87. Also see Leibniz's 'Discourse on Metaphysics' § 36.
29 Origen, *Homélies sur Jérémie*, ed. Pierre Nautin, trans. Pierre Husson and Pierre Nautin, Sources Chrétiennes, 2 vols (Paris: Éditions du Cerf, 1976), vol 1, IX. 2. Augustine, *The City of God*, 14, 28. Henri de Lubac offers a concise account of patristic images of heaven as a city in his *Catholicism: Christ and the Common Destiny of Man*, trans. Lancelot C. Sheppard and Elizabeth Englund (San Francisco: Ignatius Press, 1988), pp.112-19.
30 Immanuel Kant, *Groundwork of the Metaphysic of Morals*, trans. and analysed by H. J. Paton (New York: Harper and Row, 1964), p.88.
31 Ibid. p.96.
32 Ibid. p.106.
33 Ibid.
34 See Immanuel Kant, 'On the Proverb: That May be True in Theory, But Is of No Practical Use', in *Perpetual Peace and Other Essays on Politics, History, and Morals*, trans. Ted Humphrey (Indianapolis: Hackett Pub. Co., 1983), p.67.
35 See Immanuel Kant, *Critique of Practical Reason*, trans. and introd. Lewis White Beck (Indianapolis: Bobbs-Merill Educational Publishing, 1956), p.114, p.124.
36 Immanuel Kant, *Religion within the Limits of Reason Alone*, trans., introd. and notes Theodore M. Greene and Hoyt H. Hudson (New York: Harper and Row, 1960), p.125. When talking about the final end that is defined for us by the moral law, Kant observes, 'This end is the *summum bonum*, as the highest good *in the world* possible through freedom', *The Critique of Judgment*, trans. James Creed Meredith (Oxford: Clarendon Press, 1952), p.118.
37 Kant, *Religion within the Limits of Reason Alone,* pp.124-25.
38 Ibid. p.126.
39 Andrew Reath distinguishes the 'theological' and the 'secular' in this way. See his 'Two Conceptions of the Highest Good in Kant', in *Immanuel Kant: Critical Assessments*, ed. Ruth E. Chadwick, III: *Kant's Moral and Political Philosophy* (London:

Routledge, 1992), p.228.
40 Gordon E. Michalson, Jr, *Kant and the Problem of God* (Oxford: Basil Blackwell, 1999), p.108.
41 Kant, *Religion*, p.116. Modern scholarship details many allusions to Yahweh as king such as Ps. 93:1 and to the coming of the kingdom (e.g., Isa. 25-26, 40-44).
42 Kant, *Religion within the Limits of Reason Alone*, p.47.
43 Ibid. p.86.
44 Ibid. p.92.
45 Augustine, *The City of God*, 14, 4.
46 Augustine, *The City of God*, 28, 54; 19, 28.
47 Augustine, 'On Baptism, Against the Donatists', Book 5 § 38, *The Works of Aurelius Augustine*, ed. Marcus Dods (Edinburgh: T. and T. Clark, 1872), vol. 3.
48 Augustine, 'On Baptism', Book 3 § 26.
49 Kant, *Religion within the Limits of Reason Alone*, p.86.
50 Ibid. p.122
51 See Origen, 'Prayer', Ch. 20, 1, in his *Prayer, Exhortation to Martrydom*, trans. John J. O'Meara (London: Longman, Green and Co., 1954). Clement evokes 'the spiritual church' at the very end of *Stromata*, Book 7 ch. 11, *The Ante-Nicene Fathers*, ed. Alexander Roberts and James Donaldson (rpt.; Grand Rapids, MI: Wm. B. Eerdmans, 1994), vol. 2.
52 Kant, *Religion within the Limits of Reason Alone*, p.92.
53 Ibid.
54 Ibid. p.93.
55 Ibid.
56 Ibid. p.96.
57 Ibid. p.112.
58 Ibid. p.96.
59 Ibid.
60 Ibid.
61 Ibid. p.97.
62 Ibid. p.110.
63 Ibid p.105.
64 Ibid. p.106.
65 Ibid. p.125.
66 Ibid. p.54.
67 Prominent among contemporary theologians who argue for an eschatological interpretation of the βασιλεια are Johann Baptist Metz, *Theology of the World*, trans. William Glen-Doepel (New York: Herder and Herder, 1969), 94f, Jürgen Moltmann, *The Coming of God: Christian Eschatology*, trans. Margaret Kohl (Minneapolis: Fortress Press, 1996), Part III, and Wolfhart Pannenberg, *Systematic Theology*, trans. Geoffrey W. Bromiley (Edinburgh: T. and T. Clark, 1998), vol. 3. However, I would like to draw attention to Troeltsch's insightful remarks on nature in *The Christian Faith*, §17.
68 Jacques Derrida, 'Faith and Knowledge: the Two Sources of "Religion" at the Limits of Reason Alone', trans. Samuel Weber, *Religion*, ed. Jacques Derrida and Gianni Vattimo (Cambridge: Polity Press, 1998), p.8.
69 Ibid.

70 Ibid.
71 Ibid.
72 I explore this essay in more detail in '"Absolute *Interruption*": On Faith' in *Questioning God*, ed. John D. Caputo (Bloomington: Indiana University Press, 2001). I take up the question of the kingdom in a more theological setting in 'The Kingdom and the Trinity', forthcoming in *The Australasian Catholic Recorder*.
73 Derrida, 'Faith and Knowledge', p.18.
74 Jacuqes Derrida, 'Circumfession', in Geoffrey Bennington and Jacques Derrida, *Jacques Derrida*, trans. Geoffrey Bennington (Chicago: University of Chicago Press, 1993), p.155.
75 Johannes Weiss, *Jesus' Proclamation of the Kingdom of God*, trans., ed. and introd. Richard Hyde Hiers and David Larrimore Holland (London: SCM Press, 1971), p.133. Albert Schweitzer underscored the importance of Weiss's insight: 'The Jesus of Nazareth who came forward publicly as the Messiah, who preached the ethic of the Kingdom of God, who founded the Kingdom of Heaven upon earth and died to give His work its final consecration, never had any existence', *The Quest of the Historical Jesus: A Critical Study of its Progress from Reimarus to Wrede*, trans. W. Montgomery, 3rd ed. (London: Adam and Charles Black, 1954), p.396.
76 Richard Rand, 'Canons and Metonymies: An Interview with Jacques Derrida', *Logomachia: The Conflict of the Faculties*, ed. Richard Rand (Lincoln: University of Nebraska Press, 1992), p.210.
77 In a quite different way, the distinguished Kantian scholar Nathan Rotenstreich also develops an account of faith that is not reducible to religious faith. See his *On Faith*, ed. and foreword Paul Mendes-Flohr (Chicago: University of Chicago Press, 1998).
78 Caputo, ed., *Deconstruction in a Nutshell: A Conversation with Jacques Derrida* (New York: Fordham University Press, 1997), p.22.
79 Adolf von Harnack, *What Is Christianity?*, trans. Thomas Bailey Saunders, introd. Rudolf Bultmann (Philadelphia: Fortress Press, 1986), p.67.
80 Derrida, 'Faith and Knowledge', pp.64-65.
81 See my essay '"Absolute *Interruption*": On Faith'.
82 Jacques Derrida, *On the Name*, ed. Thomas Dutoit, trans. David Wood, John P. Leavey, Jr. and Ian McLeod (Stanford: Stanford University Press, 1995), p.43.
83 Derrida, 'Faith and Knowledge', p.18.
84 Jacques Derrida, *Politics of Friendship*, trans. George Collins (London: Verso, 1997), p.104.
85 Ritschl, *The Christian Doctrine of Justification and Reconciliation*, p.33.
86 Ernst Bloch, *Atheism in Christianity: The Religion of the Exodus and the Kingdom*, trans. J. T. Swann (New York: Herder and Herder, 1972), p.82.
87 Ritschl, *The Christian Doctrine of Justification and Reconciliation*, p. 11, Derrida, 'Faith and Knowledge', p.36.
88 I am thinking of Caputo's pages on the kingdom in his *The Prayers and Tears of Jacques Derrida: Religion without Religion* (Bloomington: Indiana University Press, 1997), pp.222-29. Also see his 'Reason, History, and a Little Madness: Towards an Ethics of the Kingdom', in *Questioning Ethics: Contemporary Debates in Philosophy*, ed. Richard Kearney and Mark Dooley (London: Routledge, 1999).
89 See Jacques Derrida, *The Gift of Death*, trans. David Wills (Chicago: University of

Chicago Press, 1995), p. 49.
90 Derrida, 'Faith and Knowledge', p.50. (Derrida's emphasis)
91 Ibid.
92 Ibid.
93 Ibid. p.13.
94 Ibid. p.11.
95 Ibid. pp.64-65.
96 Emmanuel Levinas, 'Desacralisation and Disenchantment', in *Nine Talmudic Readings*, trans. and introd. Annette Aronowicz (Bloomington: Indiana University Press, 1990), p.141.
97 Derrida, 'Faith and Knowledge', p.64.
98 Emmanuel Levinas, *Otherwise than Being, or Beyond Essence*, trans. Alphonso Lingis (The Hague: Martinus Nijhoff, 1981), p.183.
99 Levinas admits that 'the sacred is the ambience in which holiness often dwells', Raoul Mortley, 'Emmanuel Levinas', *French Philosophers in Conversation* (London: Routledge, 1991), p.17. Also see Lévinas, 'Desacralization and Disenchantment'.
100 Derrida, 'Faith and Knowledge', p.65.
101 Ibid.
102 Ibid. p.8.
103 Ibid.
104 Ibid. p.15.
105 Ibid.
106 Ibid. p.16.
107 Derrida, *Politics of Friendship*, p.25, n.26.
108 Derrida, 'Faith and Knowledge', p.16.
109 Ibid.
110 Caputo, ed., *Deconstruction in a Nutshell*, p.24.
111 Derrida, *The Gift of Death*, p.49. Also see 'On the Gift: A Discussion between Jacques Derrida and Jean-Luc Marion', *God, the Gift, and Postmodernism*, ed. John D. Caputo and Michael J. Scanlon (Indianapolis: Indiana University Press, 1999), esp. pp.59-60.
112 See Jacques Derrida, 'Scribble (writing-power)', abr. and trans. Cary Plotkin, *Yale French Studies*, 58 (1979), p.125.
113 Derrida, 'Faith and Knowledge', p.8.
114 Richard Kearney and Joseph Stephen O'Leary, ed., *Heidegger et la question de Dieu* (Paris: Bernard Grasset, 1980), p.335. My translation.
115 Kearney and O'Leary, *Heidegger et la question de Dieu*, p.334. My translation.
116 Derrida, 'Faith and Knowledge', p.16.
117 Kearney and O'Leary, *Heidegger et la question de Dieu*, p.334. My translation.
118 See Maurice Blanchot, 'The "Sacred" Speech of Heidegger' in *The Work of Fire*, trans. Charlotte Mandell (Stanford: Stanford University Press, 1995), p.121.
119 See Henri de Lubac, *Surnatural* (Paris: Aubier, 1946), p.483, and *The Mystery of the Supernatural*, trans. Rosemary Sheed (London: Geoffrey Chapman, 1967), pp.176-77.
120 See Heidegger, *Ontology - The Hermeneutics of Facticity*, trans. John van Buren (Indianapolis: Indiana University Press, 1999), p.22.

121 Derrida, 'Faith and Knowledge', p.8.
122 Ibid. p.64.

9
Kant and Derrida: Inventing Oneself Out of an Impossible Choice

Olivia Custer

September 2001. George W. Bush challenges every person on the planet to choose sides: 'you're either with us or against us'. Joining the war against the 'evil-doers', he tells us, is a duty for those who choose freedom. This is echoed on the other side of the planet by the affirmation that everyone must be either a good Muslim or an infidel, the former being duty bound to war against the latter. The only difference between the two calls to holy war seems to be one of inflection: the first framing a choice, the second appealing to identities. Neither of these discourses offer much of a choice, each calling for an equally determined operation of 'infinite justice'. Is there a choice of freedom? Can one choose freedom any more than identity? Choosing freedom, as Bush presents it, turns out to be a choice of a certain philosophical heritage, a certain Enlightenment interpretation of the Christian mission. And this choice is not a choice, but a duty. Unless it is a duty because a choice, a desire. Or a duty some have been chosen for. Duty and choice. Duty and desire. Desire to do one's duty. Desire to choose one's duty. Desire for a duty one desires. Duty to desire one's duty. Desire or duty for one's duty and desire to coincide. Duty to face the question of possible antagonism between duty and desire. Or to wonder about the conditions of possibility of their coincidence. How are we to respond to this summation to choose sides? One would like to find a responsible response, which yet refuses the proposed calculation. Perhaps one must start by returning to one of the important elements of this heritage westerners are being asked to defend, the very concept of duty and its relation to the possibility of choice. It is then not so much a choice as a duty, a choice without choice, from which one may perhaps hope for choice, to read Kant on the question of duty, a choice which might also be based on a desire to first experience the peculiar conflict and complicity between duty and desire in an experience of reading, a reading which will attempt to trace conflict and complicity in desire and on duty, between Kant and Derrida.

Kant before Derrida: a mere preliminary

Guided by desire, I turn to *Passions* for one of Derrida's descriptions of the conception of duty he has sought to develop in recent years. As the very title of the book warns, duty here will have to be considered not as a duty which is safely in the realm of reason but one which may also belong to the realm of passions, a duty which may have to come to terms with passions, come to find the terms for a duty not without passion. Derrida declares that to even express duty, in the sense he wishes to ascribe to the term, we may have to work against 'the very language of duty'. In a discussion of the rites governing reading, and critical reading in particular, the term 'duty' surfaces first as that which avoids submitting to rites at all costs. Derrida then insists that:

> A gesture 'of friendship' or 'of politeness' would be neither friendly nor polite if it were purely and simply to obey a ritual rule. But this *duty* to escape the ritualised rule of decorum demands equally to be extended to the other side of the very language of *duty*. One must not be friendly or polite out of duty. We risk such a proposition, to be sure, against Kant [my translation].[1]

Duty, according to Derrida, will be duty also to escape from the language of duty. Dutiful reading must escape from the ritual reading. Duty as we should now think of it, must be beyond duty as it has come down to us in the philosophical language. Duty beyond duty – what is Derrida thinking? Whatever he is considering here, it is described as a proposition 'against Kant.' According to Derrida here, it is our duty to escape from the rules of duty, to escape from the very language of duty, to escape from Kant. Or rather to go against Kant, or to go without Kant.[2]

To clarify why thinking duty is for Derrida irrevocably linked to trespassing against Kant let us turn to the difficulty which not only haunts, but also engenders Derrida's conception of duty.[3] In the final pages of *Adieu*, Derrida puts forward a general formulation of the difficulty which is constitutive of his conception of duty in terms of the problematic relation between ethics and politics or right:'*Il faut déduire une politique et un droit de l'éthique.*'[4] This is not only a pragmatic necessity, but a formal one. One needs to deduce a set of rights or rules from ethics both because one needs rules and because one needs them to originate in ethics. This demand that we require that a politics be determined by ethics could simply be taken as common sense, and the common basis for giving a sense to ethics: ethics is that from which we draw out rules of conduct. But however much this may look like common sense[5], it is in fact the beginning of the difficulty:

> The *formal* injunction of deduction remains incontestable, and it awaits only the third or justice. Ethics enjoins a politics and a right: this dependence and this conditional derivation are as irreversible as they are unconditional. [my translation][6]

There is an injunction to deduce politics from ethics. There must be a deduction of politics, or right, from ethics. '*Il faut un rapport*' and there can be no doubt about the direction of this derivation. This is the starting point here. But, '*mais*', there is a difficulty :

> But the political or juridical *content* so assigned remains on the other hand undetermined, always to be determined on the other side of knowledge (*savoir*) and of all presentation, of all concept and of all possible intuition, singularly, in the word (*parole*) and responsibility taken by each individual, in each situation, and after an analysis which is unique each time - unique and infinite, unique but *a priori* exposed to substitution, unique and nevertheless general, interminable despite the urgency of the decision. [my translation][7]

We have no method for such a derivation. Derrida's description of the indeterminacy of the content hinges on his point that counting on a method of derivation of particular laws (and especially counting on the logical method of deducing particular cases from a general concept as one does for knowledge) is tantamount to avoiding responsibility. Perhaps the easiest way to understand Derrida's insight is in the terms of choice and calculation: if when faced with a decision (a choice) one resorts to having a machine, or the mechanism of a logical proof, or any from of calculation, make the choice, then one is not actually choosing. In this perspective, trying to 'know' what to do is equally counterproductive: if knowledge dictates the decision, then there is no decision in the strong sense, only submission to the dictates of knowledge. A decision, responsibility, only occurs where neither knowledge, nor reasoning, nor any other procedure for weighing and comparing the alternatives can produce the decision.[8] As Derrida says in the final pages of *Adieu:*

> without silence, without hiatus, which is not the absence of rules but the necessity of a leap at the instant of the ethical, juridical or political decision, we would only have to roll out knowledge (*savoir*) in a programme of action. Nothing could be more undermining of responsibility and more totalitarian. [my translation][9]

There is no smooth, continuous path from ethics to politics. At some point there has to be a leap: when knowledge and logic can no longer guide there must be a leap. The gap in the path between ethics and politics must be passed over, transgressing the general principle which requires that you have a method for such a translation. Daunting as the perspective of such a 'hiatus' may be, it is only part of the difficulty Derrida associates with duty. Or rather it only becomes a difficulty because the impossibility of finding a way to operate the deduction successfully does nothing to temper the 'injunction to deduce'. The real difficulty is that we cannot resign ourselves to the impossibility which must at the same time recognise. *Il faut. Despite* the impossibility, we must deduce. There can be no appeal to the impossibility of the process to justify not accomplishing the deduction. The '*il faut*' remains irrecusable exactly when it is impossible to obey this command.

Let us note that Derrida's '*il faut*' reflects, and hopes to provoke, a mixture between resignation and hope, passivity and activity, neutral anonymous necessity and urgent ethical necessity. The purpose of the utterance is thus as ambiguous as its content, or rather the ambiguity derives from the multiple utterances it combines : 'we must accept that we must', 'we must accept that we have no choice but to', 'we have no choice but to accept that we have no choice but to', 'we have no choice but to accept that we must'. It seems to be imbued with the force both of an imperious command from on high, and the force of blind necessity. Or rather its force cannot be described by analogy with either, only some combination of both. We must deduce politics from ethics. We cannot know how to accomplish this deduction. Nevertheless we must/it must be done. This is the difficulty which determines Derrida's conception of duty. It is because of this insoluble difficulty - a difficulty that cannot be solved and that must not be dissolved - that no ethical decision comes to pass without some form of transgression: political laws are always transgressions of the impossible deduction. The deduction is always a transgression both of the rules of proper deduction, and of their limits since we deduce, as we must, where we cannot.

Repeatedly in the publications of the nineties, as Derrida develops this conception of duty, he explicitly marks a difference with Kant, presenting his own notion of duty as being precisely a reinterpretation of Kant's. Although eager to claim that his thought is to be inscribed in the critical tradition, Derrida repeatedly presents his divergence from Kant as central to his conception of duty. [10] His quarrel with Kant seems to come from the fact that Derrida takes the impossibility of deducing politics from ethics on which he insists to be unthinkable for Kant. As we have seen, Derrida marks his objection to Kant's duty in terms of the question of rules: it is because, according to Derrida, duty must be thought of outside the language of rites, rituals, procedures, protocols or rules that we must move 'against Kant'. Derrida's argument is that, if there is a rule to determine what duty demands, then there is no occasion for duty in the strong sense, as there is no occasion for a real choice. Insofar as it is committed to the principle of rules, of principles from which specific duties can be derived, Kant's conception of duty is, for Derrida, too tied to thinking of it in terms of rules for it to be adequate to thinking a duty. Derrida offers a shorthand for the problem in terms of the issue of the possibility of deducing politics from ethics. For Derrida, Kant remains committed to the possibility of deducing rights from ethics without understanding that for duty to be duty, for duty to be an act of responsibility, this deduction must remain impossible, even as it may be urgent according to the logic outlined above.[11] Now of course the very distinction between ethics and politics, or as Derrida sometimes says between ethics and right, is Kantian, indeed comes to us from Kant. That there is a heterogeneity between the realm of ethics and the juridical realm is a fundamental supposition for Kant's practical philosophy, indeed its starting point.[12] There is no question that for Kant the radical distinction between morality and mere legality must never be forgotten and Derrida knows this as well as anyone. His suggestion, however, is, insofar as he suggests that it is possible to find an adequate passage between virtue and right, insofar as it is for him possible to deduce politics from ethics, that Kant in some sense effaces this distinction, or at least is not willing to take on the consequences of radical heterogeneity. According to Derrida, Kant does not recognise that this passage must be *in principle* impossible. Failing to recognise this impossibility, Kant stays on the side of a duty which can be cast in terms of rules, procedures, protocols and does not move, as Derrida does, to consider duty 'beyond' the limits of rule-bound duty. Kant thus does not approach or confront a duty which would be in principle inaccessible by/to rules. Thus Derrida can argue that, although of course the distinction between ethics and law is Kantian, to be faithful to this distinction requires going beyond Kant. For, while he may indeed have marked the distinction between ethics and right (or politics), between the universal laws of morality and the particular juridical laws, Kant failed to see that the derivation of the latter from the former is not just problematic, but must remain in principle impossible. As Derrida sees it, where Kant does recognise that particular empirical laws are often, perhaps always, inadequate translations of the moral law, he nevertheless takes this inadequacy to be accidental, an empirical fact rather than a necessity. Kant is held to suppose that this inadequacy can be progressively corrected (so that in principle the particular laws of government can be modified to an ever greater coincidence with the moral law) and to assign to practical philosophy the task of developing an adequation between right and ethics. Derrida contrasts this belief in the perfectibility of particular laws with his own suggestion that the discrepancy between ethics and politics is inevitable not simply empirically, but as he says, in principle. Derrida thus situates his 'transgression' of Kant as a difference in the *status* of the inadequacy of politics to ethics: where the inadequacy is for Kant an empirical problem which can be remedied by good philosophy, for Derrida the inadequacy cannot be overcome.[13] To escape from a thinking which suppresses the impossibility will require escaping from Kant:

> a duty as *over-duty* whose hubris and essential excess dictate transgressing not only the action that *conforms to duty* (*pflichtmässig*) but also the action undertaken *out of the sense of duty* (*aus Pflicht*), that is, what Kant defines as the very condition of morality. Duty must be such an over-duty, which demands acting without duty, without rule or norm (therefore without law) under the risk of seeing the so-called responsible decision become again the merely technical application of a concept and therefore of a presentable knowledge.[14]

Duty, claims Derrida, must be duty without a rule, without then a law – even the moral law. To insist that an ethical decision must be made without a rule is presented by Derrida as a transgression against what Kant defines as the condition of morality. As Geoffrey Bennington so concisely explains, Derrida's ethics require going 'further' in Kant's logic than Kant himself did:

> Kant famously says that I must act not just *in accordance with* duty but *from* duty, for the sake of duty (otherwise I always might simply be aping what I take to be dutiful conduct) ; but the further logic of this is that I must in fact, in the name of duty, act not just *from* duty, but *out of duty* in the sense of inventing something that falls outside what duty might be taken to dictate or to prescribe.[15]

This third position is presented as Derrida's, not Kant's. Thus Bennington reproduces the schema Derrida has so often put forward and reminds us that the specificity of Derrida's conception of duty, and that which distinguishes it from Kant's conception, is taken to be that this duty demands an invention. A duty which calls for invention, this is supposed to mark the novelty with respect to Kant, on this path beyond Kant which is always inscribed in a very Kantian logic of betraying to be faithful.[16] As is marked by the apparent equivalence of 'against' and 'beyond' in this context, Derrida is claiming to radicalise Kant, as though his notion of duty were hyperbolically Kantian[17].

Duty, if it is to mean anything, must be thought against Kant because beyond Kant. What is the radicalisation Derrida is proposing ? Indeed is it a radicalisation of Kant ? Are we to take Derrida at his word when he says that the duty he calls on us to consider is a duty against Kant because beyond Kant ? Do we have a choice but to read Kant after Derrida as simply the Kant who came before Derrida, the Kant after whom Derrida can be Derrida?

Kant before Derrida: no model for duty

Is the duty to which Kant aspires – 'Duty ! Sublime and mighty name'[18] – necessarily yet another irresponsible escape from responsibility as Derrida implies? To begin to answer such a question, we return to the formal problem of the heterogeneity of right and ethics in Kant's work. In particular we must try to establish whether the impossibility *in principle* to deduce rights from ethics necessarily constitutes a move 'beyond' or 'against' Kant. Although the reference to Kant (and in particular to Kant's political writings where he is specifically grappling with the task of perfecting legal rules in view of increasing adequacy with the moral law) certainly does serve to clarify the peculiar incommensurability of politics to ethics Derrida is concerned about, one may not simply accept Derrida's claim he is assuming a position 'against Kant' or, as he puts in more strongly, 'without Kant'.

Does Kant's conception of the act of duty really leave no occasion for a choice in the strong sense developed by Derrida? As we have seen, Derrida can argue that there is no such choice in Kantian morality, insofar as Kant believes that the action duty dictates can be deduced from moral principles. Such a deduction reduces any act of duty, even that for the sake of the moral law, to the result of following a procedure and not a responsible act. Thus in Derrida's eyes, Kant's faith in the possibility of determination would be precisely what precludes any possibility of choice and, therefore, of responsible duty. It is certainly easy to make the case that Kant *does* believe in the possibility of a deduction of laws from the moral law. His political writings, his *Doctrine of Right*, his elaboration of the details of a cosmopolitical constitution offer so many examples in which he argues from the moral law, from duty, to specific rights. Kant does seem to presume that the action duty dictates can be firmly and unequivocally established from ethical principles. To put it in Derrida's terms, Kant does seem to believe in the possibility of deducing politics from ethics. Not only does he believe in this possibility, he systematically argues that this is an almost trivial operation, insisting that any child can determine the action duty dictates. To demonstrate his point that the concept of duty is 'incomparably simpler, clearer and more natural and easily comprehensible to everyone,'[19] than any other motive for an action, Kant suggests turning to an example which involves a choice concerning a debt and an inheritance. Having set out the case – someone has possession of a fortune when the owner dies and faces the question of keeping the money of which he and his family have a pressing need or returning it to the rightful heirs who will not notice or squander it – Kant argues that 'if this case is explained even to a child of around eight or nine years old' the child will 'undoubtedly' answer that the money should not be kept.[20] 'Nothing can be clearer than this.'[21] If, on the other hand, one tries to reason in terms of greatest happiness, the reasoning leads to conflicting conclusions and the very possibility of determining the correct action becomes 'highly uncertain'.

> Thus a will which follows the maxim of happiness vacillates between various motives in trying to reach a decision. For it considers the possible results of its decision, and these are highly uncertain; and it takes a good head to find a way out of the host of arguments and counter-arguments without miscalculating the total effect. On the other hand, if we ask what duty requires, there is no confusion whatsoever about the answer, and we are at once certain what action to take. We even feel, if the concept of duty means anything to us, a revulsion at the very idea of calculating the advantages we might gain through violating our duty, just as if the choice (*Wahl*) were still a real one.[22]

If we look at things from the point of view of duty, says Kant, there is no uncertainty as to the action which must be taken, there is no risk of miscalculation, indeed even an aversion to the very idea of calculation as a misplaced complication. The mere suggestion that there is a real choice is then a sign that the problem is not being considered from the point of view of duty. From the point of view of duty, there is no possible choice. It is only when we look at the situation and ask about happiness that determining a course of action becomes problematic; the calculations are complicated, so complicated it seems as though it is impossible for them to be decisive. At first glance, this passage seems to confirm Derrida's contention that for Kant, duty does not seem to involve an impossible choice but rather no choice at all. Kant maintains that the only course of action which could be taken in the name of duty would be distinguished even by a child, without difficulty and without doubt. Furthermore, 'if the concept of duty means anything to us' we will feel 'revulsion' at the prospect of treating the situation as though it involved a real choice; no deliberation is required to determine a course of action if one is not driven by motives involving happiness but simply by duty. Such passages lend easy confirmation to Derrida's claim that Kant's duty is a duty which is pre-programmed, and that therefore ultimately one submits to it, as to any other protocol, irresponsibly. The lines seem to be drawn. On one side, Kant holds that there is no real choice involved in duty and that choice is only difficult, and therefore necessary and possible, for those who are determining actions from other motives than submission to duty. On the other side, Derrida argues that it is only where there is a real choice that there is an occasion for duty. However distinct this opposition seems to be, a closer reading suggests that it is not so clear that Derrida's insistence that duty requires an impossible choice and Kant's contention that duty requires no choice at all are so far apart.

We must here be careful to avoid formulating an opposition between Kant and Derrida which confuses the different senses of the word *choice* which Derrida so adamantly insists we must distinguish. Indeed, closer consideration shows that the 'choice' Kant anticipates in a choice of action based on search for happiness, is precisely what Derrida would call no choice at all: is a 'choice' (*Wahl*) which is the result of a calculation. Granted, such a choice may involve a very difficult calculation, one that may in any given instance appear impossibly complex – it takes a good head ! - but the weighing of options in terms of consequences for happiness is a calculation nonetheless. In principle, with a good enough head one could use procedures of evaluation, measurement and comparison to determine the correct course of action. The choice Kant is talking about, choice which duty cannot resolve is an election based on calculation (*Wahl*). So when Kant says of duty that we cannot treat it as though there were a 'real' *Wahl* involved, he is not so much contradicting Derrida's position as agreeing with it. If duty is to mean anything to us, it cannot be of the order of what is in principle calculable. Kant and Derrida thus agree at least this far, that duty must be of another order than *Wahl*. Of course, this is not to assume too quickly that Derrida and Kant therefore 'agree' on what type of act would *not* be determined by such calculation. But this does serve to underline that what will determine their agreement or disagreement is not whether or not duty is subject to calculation, but what type of decision might *not* be reducible to a calculation.

Both Derrida and Kant will argue that there can be no talk of duty where calculations of happiness are determinant. For Kant, instead of a calculation an act of duty must result from a free choice, a choice of freedom, instead of submission to the laws of nature. An act of duty must be an autonomous decision to affirm the rational self, to make reason that which determines the action. Derrida, however, will object that the free choice Kant posits as a rational choice of determining grounds for action is but yet another determination by rules. The determining grounds may be said to be rational rather than sensible but they offer determination of the action in the determined order of submission to a law. According to Derrida then, although Kant may assert the logical requirement that duty, if it is to mean anything, must be determined beyond any calculation, his thinking shies away from the most rigorous confrontation with the consequences of this requirement, simply substituting one regime of rule for another. From this perspective, Kant's contention that even a child knows which act the moral law dictates in a given set of circumstances marks a belief that the moral law provides a rule, a protocol, a procedure which can ensure an act of duty. Before acknowledging too quickly that Kant's reference to the moral law does reduce the act of duty to a following of a protocol, let us note that for his duty to be assured by a calculation or protocol, Kant would have to hold *both* that it is possible to deduce rules from morality, to fix the rules which morality would dictate *and* that such rules, when followed, would *ensure* an act of duty. For the deduction of rules from duty does not *in itself* constitute the object of Derrida's quarrel with Kant. That one thinks rules may be deduced from ethics does not necessarily commit one to the position that following the rules, executing the procedures is *enough* to guarantee an act of duty ensues. Derrida himself never fails to note that the impossibility of a deduction of politics from ethics in no way reduces its necessity, or indeed its urgency. Thus Kant's efforts to deduce rules/right from ethics do not in and of themselves demonstrate that his thought does not encompass that of a duty beyond all calculation and all rules. On the contrary, it is possible to find Kant not only recognising that these deductions are never definitive in the sense that they can be perfected (better deductions can be made) but even arguing that any deduction must remain open to question – not just indefinitely but also infinitely. That Kant advocates not only the possibility, but also the necessity, of extracting specific rules from the very concept of duty should not too quickly induce us to relegate him to some insufficiently radical appreciation of the heterogeneity of ethics to procedures and rules. We must instead consider the relation he posits between duty and rules in all its complexity.

Alongside the Kant who lays down a specific constitution as a necessary condition for the moralisation of humanity, alongside the Kant who offers detailed analyses of the criminal and civil laws which are necessary consequences of correct practical thinking, there is a Kant who explicitly argues that any rules imposed in the name of duty must in principle remain indefinitely open to modification. In 'What is Enlightenment?', Kant characterises it as 'a crime against human nature' to presume to establish definite rules. To the question of whether a society of clergymen should 'be entitled to commit itself by oath to a certain unalterable set of doctrines, in order to secure for all time a constant guardianship over each of its members, and through them over all people?' Kant replies:

this is quite impossible. A contract of this kind, concluded with a view to preventing all further enlightenment of mankind forever, is absolutely null and void, even it if is ratified by the supreme power, by Imperial Diets and the most solemn peace treatise. One age cannot enter into an alliance on oath to put the next age in a position where it would be impossible for it to extend and correct its knowledge, particularly on such important matters, or to make any progress whatsoever in enlightenment. This would be a crime against human nature, whose original destiny lies in such progress. Later generations are thus perfectly entitled to dismiss these agreements as unauthorised and criminal.[23]

Just as one age cannot presume that a latter one will not perfect the knowledge it has acquired, one age cannot determine the rules of conduct for the next. Just as to limit knowledge would be absurd, to limit progress in Enlightenment would be a crime against human nature. In the name of progress, as human nature, the possibility of progress must remain open and this is as true for rules of conduct as it is for knowledge. Thus, however firm his commitment to certain laws, to the content he gives to his *Doctrine of Right*, Kant insists we remain open to the substitution of this content. Indeed, the possibility of such a substitution is a condition for the coherence of his thought which would otherwise participate in a criminal frustration of human nature.

It is important to remember this requirement that rules never be fixed definitively in order to avoid caricaturing Kant's faith in the possibility of settling ethics into rules. However this does not yet answer Derrida's complaint. For Kant to recognise that the content of the rules deduced from ethics must in principle remain open to revision is not the same as recognising that their deduction from ethics is in principle impossible. When Kant argues that a revision of the deduction must always be possible, he is concerned with an inadequacy of the deduction which is open to correction. Kant then leaves room for a progressive approach to an adequate translation of ethics into politics, suggesting an asymptotic approach to perfection rather than its immediate accomplishment. However requiring that the deduction remain open to revision is quite different from claiming, as Derrida does, that the deduction is impossible *in principle*. Derrida's 'impossible in principle' is to mark a more radical difficulty: the problem is not that any given deduction is not good enough, but that, insofar as it presumes to transpose the decision to a problem of logic and knowledge, *any* deduction can only serve to efface the impossibility of the choice or the ethical dimension of the decision of ethics. According to Derrida then, what Kant fails to grasp here is that duty can, in principle, never be chosen by knowledge and/or logic. Logic as always determinate and determinant, will always be antagonistic, hostile to letting a responsible decision come to pass. To hope to establish rules, even rules which will be progressively refined, risks supressing the possibility of thinking about duty in its most specific and radical sense. Derrida then does seem to have a formal objection to Kant, precisely an object to the formalism of his thinking of the relation between ethics and right: Kant is, for Derrida, too close to logical formalism, the formalism necessary for thinking logic instead of moving radically away from the logical principles which organise knowledge.

Is this enough to dismiss Kant as that 'beyond' which we must move? Derrida's challenge to Kant must rest on a double point: that Kant thinks he can deduce rules from ethics and that such rules are adequate in principle to determine an act of duty. While Derrida easily establishes the first point, the second is more problematic and requires that we take into account Kant's thought where it demands on the contrary that no rules be sufficient to determine an act of duty. There are indeed moments where Kant is not as far from Derrida as the latter would have us think. Kant's practical philosophy does not just demand that the rules one purports to deduce from ethics be indefinitely open to revision, it also insists that an act of duty in the strongest sense, the sense which indeed gives any meaning to the term, remains outside the logic of progressive refinement of rules and procedures. Not only does Kant insist on the necessity of leaving open the possibility of progress in the deductions we make, he also at times makes clear that this logic of progress, which is also a progress of logic, cannot be the correct language for describing an act of duty in the purest of senses, an act of virtue.

'Virtue is always *in progress* and yet always starts *from the beginning.*'[24] With this rather paradoxical claim the Introduction to the *Doctrine of Virtue* marks that, although progress may be a useful way of thinking of virtue in its objective manifestations, from the point of view of the event which is the choice of duty, virtue always starts from the beginning. The choice of duty cannot be made progressively, but only ever from the beginning and all at once. The act of free choice is not subject to progress: it either takes place or does not. And all the progress Kant foretells for humanity is progress of *legality*, not morality proper. 'The profit which will accrue to the human race as it works its way forward will not be an ever increasing quantity of morality in its attitudes.'[25] There will be a generalisation of legality, of the conformity of actions to the dictates of the moral law, but this says nothing of morality in the strong sense. Progress is a relevant notion for legality, not morality and indeed the relevance of the notion of progress is a good indicator of the heterogeneity of legality to morality. Legality is a measure of an action's conformity to juridical laws, morality is the moral worth which can only be attributed to an act motivated by the command of duty. 'The mere conformity or non-conformity of an action with law, irrespective of the incentive to it, is called its legality (lawfulness); but that conformity in which the Idea of duty arising from the law is also the incentive to the action is called its *morality*.'[26] There is a rule and measure for legality; legality can be increased progressively. But there is no measure for the morality of an act: morality is not subject to degrees and therefore not susceptible to progress.[27] We have no means of even conceiving a measure of morality because the morality of an act is precisely that which lies outside the world of measure, the phenomenal world in which measuring makes sense.[28] Whereas we can *know*, we can decide theoretically, whether an act conforms to the law, we can never *know* whether a given act is a moral act. 'In actual fact it is absolutely impossible for experience to establish with complete certainty a single case in which the maxim of an action in other respects right has rested solely on moral grounds and on the thought of one's duty.'[29] The moral value of an act is not measurable, not knowable. Duty, in the strong sense of an act for the sake of duty, a virtuous act, is heterogeneous to knowledge. We must therefore note that, although Kant seems to say that we 'know' what duty dictates, this has to be complicated: strictly speaking, Kant must insist that we can never *know* that a given act is adequate to duty. Although Kant can claim that even a child knows what to do, this does not mean that we can ever 'know' how to act virtuously.[30] We must temper the accusations that Kantian duty is of the same order as knowledge.

Although such claims as 'virtue always begins again from the beginning' are perhaps not the most familiar ones to readers of Kant, these are crucial parts of Kant's thought.[31] Indeed, that virtue *not* be knowable or measurable by concepts and rules is critical for it not to be reduced to an empirical concept, which is itself a condition for the possibility of a philosophical account of duty. It must, for Kant, remain impossible to know particular instances of acts which are acts of virtue in the strict sense, acts performed for the sake of the moral law. It is in the name of this rigorous distinction between legality and morality that Kant will insist that 'Imitation has no place in morality.'[32] Since we have no way of recognising a model of morality, one cannot hope to have a model to imitate. There is no act of which we could say that it can furnish a model of virtue, a model of duty accomplished for the sake of the moral law. Accepting a model of virtue for Kant would imply accepting an implicit rule: any model 'contains' its own rule. To be consistent in distinguishing virtue from that which can be prescribed, or described, by rules, Kant will break with a long tradition of education by imitation.

'Virtue is always *in progress* and yet always starts *from the beginning*.'[33] When we read the Kant who talks about progress and revision of right, we should never forget that then he is talking about legality. When he talks about virtue in the strong sense, he will instead claim that one must always start from the beginning. According to Kant, there can be no morality comfortably guided by rules, 'virtue can never settle down in peace and quiet with its maxims adopted once and for all.'[34] Virtue cannot be the confident execution of a programme or routine. It can never become a habit.[35] Rules, knowledge, protocols, ritual – all these will never allow one to settle confidently and assuredly, with a good conscience, into virtue. 'For a man cannot carry his giving an example of the respect due others so far as to degenerate into blind imitation (in which custom, *mos*, is raised to the dignity of a law), since such a tyranny of popular mores would be contrary to a man's duty to himself.'[36] When he is considering morality and not legality, when he attempts to describe duty in what must be its proper sense for the philosopher, Kant's language is not far from Derrida's: the act of duty, if there is such a thing, cannot come from habit or custom. An act of duty, if it is to be duty in any sense which would distinguish the act from the run of natural causality, must remain heterogeneous to calculation, to knowledge, to rituals and established procedures. However necessary it is to use reason to establish the specific rights which conform to the moral law, the language of rites, or of rights, cannot allow us to think duty in the strong sense.

Enduring

To think duty, we must think against or beyond Kant, says Derrida. We must move beyond the traditional accounts of duty, not only beyond ritual associations of duty with specific rites, but even beyond the very language of duty which will always tend to reduce the specificity of duty to a more manageable quantity, reduce it indeed to a quantity which can be manipulated by known procedures of conceptual calculation. Kant himself does not avoid positing a procedure which banishes the necessity of considering a duty which would not be a simple submission to particular rules. However, against Derrida's account – that is in opposition to Derrida's picture, but also taking his account as our backdrop – we can read a Kant who not only demands that rules imposed in the name of ethics must remain open to constant revision, but also, more importantly, defines morality as that which remains inaccessible by/to imitation, knowledge, habits, and rituals. We find Kant struggling with the fact that it is only if virtue does remain impervious to rules (either prescriptive or descriptive) that philosophy can have anything to say on the subject; virtue must not, if it is to mean anything at all (and not be simply another word for an empirical concept), be governed by logic or any other rules. Derrida *himself* seems to acknowledge the force of Kant's distinction between right and ethics when, in 'Force of Law', he describes the heterogeneity he is eager to insist on not *against* Kant, but *in Kant's very terms*. Having stipulated the need to think justice through an experience of *aporia*, Derrida explains that following rules does not ensure justice:

> If I were content to apply a just rule, without a spirit of justice and without in some way inventing the rule and the example for each case, I might be protected by law (droit), my action corresponding to objective law, but I would not be just. I would act, Kant would say, *in conformity* with duty, but not *through duty* or *out of respect* for the law.[37]

Derrida here takes up Kant's distinction between acting in conformity with duty and out of duty not as simply a first step in the clarification of the specificity of duty but as sufficing: Kant's distinction here is credited with being precisely the distinction which Derrida wants to draw between applying a rule and inventing a just response. In 'Force of Law', Derrida then leads us to assume that the just act, that which would be the occasion for an invention, proper to each occasion, is precisely what Kant was considering when he referred to acts through duty. Yet in later texts Derrida will repeatedly exhort us to think a duty *against* and *without* Kant precisely because the latter does not leave room to think duty as beyond all rules in this radical sense. Why does Derrida come to demand a move beyond Kant? His ultimate formulation of the quarrel with Kant seems to hinge on the requirement that a thought of duty must *endure* the impossibility of being determined by rules. It is not enough, according to Derrida, to accept that, for a responsible decision to be such, it cannot be determined by a rule or a procedure. Nor is it enough to recognise that rules which determine actions in the name of duty are necessary despite the impossibility of deducing rules from ethics. Derrida formulates an extra condition for thinking a duty worthy of the name: that such thinking 'endure' the impossibility of having rules for duty even as it accepts their necessity.[38] It is not enough to *recognise* even the double bind duty is in with respect to respecting rules, one must 'endure' this. This is where, according to Derrida, Kant fails us. Derrida will claim that, although he may have recognised that duty must be beyond rules, Kant undermines the possibility of enduring this thought. Kant ruins the possibility of having this impossibility endure in his thought. Noting that when Kant sets forth a Universal Hospitality he immediately modulates the universality of such a right, reducing it to certain conditions, Derrida asserts:

> the thinker of the cosmopolitical right to universal hospitality, the author of the Third Article towards perpetual peace is also, without there being here anything coincidental, he who destroys at the very root what he poses

and determines thereby. And this stems from the juridicity of this discourse, from the inscription in a right of that principle of hospitality of which the infinite idea would have to resist right itself - in any case to go beyond it exactly there where the idea demands it. [my translation][39]

Kant thus destroys the very ethics he puts forward, by his inscription of an ethical principle in juridical laws. This is how Derrida can continue to take issue with Kant, arguing that although Kant may have indeed recognised that a deduction of rules must remain impossible, he could not long endure this. The more radical conception, the heterogeneity of morality and legality is banished, controlled, or even denied, by the rest of Kant's text. According to Derrida, Kant's text destroys the thought of the impossible choice of duty, shying away from an experience of enduring the impossibility. It is of course hard to establish what exactly it would entail for a thought to have risen to this challenge of enduring the contradiction between the necessity and the impossibility of deducing rights from ethics. The endurance Derrida is invoking is not simply a passive endurance which would be the capacity to be inured to the difficulty, to emerge unscathed. Rather than avoiding the difficulty, enduring it requires attempting an experience of the impossibile. A proper conception of duty, Derrida asserts, must be a response to the challenge to think *together* the impossibility in principle of a deduction and the necessity for particular rules which could claim a relationship to ethics. This response would be the condition of a responsible thought of duty as responsibility.

We have seen that Kant's work offers two apparently contradictory answers to the question of whether there can be rules legitimately claiming to translate the moral law, two answers to the question of whether a deduction of law from ethics is possible. On the one hand there is the Kant who confidently deduces rights from morality. These rights dictate, set out, say what is to be done; they formalise and fix the knowledge which can determine an act of duty. On the other hand, we have a Kant saying that taking any model as a model for duty is to fall short of morality proper. Any imitation, any following of a model, and indeed *any* following of pre-existing rules will condemn the action to fall short of being an act of duty. To ask whether the heterogeneity of duty to rules is endured by/in Kant's thought is to ask whether, and how, the two strands of thought are linked. Does Kant's text offer a thought of, or an occasion for, enduring the tension between these two strands of thought?[40] Does his text allow us to read *together* Kant's prescription of a specific constitution in the name of his ethics and his explanation that a virtuous act *must* be of a different order from calculation or knowledge? For Kant's thought to offer us a thought which endures the antinomy, as Derrida would say, it must offer us an experience of thinking the two antinomic conditions. Kant does demand that we think *both* that an act of duty, a virtuous act, cannot be determined by any rules *and* there must be rules which can be extracted/deduced from morality, rules which would determine an ethical act. I would like to suggest that he also offers us a chance to think these 'together'. Or rather, to be more precise, I would like to suggest that there is an occasion in Kant's work, specifically in the first half of the *Critique of Judgment*, for thinking an act which would have to follow the rules, and yet not be determined by them. This being precisely the same formal double constraint as must be endured by an act of duty, we may find here in Kant's text the elements of a response to the antinomy. That the conceptual constructions Kant offers us in this perspective are precisely developed as a description of the experience of responding to the impossibility of presenting what must nevertheless be presented can but facilitate an association of the proposed reading with what Derrida seems to envisage as an experience of enduring the antinomy of duty. Before following Derrida in his dismissal of Kantian duty as incapable of making room for a duty which would be an invention, let us then consider how the *Critique of Judgment* opens up a possibility for reading Kant's theory of duty.

The first characteristic of genius is originality: 'genius is the exemplary originality of a subject's natural endowment in the *free* use of his cognitive powers.'[41] That a genius must be original means for Kant that the genius does not imitate, does not follow a model and does not follow any given rule. Indeed Kant insists that 'imitation' describes all that *could* be done in imitation, thus encompassing everything that 'lies in the natural path of an investigation and mediation by rules'[42]; following a rule and copying a model are equivalent because copying a model must involve following the rules the model gives. Coining a term for the non-imitative work of the genius, Kant defines *Nachfolge* in opposition to *Nachahmung*.[43] What is interesting here is that precisely when Kant claims to need a new term to describe the manner in/by which genius distinguishes himself, sets his work apart from all that goes before,[44] he coins a term which is reinscribed in a language of following – 'nach'. To affirm that the genius' work is not imitation is to say that it is not determined by anything which precedes it (in what seems to be the most rigorous extension of the idea of precedence) and yet the genius' act is defined as a 'nach' of *some* sort. The choice of *Nachfolge* as a term to distinguish the work of genius from anything which is the result of imitation thus marks some sort of succession; the work of genius cannot be the result of an imitative following of a pre-existing model *and yet* it is defined by some relation to a predecessor. The genius, in other words, must exceed any pre-existing models/rules *and yet* have a relation to pre-existing models/rules.

Commentators never fail to insist on the originality which defines genius (there is no rule for the work of genius), but sufficient attention is not always paid to the fact that Kant *also* insists that the work of genius *needs* to follow *rules*. Granted, 'genius must be considered the very opposite of *spirit of imitation*,'[45] but, if the genius can thus produce works of art precisely because he is doing something which does 'differ in kind' from that for which there are rules, *nonetheless,* as the second part of this section specifies, 'there is no fine art, that does not have as its essential condition something mechanical, which can be encompassed by rules and complied with, and hence has an element of academic correctness.'[46] We must never fail to remember this or we will risk the ridicule Kant heaps on shallow minds.[47] According to Kant, completely renouncing all rules would simply result in nonsense.[48] Nonsense or mere product of chance, haphazard without sense rather than invention of a new sense, such would be the result of proceeding without rules: 'something must be thought, as purpose, since otherwise the product cannot be ascribed to any art at all, but would be a mere product of chance.'[49]

That the genius does follow the rules of academic correctness turns out then to be as important a condition of possibility of a work for genius as is the condition that the work not be the product of simply following rules. Kant proposes to think these two conditions together by doubling the double relation to rules. As he explains in §49, the relation of a work of genius to rules is actually fourfold:

> the product of genius (as regards what is attributable to genius in it rather than to possible learning or academic instruction) is an example that is meant not to be imitated, but to be followed by another genius. (For in mere imitation the element of genius in the work - what constitutes the spirit – would be lost.) The other genius, who follows the example, is aroused by it to a feeling of his own originality, which allows him to exercise in art his freedom from the constraint of rules, and to do so in such a way that art itself acquires a new rule by this, thus showing that his talent is exemplary. But since a genius is nature's favorite and so must be regarded as a rare phenomenon, his example gives rise to a school for other good minds, i.e., a methodical instruction by means of whatever rules could be extracted from those products of spirit and their peculiarity.[50]

Let us note how many affirmations are condensed into this passage :

1. The work of genius must be original: his product, as regards what is attributable to genius, must differ in kind from what can be

produced by rules, what is due to possible learning or academic instruction is not attributed to the product of genius as such.
2. The work of genius must respect academic correctness, in other words follow a set of rules.
3. The work of genius must have the power to arouse another genius who can follow him, meaning that there would be a relation between the two but, insofar as this succession is not simply imitation but following, the first does not give a rule to the second (the successor 'is aroused by it to a feeling of his own originality, which allows him to exercise in art his freedom from the constraint of rules').
4. However the work of genius is also a source of rules since it 'gives rise to a school', a methodical instruction by means of rules 'extracted' from the work.[51]

Kant thus posits simultaneously that, to be a product of genius, the work of art needs to follow rules and go beyond them, *and* that it needs to provoke another genius to go beyond all rules while also providing the rules for academic correctness which are the minimum condition for the successor's work.[52] The double relation to rules (follow them, and go beyond them) is doubled again: from the work of genius comes both an awakening to go beyond rules and the possibility of extracting new academic rules. Thus to contemplate the double relation to rules which originality imposes – original and yet not nonsense, not determined by rules and yet not without following rules – Kant suggests that the work of genius must respond to the double condition by enduring in two ways : enduring as a source of rules and enduring as that which offers a new chance of going beyond the rule of (even the new) rules. By considering the relation of a work of genius to a successor in time, Kant can articulate how an act might both bear a relation to rules (following them, and being a source for rules) and be different in kind from anything which rules could dictate in its legacy. The logic of a double legacy in return provides a model for considering the original work's double relation to rules. The work of genius must endure in two ways to be said to have endured the double condition of following rules and having been invented beyond all rules.

This reminder of the complex relation to rules endured by Kant's genius highlights that there is at the very least an interesting parallel between the genius' relation to rules and the relation of morality to rules. Both Kant's theory of the act of virtue, and his theory of the genius must work with the necessity of a double relation to rules: the act must follow rules and the act must be different in kind from anything rules can dictate. Both the work of genius and the act of virtue must follow a certain number of rules in the sense of not breaking them and yet they cannot, if they are to have any sense, be determined by them. A work of genius must, as a minimum condition, have an element of academic correctness, and yet not be such that it might have been the result of following any academic program. An act of virtue must, as a minimum condition, conform to legality and yet it cannot be such that it might have been determined by judicial laws. Neither the work of genius, nor the act of virtue, can be the result of imitation but both must conform to rules. Furthermore one must 'extract' rules, however inadequate to the original from both the work of genius, and the act of virtue.[53] There is perhaps more here than a parallel. Perhaps Kant's theory of the work of genius should be taken not just as a clarification of that which is involved in the production of works of art but also as a proposition for a vocabulary suited to describing the act of virtue. The *Critique of Judgment* can indeed be read as supplying Kant's best attempt at finding a conceptual description of what distinguishes an act of duty in the strong sense from an act which simply conforms to duty.

If we do read the *Critique of Judgment* as providing an occasion for rethinking what an act of duty would have to be,[54] if the term is to mean anything, then perhaps we do have a thought which might be said to endure the difficulty: we find Kant's thought (of) enduring an antinomy, an antinomical relation to rules, an impossibility of presenting what must be presented. Kant's theory of genius is indeed a theory of enduring the impossibility of presenting. The work of genius does nothing to reduce impossibility of presenting and yet does not submit passively to this impossibility.[55] Rather it endures the impossibility, it endures a paradoxical relation to rules and indeed makes the paradox endure by provoking both good minds (those good heads for calculation) and other geniuses. Insofar as it is precisely such a non-determinant role of rules as this which Kant seems to be at pains to conceive (in both senses of the word) for duty, Kant's aesthetic theory may provide the best answer to the challenge of providing a positive description of the act of virtue, an act from duty.

What now of Derrida's claim that Kant's conception of duty fails to leave room for a decision in the strong sense?[56] If we do develop a reading of his conception of duty which appeals to the theory of genius, we would be led to conclude that in Kant's account, an act of duty must be an *invention*: not without rules but beyond them, not to be imitated and yet source of rules for a new school, before another explosion of freedom/duty/genius. An act of duty (if there is such a thing, which we will never know) must be an invention which interrupts the rules (of the academy). The event which interrupts all rules must nonetheless bear some relation to them (both to the rules from which it breaks away, and to rules it may provide), otherwise it would remain sheer nonsense. Yet the relation of the invention to a rule or model can not be one of logical deduction or any other procedural extrapolation. An act of duty, if there is such thing, if that is to mean anything, cannot be determined by any rule, or any programme. And yet, if duty is to mean anything, it must be possible to derive rules and protocols from duty (it must be possible to deduce rights from ethics). Indeed 'good minds' (the same *güte Köpfe* who produce academic art and who determine their course of actions by calculations of happiness)[57] need rules and a good mind will always be a necessary, although not sufficient, condition for either a work of genius or a truly virtuous act. A deduction of rules must therefore always be possible – it must always be possible to extract rules (legality) from an act of duty (morality) - and yet to act out of duty requires an invention beyond rules; the act of duty cannot be the result of any deduction. If we take Kant's theory of aesthetic judgment to be an essential component of his theory of moral judgment, the choice which is involved in duty according to Kant, that which is no *Wahl* at all, may turn out to be an impossible choice according to Derrida's definition. One of Derrida's ways of qualifying of a decision in the strong sense of the term is that such a decision would be neither active nor passive. If we do read Kant's theory of genius as proposing a formulation of what an act of freedom would look like, we find that Kant too withstands the thought that the act of duty is neither simply active nor simply passive. The work of a genius is his own production, there is an active element but the active element is the moment of judging what he has produced despite himself. Indeed, Kant suggests that the genius finds the form of his work by taste,[58] which is 'merely an ability to judge'.[59] And even the act of judgment which might most properly be called the genius' active accomplishment is both active and passive: the talent which makes possible a pure judgment of taste is both a gift of nature (passive), and the result of cultivation (active). The genius chooses, judges, that which comes to him; he elects to pick up on it, chooses to have chosen it. But such a judgment of taste is only possible because the genius has been chosen. If we take this as a cue to thinking about duty, the choice of duty will be, according to Kant's text, choosing it and being chosen.[60] For Kant we must always try to choose in the name of freedom, but choice is a hope to choose/be chosen by freedom. Invention is the name for the active dimension of the judgment of taste, or, by extension, of duty.[61] The act of invention, the act which is the only choice worthy of the name, is at the limit where active and passive cannot be distinguished: it is a being chosen as much as, even as, it is an act of choice. Or rather it is a response to (a taking of responsibility for?) one's election. It is also always inventing a duty to choose.

The act of duty, as the work of genius, can only be an event which invents a new response to an impossible challenge, the challenge of a choice in the strong sense of choosing where there are no criteria for choice, of deciding where no rules can help. To act out of duty would then have to be a choice only through the invention of a new possibility, the novelty of which does not preclude, on the contrary requires, a relation to the past and to a future. Such is the thought of duty which emerges from an experience of reading Kant on duty, taking the theory of aesthetic judgment to be the occasion for thinking an act which is in a double bind with respect to respecting rules. The resonance with Derrida's propositions is striking. In their respective insistence that an act of duty, if there is such a thing, would have to interrupt the rules of nature and the rules of logic,[62] Derrida and Kant both posit an act of invention which might be thought of as the duty to invent oneself out of an impossible choice. They evoke a duty to invent *a way out* of the impossibility of choice, to invent a way out of impossibility, to invent a way to choose where it is impossible to choose but theirs is also a duty to invent the *self*, that is the self capable of choice, out of the experience of this impossibility.[63] The act of duty will have to have invented a choice, a possible choice and the possibility of choosing. Such would be the duty Derrida, after Kant, leaves us: a duty to invent *ourselves* out of an impossible choice.

Unless this is not so much the duty both Kant and Derrida have passed on to us, as an invention of my desire not to have to make an impossible choice between them ...

The reading I have been sketching suggests that Derrida trespasses *on* Kantian ground precisely where he claims to be trespassing *against* Kant. It suggests that Derrida's conception of duty which goes against Kant because beyond Kant, is perhaps not altogether 'beyond' Kant, if we learn to read together the different parts of the Kantian text. By insisting on the *Critique of Judgment* as an essential element of Kant's thought, we find a Kant who can endure the criticism Derrida has sometimes levelled at him. We find a Kant who cannot simply be taxed with insufficient rigour, charged with having left his logic halfway, leaving it to Derrida to complete the task. After Derrida we must not simply, as some of his formulations suggest we do, look back at Kant as the one who came before, according to a model of progress they have both given us reason to complicate.[64] That the relation between these two thinkers can then no longer be thought of in terms of a linear succession, is no doubt due to the fact that it is, of course, Derrida who has opened the possibility of reading Kant's text as offering more than a simple preparation to Derrida. It is only *after* Derrida that we realise that Kant is not simply a predecessor of Derrida's. Kant after Derrida is not Kant before Derrida. It is only possible to read the Kant who is proposing duty as invention after Derrida, even if this is not Kant *d'après* Derrida. Thus Derrida will have given us to read not only the Kant against whom he argues for an impossible decision, but also the Kant who already attempts to express a philosophical response to the challenge of thinking decisions, original scissions, judgments, which are not governed by rules or logic. Derrida will have given us to read not only the author of *Perpetual Peace* who, deducing conditioned rights from unconditional ethical principles, destroys at its root what he posits, but also the author of the third *Critique* who struggles to find an expression for an act which could exceed all determination by rules while enduring a necessary relation to rules.

I have tried to show that one can pursue a reading of Kant's theory of duty, through a reading of the *Critique of Judgment*, to find Kant closer to Derrida than might be expected. But why read Kant this way? I cannot avoid a suspicion that, although it may hold up to the rules of academic correctness, that it is not wrong or impossible, such a reading may also be a way of avoiding a choice between Kant and Derrida. How reassuring to have them both describing the same impossible duty! Although I would defend the possibility, and even the necessity, of following such a reading,[65] the very coincidence it reveals between Kant and Derrida serves to indicate that we must also start again, perhaps from the beginning: if we contest Derrida's contention that he is separated from Kant by a different degree of rigour in the distinction between right and ethics, we must search for another way of expressing what *does* separate Derrida from Kant on the question of duty. The issue which separates them may not be in the fact of positing a radical heterogeneity between ethics and politics, nor even the recognition that to be consistent a thought of duty would then have to attempt to endure the heterogeneity without resignation. One cannot however say there is simply no difference between them. There is unquestionably a difference in manner, precisely as they approach the problems where the arrangement of thoughts owes more to the *modus aestheticus* than the *modus logicus*.[66] The specificity of Kant's thought with respect to Derrida's may not be a question of logic, not even of the degree of logic, but rather of some standard of measure for thought which is not logical.

In his recent seminar on the death penalty, Derrida has once again been confronting Kant on a question concerning rights and ethics. As Derrida searches for an ethics in the name of which to argue for abolition, he has repeatedly suggested that all the arguments usually put forward to defend the abolitionist stance actually participate of the logic which, when most rigorously pursued, lead Kant to provide the strongest philosophical arguments on the subject – in favour of the death penalty.[67] The impossible choice out of which Derrida wants to invent himself comes to look like a choice between abolitionist sympathies and the possibility of defending one's position philosophically. Indeed, Derrida has been explicitly worried by what he calls the fact that, to this day, *all* philosophical defences of a position on the issue of the death penalty can be seen to condone it in principle, no matter which side they claim to be on. He has come to hypothesise that philosophy may properly always lead to a support of the death penalty.[68] Arguing philosophically, there has yet been no choice but to follow Kant on this question – for in this issue Kant has become the exemplary philosopher, the most rigorous of them all (*'Kant ... étant sans doute le plus rigoureux de tous'*).[69] Derrida thus faces the prospect that *any* faithfulness to Kant, any faithfulness *even* to betray Kant by working for abolition, may entail a betrayal in principle of the attempt to cast the abolitionist case in terms of a right deduced necessarily, although impossibly, from an ethics. Kant becomes the name for philosophy's opposition to Derrida's *desire* for a philosophical defence of abolitionism. Derrida's justification for his position on the death penalty is indeed justified in terms of a desire which precedes philosophical justification: his sympathy for the abolitionist cause is what first pushes him to consider how such a right might be defended philosophically.[70] Derrida then hypothesises that philosophy has never yet left room for a specific choice against a system of right comprising the death penalty. He raises the possibility that any appeal to philosophy, and to Kant as its exemplary representative, to develop the rigour of the abolitionist discourse may be counterproductive.

There has thus been a shift in Derrida's confrontation with Kant. On the issue of the death penalty, Kant is no longer reproached for being insufficiently rigorous but rather admired for his very rigour in developing a reciprocal relation between ethics and politics, even if this relation seems to exclude *in principle* a specific right Derrida desires to defend. The admiration Derrida professes for Kant's rigour only confirms that to follow his duty, to follow the duty of inventing a defence of abolition as a duty, Derrida can no longer contemplate a move *beyond* Kant. Rather he feels compelled to avoid even beginning to follow Kant's elaboration of ethics and rights.[71] Thus whereas in a discussion of the possibility of the deduction of rights from ethics, Derrida invites us to prolong Kant *beyond* Kant, when he considers first a specific question of right, Derrida warns that *any* concession to Kant may preclude the possibility of a certain choice, that which reflects Derrida's own chosen duty; any concession to Kant's rationality is a concession to a devastating if insidious (pathological, one might say) opposition to the abolitionist cause.

Derrida seems thus to find two lines of objection to the concept of duty inherited from Kant, both of which involve a decision which is a choice beyond all rules. The first line of objection involves a demand that a non-logical (i.e. impossible according to logic) decision be *posited* beyond the decision Kant envisages; a choice, in the strong sense, beyond Kant. The second line contemplates a non-logical decision which must have been *taken* before entering into logic, before beginning to use conceptual/philosophical tools to construct an expression of the relation between rights and ethics. As we continue to read Kant, in the perspective of trying to elaborate our own way of inheriting his Enlightenment, we must continue to read in both of these directions Derrida. On the one hand, we can continue, or begin again, as I suggested earlier to read Kant after Derrida by reconsidering Kant's theory of aesthetic judgment – that peculiar site in critical philosophy where the distinction between the pathological and the rational can only be upheld by enduring the impossibility of separating them, or the necessity of imagining their necessary complicity. We should return to the delicate question of the position of the aesthetic judgment in the Kantian system, and in particular the role of something like an aesthetic judgment in a full account of Kant's conception of duty, in order to refine the reading of Kant's account of duty which seems closest to Derrida's. On the other hand, we must consider the possibility that something like an aesthetic judgment is precisely what keeps Derrida and Kant apart. It may be that we have to take seriously a certain judgment, a judgment without the guidance of concepts or rules, which determines the very choice of putting concepts and rules to work in the formalisation of philosophical thought and argument. We need then to read Kant after Derrida in both these directions, with the double risk of collapsing their accounts onto one another or finding them separated too far for any philosophical discussion between them. One must read knowing that work of 'clarifying' these questions is a necessary precondition for being able to think/read responsibly, although it is only perhaps a preliminary exercise. By following this double task, a double duty of reading, one can perhaps hope to find conceptual tools for choosing a new way to inherit Kant – conceptual tools which are necessary to, but will never ensure the possibility of, inventing a way of reading Kant after Derrida.

Notes:

1 *Un geste 'd'amitié' ou 'de politesse' ne serait ni amical ni poli s'il obeissait purement et simplement à une règle rituelle. Mais ce* devoir *d'echapper à la règle de la bienséance ritualisée commande aussi bien de se porter au-delà du langage même de* devoir. *On ne doit pas être amical ou poli par devoir. Nous risquons une telle proposition, sans doute, contre Kant.*, Jacques Derrida, *Passions* (Paris: Galilée 1993), p.21.

2 See also *Passions* 88ff, where Derrida marks his objections to Kant's conception of duty; and Anne Dufourmantelle and Jacques Derrida *De l'hospitalité*, (Paris: Calmann-Lévy, 1997). *'Il ne s'agit pas ici ... si on veut bien lire, de répéter l'argument kantien au sujet de ce qui est "conforme au devoir"* (pflichtmässig*) mais bien au contraire, contre et sans Kant, de se porter au dela de la dette et du devoir, et donc même de ce qui se fait par pur devoir* (aus reiner Pflicht*). A suivre.'* (p.77). If only one reads what he is saying, one should see that Derrida is not repeating a Kantian distinction, but rather going against and without Kant. Thus does Derrida, in advance, dismiss part of the reading proposed here which will insist that there may be a repetition of a Kantian distinction, if one is willing to read Kant's distinction in a certain light. But such a dismissal can never be definitive – and must depend on what might be taken to be a 'repetition' here. Is it not possible to rehearse Kant's distinction without simply repeating it?

3 The transgression against Kant which Derrida is called to is exemplary of the transgression he considers to be a condition of possibility for duty at all. As he says in *Apories* (Paris: Galilée, 1996), '[p]erhaps nothing ever comes to pass except on the line of a transgression, the threshold of some "trespassing".' (p.66) [my translation], 'nothing ever comes to pass except ...'. For Derrida this very sparse expression encompasses a great deal: no decision comes to pass, no duty, no responsibility, no event. All these claims are somehow encompassed in this 'rien ne se passe-t-il jamais'. This is not to say that 'nothing comes to pass' is the most general form of the statement and that, for instance, 'no duty comes to pass' is a specific case of the more general statement. Neither is the transgression a specific case of the more general term transgression. What operate here are not the logical rules of generalisation but instead exemplary relations, those exemplary relations which Kant will describe in his critique of aesthetic judgment.

4 'It is necessary to derive a politics and a right from ethics.' [my translation], Jacques Derrida, *Adieu à Emmanuel Levinas*, (Paris: Galilée, 1997), p.198.

5 As so often, Derrida finds in common sense a certain paradoxical difficulty. Paradoxes we must live with are hidden, made liveable, in common sense – in the *doxa*.

6 *l'injonction* formelle *de la deduction reste irrécusable, et elle n'attend pas plus que le tiers ou la justice. L'éthique enjoint une politique et un droit ; cette dépendance et la direction de cette dérivation conditionnelle sont aussi irréversibles qu'inconditionnelles.*, Derrida, *Adieu*, p.199.

7 *Mais le* contenu *politique ou juridique ainsi assigné demeure en revanche indéterminé, toujours à déterminer au dela du savoir et de toute présentation, de tout concept et de toute intuition possibles, singulièrement, dans la parole et la responsabilité prises par chacun, dans chaque situation, et depuis une analyse chaque fois unique - unique et infinie, unique mais* a priori *exposée à la substitution, unique et pourtant générale, interminable malgré l'urgence de la décision*, Ibid.

8 'To protect the decision or the responsibility by knowledge , by some theoretical assurance, or by the certainty of being right, of being on the side of science, of consciousness or of reason, is to transform this experience into the deployment of a programme, into a technical application of a rule or a norm, or into the subsumption of a determined 'case.' All these are conditions that must never be abandoned, of course, but that, as such, are only the guardrail of a responsibility to whose calling they remain radically heterogeneous. The affirmation that announced itself through a negative form

was therefore the necessity of *experience* itself, the experience of the aporia (and these two words that tell of the passage and the nonpassage are thereby coupled in an aporetic fashion) as endurance or as passion, as interminable resistance or remainder.' *Aporias*, p.19.

9 *[s]ans le silence, sans le hiatus, qui n'est pas absence de règles,mais nécessité d'un saut à l'instant de la décision éthique, juridique ou politique, nous n'aurions qu'à dérouler le savoir en programme d'action. Rien ne serait plus irrésponsabilisant et plus totalitaire.*, Derrida, *Adieu*, p.201

10 In *L'autre cap*, a long sequence describing the duty Derrida advocates insists on the impossibility of deduction: 'To lay out in advance the generality of a rule as a solution to the antinomy...to lay it out as a force or a given science, as a knowledge or a power which would precede the singularity of each decision in order to regulate it...this would be the most sure and reassuring definition of responsibility as irresponsibility.' [my translation] (p.71). But a few pages later, Derrida reminds us that 'The *same duty* dictates cultivating the virtue of such critique, of the critical idea, the critical tradition, but also to submit it, beyond critique and questioning, to a deconstructive genealogy that thinks and exceeds it without yet compromising it.' (English version from *Aporias*, trans.Thomas Dutoit, Jacques Derrida (California: Stanford University Press, 1993), p.18, in *L'autre cap*, p.76). Thus for Derrida, to think duty we must go beyond the critical tradition but without compromising it. When Derrida quotes this passage later in *Apories* (p.40) he will add an explicit reference to Kant, underlining that it is '*Kant par excellence*' who must be submitted to this deconstruction.

11 The objection that Kant's commitment to right undermines the very possibility of an ethical act was perhaps expressed most clearly by Derrida in his analyses of hospitality. The third article of Perpetual Peace, 'Cosmopolitan Right shall be limited to Conditions of Universal Hospitality' is, for Derrida, emblematic of Kant's subordination of 'universal hospitality' to conditions. Cf infra note 39.

12 It is only because there is a realm of ethics which is not tainted with the empirical that there is the possibility of moral philosophy. It is only insofar as ethics is *not* simply a matter of juridical laws that a critique of practical reason is possible.

13 'The hiatus, the silence of this non-response to the schemas between ethics and politics, remains. It is a fact that it remains, and this fact is not an empirical contingency, it is a *Faktum*.' [my translation], Derrida, *Adieu*, pp.200-1.

14 Derrida, *Aporias*, p.16.

15 Geoffrey Bennington, *Interrupting Derrida* (London and New York: Routledge, 2000), pp.37-8.

16 This paradoxical logic is made to play a critical role in the *Critique of Judgment*, where it is crucial to Kant's account of genius. Kant is of course not the first to insist on what Derrida calls the well known paradox of the possibility of betraying to be faithful. There are however particularly strong Kantian associations when Derrida speaks of betraying to be faithful and this is perhaps an indication that Derrida's confrontation with Kant on the question of duty must also be a confrontation with the third *Critique*.

17 It is Derrida's faithfulness to a Kantian method which makes his transgressions into radicalisations. Note the Kantian structure of Derrida's argument: when he argues that the deduction of right from ethics must remain in principle impossible, the neces-

sity of the 'must' is that of a condition of possibility. Duty 'must' not involve a simple deduction if duty is to mean anything; such is precisely for instance the argumentative structure of the critique of aesthetic judgment: beauty, if it is to mean anything (i.e. to have a *specific* meaning in the sense of being distinct from everything else), must be not the agreeable etc.

18 Immanuel Kant, *Critique of Practical Reason*, trans. M. Gregor (Cambridge: Cambridge University Press, 1997), p. 73. Ak V 86.

19 Immanuel Kant, 'On the Common Saying: "This May be True in Theory, but it does not Apply in Practice"', in *Political Writings* 2nd ed. (Cambridge: Cambridge University Press, 1991), p.70. (henceforth 'Theory and Practice')

20 While Kant can be taken to be suggesting that what duty dictates can be 'known', we should note that this 'knowledge' is not as determinate as might seem. Strictly speaking the child does not so much 'know' what the moral law dictates as 'know' what it forbids: that keeping the money is incompatible with an act of duty here does not mean that simply returning it will ensure an act of duty. Furthermore, given Kant's insistent identification of reaching majority as a condition for acting from duty, the reference here to the distinctions a *child* draws would require careful interpretation but certainly should caution us against taking this child's discernment as a model for duty in the strong sense Kant will develop.

21 Kant, 'Theory and Practice', p.70.

22 Ibid. p.71.

23 Immanuel Kant, 'An Answer to the Question: "What is Enlightenment?"' in *Political Writings,* p.57.

24 Immanuel Kant, *The Metaphyics of Morals*, trans. M. Gregor (Cambridge: Cambridge University Press, 1991), p.209; Ak VI 409.

25 Immanuel Kant, 'The Contest of the Faculties', in *Political Writings*, p.187; Ak VII 91.

26 Kant, *The Metaphysics of Morals*, p.46; AkVI 219.

27 'The distinction between virtue and vice can never be sought in the degree to which one follows certain maxims.' *The Metaphysics of Morals*, p. 204; AkVI 404.

28 The moral worth of an act of duty is, to some extent, independent of the action which is the effect of the act in the phenomenal world: there can be no phenomenal distinction between acts which are legal and acts which are the result of an act of virtue.

29 Immanuel Kant, *Groundwork of the Metaphysics of Morals*, trans. H. J. Paton, (New York: Harper Torchbooks, 1964), p.74. Ak IV 407.

30 Note that what Kant actually says of the child in the example of 'Theory and Practice', is that he will undoubtedly know *not* to keep the money. What goes against the moral law can, for Kant, be a matter of knowledge but one cannot conclude that duty which coincides with the moral law can be an object of knowledge.

31 Although the necessity for such a thought of virtue is traceable throughout Kant's work, the explicit formulations of what amounts to an attempt to give a positive account of an ethical act are to be found essentially in the works from the nineties. It is then that we find the event of a virtuous act described in such a way as to insist on the discontinuity with the phenomenal world (and the laws associated with it). In the *Anthropology* (US: Southern Illinois University Press, 1996), Kant speaks of a metamorphosis, which cannot be brought about progressively but must occur as an explo-

sion (AkVII 294).
32 Kant, *Groundwork*, p.76, Ak IV 409.
33 Kant, *The Metaphysics of Morals*, p.209; Ak VI 409.
34 Ibid.
35 Kant, *Anthropology*, §12, Ak VII 147.
36 Kant, *The Metaphysics of Morals*, p.256; Ak VI 464.
37 Jacques Derrida, 'Force of Law: "The Mystical Foundation of Authority"' in *Deconstruction and the Possibility of Justice*, eds. Drucilla Cornell, Michael Rosenfeld, David Gray Carlson (New York, London: Routledge, 1992) p.17.
38 Cf for instance: 'The invention of the new which could not pass through the endurance of the antinomy would be a dangerous mystification, immorality plus clear conscience, and sometimes clear conscience as immorality.' [my translation], Derrida, *L'autre cap*, (Paris: Les Editions de Minuit, 1991), p.71. Or another passage in which the enduring is described as an ordeal: 'A decision which didn't go through the ordeal of the undecidable would not be a free decision, it would only be the programmable application or unfolding of a calculable process. It might be legal; it would not be just.', Derrida, 'Force of Law: "The Mystical Foundation of Authority"', p.24.
39 *le penseur du droit cosmopolitique à l'hospitalité universelle, l'auteur du Troisième Article en vue de la paix perpétuelle est aussi, sans qu'il n'y ait là rien de fortuit, celui qui détruit à sa racine même ce qu'il pose et détermine ainsi. Et cela tient à la juridicité de ce discours, à l'inscription dans un droit de ce principe d'hospitalité dont l'idée infinie devrait résister au droit lui-même – en tout cas l'excéder là même où elle le commande.*, *De l'hospitalité*, pp.66-7.
40 There is a standard Kantian response to this challenge which relies on distinguishing morality at the level of humanity and at the level of individual. This distinction allows Kant to talk both of morality in progress (a cumulative, rule governed progression) and of that morality which always starts again at the beginning. But appealing to this distinction is indeed a way of avoiding the problem of thinking them together in the sense Derrida is pursuing. Precisely because it serves to dissolve the problem, this distinction is indeed a way of avoiding the impossibility rather than confronting it. To establish whether Kant can be seen to be rising to the challenge of enduring the impossibility one must ask whether Kant offers us an occasion to read/think together at the same level, as an account of the singular act of duty, the two strands of thought.
41 Immanuel Kant, *Critique of Judgment*, trans. Werner S. Pluhar (Indianapolis/ Cambridge: Hackett Publishing Company, 1987), p.186; Ak V 318.
42 Ibid. p. 176; Ak V 308.
43 For the distinction between *Nachfolge* and *Nachahmung* see *Critique of Judgment* §49, pp. 186-7; Ak V 318. In §47 the opposition is set up as between *Nachmachung* and *Nachahmung*. The term which is opposed to *Nachahmung* still contains a reference to '*nach*'.
44 That the genius' work must be independent of all which comes before is, of course, a transcendental and not an empirical requirement. The independence from what is 'pre-existing' is not a temporal or empirical condition, but a logical one. The genius follows neither predecessors nor rules, even rules as yet unformulated.
45 Kant, *Critique of Judgment*, 176; Ak V 308.
46 Ibid. p. 178; Ak V 310.
47 'Now since originality of talent is one essential component (though not the only

one) of the character of genius, shallow minds believe that the best way to show that they are geniuses in the first bloom is by renouncing all rules of academic constraint.', Kant, *Critique of Judgment*, p.178; Ak V 310.

48 A work of genius can only be produced by an imagination which submits to rules: 'if the imagination is left in lawless freedom, all its riches [in ideas] produce nothing but nonsense' (*Critique of Judgment,* p.188; Ak V 319). Furthermore, the work of genius can be, indeed must be a source of rules, or even as Kant says sometimes it must itself serve as a rule. Cf. the second condition for genius §46: 'Since nonsense too can be original, the products of genius must also be models, i.e., they must be exemplary hence though they do not themselves arise through imitatio, still they must serve others for this, i.e., as a standard or rule by which to judge.' (*Critique of Judgment* p. 175; Ak V 308). The work of genius must serve as a rule.

49 Kant, *Critique of Judgment* p.178; Ak V 310. Demanding that the original production of the genius be neither nonsense nor a product of mere chance is a demand both for rules to allow for judging the work, and for rules which prescribe the work.

50 Ibid. p.187; Ak V 318.

51 Rules are extracted, *ausgezogen* from the work, one might say they are deduced, despite the impossibility of such a move.

52 The double relation to rules is here expressed as it governs the work of genius. But of course, this is also the double relation which an aesthetic judgment must negotiate a way through. See §17 of the *Critique of Judgment* where the double relation to rules is set up the other way around: whereas in the discussion of genius, the insistence is on the independence of the genius from rules, and the need for rules as minimum conditions is simply noted, in §17 the emphasis is reversed to underscore the necessity of rules of academic correctness whereas the necessity of breaking the rules, ruining standard proportions is explained only in a footnote. The standard idea is 'the form that constitutes the indispensible condition of all beauty, and hence merely the correctness [*Richtigkeit*] in the exhibition of the kind'. The standard form is not itself a beautiful exhibition, but it is a minimum condition for it. Following the standard form does not guarantee beauty, but seems to be a minimum condition: 'the exhibition is merely academically correct.', Kant, *Critique of Judgment*, p.83; Ak V 235.

53 The work of genius breaks with the rituals of academic correctness but does not break with the principle of having a play between the rules of academic correctness and the gesture of moving beyond all rules. The work of genius breaks both the rule of the academy and founds the (following) academy.

54 This is tantamount to reading the *Critique of Judgment* as part of Kant's account of the conditions of possibility for an autonomous act. I am here suggesting that Kant's theory of the work of genius constitutes an attempt to conceive of the possibility of freedom positively. Whereas, for instance, in the *Critique of Pure Reason* Kant claims to be satisfied with dissolving the objections to the possibility of freedom, I would contend that he eventually feels it necessary to attempt a positive account of this possibility. To put it very briefly, there is a double requirement for conceiving a causality of freedom: such a causality needs to differ in kind, to be *not even analogous* to causality of nature (i.e. not a system in which rules determine outcome; it must escape from the very model of a causality in which causes cause effects in a linear and determined way) but it also needs to qualify as a causality. The causality of freedom needs to have something like the relation between cause and

effect without having anything like it. I would like to suggest that a formally similar relationship seems to be at stake in Kant's description of the relation between various genius which is fundamental to the very definition of a genius. Indeed one genius has an effect on the next (awakens the genius, proding him towards his own productions) but is not determinant (the successor cannot take the predecessor as a model, must indeed go beyond the very rules which may have been extrapolated from predecessor's work). This is a good attempt at a positive description of a causality of freedom: enough for a relation/causality, not enough to look determinate.

55 The spirit which characterises the genius is a principle which 'is nothing but the ability to exhibit aesthetic ideas'(Kant, *Critique of Judgment*, p.182; Ak V313-4), aesthetic ideas for which no adequate presentation can be given (that is their very definition: ideas to which no intuitions can be adequate). It is the task of the genius to 'hit upon a way of *expressing* these ideas,' despite the impossibility of presenting them directly.

56 Does this formulation of a quadruple relation to rules in any way respond to Derrida's injunction : 'N'y allons pas par quatre chemins: il s'agit du concept du devoir'(*Passions*, p.25), precisely when he suggests going further than the Kantian options?

57 In 'Theory and Practice', Kant explained that 'good heads' might be able to sort through the complex calculations of happiness in order to determine an action on such grounds. Cf note 22. When Kant explains that rules can be extracted from a work of genius he uses the same expression. In both cases, the good heads are those who are determining (acts or products) through rules.

58 'giving this form to a product of fine art requires merely taste.', Kant, *Critique of Judgment*, p.180; Ak V 312.

59 Ibid. p.181; Ak V 313.

60 The accomplishment of the virtuous act can be seen as the choice to take up one's election as a finite *rational* being.

61 See Kant, *Critique of Judgment* §47 on the opposition between discovery and invention. What distinguishes the genius is that he invents. '*Nun heißt das Talent zum Erfinden das Genie*' (*Anthropology*, Ak VII 224). But also note that what makes invention in art an invention (*Erfindung*) is a reference to *Willkur* (cf. Kant, *Anthropology*, Ak VII 175)

62 Indeed, Kant and Derrida's proximity on the most rigorous conception of duty rests on their sharing, and pursuing, the argument that the rules of logic and the rules of nature are identical in their structure as rules which can be articulated systematically, and which can therefore prescribe procedures which are ensured/certain within the system.

63 It is quite easy to make the case that for Kant, the act of duty is an occasion for inventing the self, inventing the self in its fullest possibilities. It is of course much more peculiar to suggest that Derrida's duty can be thought to be an occasion for the constitution of a self. One of the major stakes for Derrida is indeed to develop a way of thinking about duty which does *not* commit one to positing a (Kantian) subject. Thus Derrida will insist that 'in order to maintain the proposition "only a decision is just," one need not refer decision to the structure of a subject or to the propositional form of a judgment' (Derrida, 'Force of Law: "The Mystical Foundation of Authority"', p.24). But perhaps this very reminder that Derrida wishes to maintain neither

subject nor propositional logic can, paradoxically, encourage us to let stand the strange suggestion that there is an invention of self involved in duty according to Derrida. This self will not be the subject, but whatever there is instead, duty will continue to be at stake. Of course the suggestion that 'self' designate whatever will come in lieu of the subject risks the objection that the subject should simply be replaced with a different self: simple substitution would not constitute the sort of rethinking of the subject Derrida calls for. And yet there can perhaps be a new use of the term 'self' but here perhaps we do have something that cannot be replaced: decision as the moment of justice survives the deconstruction of the subject.

64 If the theory of genius is taken to be an essential conceptual contribution to Kant's theory of duty, the linear model of progress which Kant often puts forward in his political writings must be complicated by the mode of development which is posited in the aesthetic realm: the relation between successive geniuses is neither linear, nor cumulative.

65 In particular, I would defend the necessity of reading the *Metaphysics of Morals* in light of the *Critique of Judgment*. One might also return to the issue of the deduction of right from ethics to reconsider it in the light of a careful analysis of Kant's use of the term. I have here been following what I take to be Derrida's use of the term which owes much to the definition of a logical procedure. Although Derrida would count as a 'deduction' any extraction of a particular (rule) from a general (principle) which followed a defined procedure, the deduction of formal logic remains the paradigm. For Kant however, the term has a different colouring. The term deduction is for him related to a use of the term current in his time to refer to deduction writings: written arguments submitted to a court which argue for the legitimacy of possession of certain territories. Deduction writings put forward the claim to territories, by showing in which sense they could be considered rightfully owned. The point in the Kantian deduction is to distinguish between fact and right (The point of the deductions Kant presents in his works is not to explain how we may have come into possession of certain concepts, but rather how their possession might be argued to be legitimate). Thus a deduction for Kant is always an argument which will be submitted to a tribunal. A Kantian deduction awaits validation; it is not, like a logical deduction, secure in its legitimacy simply by having followed the rules. For an account of deduction writings as a juridical speciality, see Dieter Henrich, 'Kant's Notion of a Deduction and the Methodological Background of the First Critique', in *Kant's Transcendental Deductions*, ed. Eckhart Förster (Stanford: Stanford University Press, 1989) pp.29-46.

66 'Whenever we convey our thoughts, there are two ways of arranging them, and one of these is called manner (*modus aestheticus*), the other method (*modus logicus*); the difference between these two is that the first has no standard other than the feeling that there is unity in the exhibition [of thoughts], whereas the second follows in [all of] this determinate principles', Kant, *Critique of Judgment* p.187; Ak V 319-20.

67 See Jacques Derrida and Elisabeth Roudinesco (Paris: Fayard/Galilee, 2001), *De quoi demain* ... 240ff for a discussion of the fragility of abolitionist positions. Derrida will show how even Beccaria can be read as one of the most efficient pleas in favour of the death penalty (242n).

68 Derrida will go so far as to call the death penalty a quasi-transcendental condition for legal systems in general, on the basis of what he calls a fact, namely that '*never*, to

my knowledge, has *any philosopher* as such, in his properly and systematically philosophical discourse, *never has any philosophy as such, contested the legitimacy of the pain of death.*' [my translation], Derrida and Roudinesco, *De quoi demain...*, p.236. 'the hypothesis which is, *subject to inventory*, mine, to know that of an essential collusion between philosophy *as such* and the pain of death.' [my translation], Derrida and Rodinesco, *De quoi demain...,* 237n.

69 Derrida and Rodinesco, *De quoi demain...*, p.236.

70 Derrida has several times in his seminar cited his 'sympathy' for the abolitionist cause as one of his points of departure (the other being the 'fact' there seems to be no philosophical defence of such a position). In *De quoi demain...*, Derrida makes it clear that he can only talk of sympathy while interrogating, and complicating the opposition between pathological and rational : 'Yes, I am *for* the unconditional abolition of the pain of death, equally for *reasons of principle* (I insist on this point; through principle and not for reasons of inutility or questionable exemplarity, I was just speaking of this) and for *reasons of the heart* (a notion that in my seminar I attempt to defend, like that of compassion, from a simple pathetic sentimentality, and that I would like to align with "reasons of principle").' [my translation],(p.149). Thus Derrida's heartfelt choice of the abolitionist cause seeks to ally principles to his heart, to his sympathies. One might say Derrida is passionate about abolition before even having an argument for it as long as one remembers that his search for a philosophical defence of abolition is not only *derived from*, but is also a search *for*, a passion: 'what is seeking itself out here, passion, according to me, would be a concept of passion not 'pathological', in the Kantian sense.' [my translation], *(Passions*, p.40).

71 It might be noted that this shift in perspective on Kant occurs with a shift of method. The death penalty also stands out after a series of themes Derrida has worked on - hospitality, friendship, pardon, perjury - as requiring a methodologically different approach: contrary to other recent themes of inquiry, the death penalty is never qualified with an 'if there is such a thing'. Perhaps for this reason, a certain form of reflection (reflection on tension between the universal if there is such a thing and the conditioned forms) did not naturally impose itself. Rather than directly tackling the issue of a deduction of politics from ethics (the problem of deducing specific rights from ethics as necessary and impossible), in his recent seminar Derrida has identified a particular cause he wishes to defend in such a way as to make it a right and is searching for a general principle, indeed a philosophical ethics, in the name of which to argue for this right. One might then consider that, in his work on the death penalty, Derrida has set himself a task which is what Kant would call a task for purely reflective judgment - precisely that kind of judgment for which the *Critique of Judgment* struggles to develop a formalism, a language, a philosophical account (it is purely reflective judgment which can look for the general law which might correspond to the particular). In other words, it is by attempting a purely reflective judgment that Derrida comes to think that the issue which divides him from Kant cannot be expressed in terms of rigour, but instead it may be a question of a particular sympathy (an aesthetic choice in the not-purely-pathological sense of aesthetic judgment?) which prompts philosophy. The sympathy in question would not be of the order of the pathological as opposed to the rational discourse, but specified as a motive for the very beginning of philosophical reflection on duty, specified as a motive for a certain ritual distinction between the pathological and the rational.

KANT AFTER DERRIDA

Select Bibliography

Adorno, Theodor, *Aesthetic Theory*, trans. C. Lenhardt (London: Routledge & Kegan Paul, 1984)

Augustine, *City of God*, trans. Marcus Dods, introd. Thomas Merton (New York: The Modern Library, 1950)

Augustine, *The Works of Aurelius Augustine*, ed. Marcus Dods (Edinburgh: T. and T. Clark, 1872), Vol. 3.

Banham, G., *Kant and the Ends of Aesthetics* (London and New York: Macmillan and St. Martin's Press, 2000)

Barth, Karl, *Church Dogmatics,* ed. G. W. Bromiley and T. F. Torrance, trans. T. H. L. Parker et al. (Edinburgh: T. and T. Clark, 1957)

Bennington, Geoffrey, *Interrupting Derrida* (London and New York: Routledge, 2000)

Bennington, Geoffrey, *La frontière kantienne* (Paris: Galilée, 2000)

Bennington, Geoffrey, 'X', in *Applying - To Derrida*, ed. John Brannigan, Ruth Robbins and Julian Wolfreys (London: Macmillan, 1996)

Bennington, Geoffrey, 'Mosaic Fragment', in David Wood, ed., *Derrida: A Critical Reader* (Oxford: Blackwell, 1992)

Bernstein, J. M., *The Fate of Art: Aesthetic Alienation from Kant to Derrida & Adorno* (Cambridge: Polity Press, 1993)

Blanchot, Maurice, *The Work of Fire*, trans. Charlotte Mandell (Stanford: Stanford University Press, 1995)

Blanchot, Maurice, *The Madness of the Day*, trans. Lydia Davis, in *The Station Hill Blanchot Reader: Fiction and Literary Essays*, ed. George Quasha (Barrytown, NY: Station Hill Press and Barrytown, Ltd., 1999)

Bloch, Ernst, *Atheism in Christianity: The Religion of the Exodus and the Kingdom*, trans. J. T. Swann (New York: Herder and Herder, 1972)

Bloom, Harold et al, *Deconstruction and Criticism* (New York: Continuum, 1984)

Bloom, Harold, *The Anxiety of Influence: A Theory of Poetry* (New York: Oxford University Press, 1973)

Bourdieu, Pierre, *Homo Academicus*, trans. P. Collier, (Cambridge: Polity Press, 1988)

Bourdieu, Pierre, *Distinction. A Social Critique of the Judgement of Taste*, trans. R. Nice (Harvard: Harvard University Press, 1984)

Borges, J. L., *'Kafka and His Precursors', Selected Non-Fictions*, ed. Eliot Weinberger, trans. Esther Allen et al. (New York: Viking, 1999)

Bubner, Rüdiger, *Ästhetische Erfahrung* (Frankfurt am Main: Suhrkamp Verlag, 1989)
Burwick, Frederick and Paper, Walter, eds., *Aesthetic Illusion: Theoretical & Historical Approaches* (Walter de Gruyter, 1990)
Caputo, John D., ed., *Deconstruction in a Nutshell: A Conversation with Jacques Derrida* (New York: Fordham University Press, 1997)
Caputo, John D. and Scanlon, Michael J., eds., *God, the Gift, and Postmodernism*, (Indianapolis: Indiana University Press, 1999)
Caputo, John D. ed., *Questioning God* (Bloomington: Indiana University Press, 2001).
Caputo, John, D., *The Prayers and Tears of Jacques Derrida: Religion without Religion* (Bloomington: Indiana University Press, 1997)
Chadwick, Ruth E., ed., *Immanuel Kant: Critical Assessments, III: Kant's Moral and Political Philosophy* (London: Routledge, 1992)
Courtine, Jean-François, ed., *Of the Sublime: Presence in Question,* trans. and afterword Jeffrey S. Librett (Albany: State University of New York Press, 1993)
Custer, Olivia, 'Ornament's work: the efficacy of Kant's "Parerga"', in *Tijdschrift voor Filosofie*, Vol 60 (3), 1998
Daval, Roger, *La métaphysique de Kant: perspectives sur le métaphysique de Kant d'aprés la théorie du schématisme* (Paris: Presses Universitaires de France, 1951)
Deleuze, Gilles, *Difference and Repetition*, trans. Paul Patton (London: The Athlone Press, 1994.)
Deleuze, Gilles, *Kant's Critical Philosophy: The Doctrine of the Faculties*, trans. Hugh Tomlinson and Barbara Habberjam (London: The Athlone Press, 1984)
Derrida, Jacques, *Margins of Philosophy*, trans. Alan Bass (Brighton: The Harvester Press, 1982)
Derrida, Jacques, *The Gift of Death,* trans. David Wills (Chicago: University of Chicago Press, 1995)
Derrida, Jacques, *Adieu à Emmanuel Levinas*, (Paris: Galilée, 1997)
Derrida, Jacques, 'Economimesis', trans. R. Klein, *diacritics*, Vol. 11 (1981)
Derrida, Jacques and Vattimo, Gianni, eds., *Religion* (Cambridge: Polity Press, 1998)
Derrida, Jacques, *Jacques Derrida*, trans. Geoffrey Bennington (Chicago: University of Chicago Press, 1993)
Derrida, Jacques, 'Force of Law: "The Mystical Foundation of Authority"', trans. Mary Quaintance, in *Deconstruction and the Possibility of Justice*, Drucilla Cornell, Michael Rosenfeld, David Gray Carlson, eds. (New

York, London: Routledge, 1992)

Derrida, Jacques, 'Scribble (writing-power)', abr. and trans. Cary Plotkin, *Yale French Studies*, Vol. 58 (1979)

Derrida, Jacques, *Dissemination*, trans. Barbara Johnson (London: The Athlone Press, 1981)

Derrida, Jacques, *'The Law of Genre'*, trans. Avital Ronell, in *Acts of Literature*, ed. Derek Attridge (New York and London: Routledge, 1992)

Derrida, Jacques, *Aporias*, trans. Thomas Dutoit (Stanford: Stanford University Press, 1993)

Derrida, Jacques, *Cinders*, trans. Ned Luckacher (Lincoln and London: University of Nebraska Press, 1991)

Derrida, Jacques, *Edmund Husserl's 'Origin of Geometry': An Introduction*, trans. and pref. John P. Leavey, ed. David Allison (Stony Brook, NY: Nicolas Hays, 1978)

Derrida, Jacques and Roudinesco, Elisabeth, *De quoi demain ... Dialogue* (Paris: Fayard/Galilée 2001)

Derrida, Jacques, *Mémoires: For Paul De Man*, trans. Jonathan Culler and E. Cadava (New York: Columbia University Press, 1986)

Derrida, Jacques, *Of Hospitality*, trans. Rachel Bowlby (Stanford: Stanford University Press, 2000)

Derrida, Jacques, *On Cosmopolitanism and Forgiveness*, trans. Mark Dooley and Michael Hughes (London and New York: Routledge, 2001)

Derrida, Jacques, *On the Name*, ed. Thomas Dutoit, trans. David Wood, John P. Leavey, Jr. and Ian McLeod (Stanford: Stanford University Press, 1995)

Derrida, Jacques, *Passions* (Paris: Galilée 1993)

Derrida, Jacques, *Points... Interviews, 1974- 1994*, ed. Elisabeth Weber (Stanford: Stanford University Press, 1995)

Derrida, Jacques, *Politics of Friendship*, trans. George Collins (London and New York: Verso, 1997)

Derrida, Jacques, *Resistances of Psychoanalysis*, trans. Peggy Kamuf, Pascale-Anne Brault and Michael Naas (Stanford: Stanford University Press, 1998)

Derrida ,Jacques, *Right of Inspection*, trans. David Willis (New York: The Monacelli Press, 1998)

Derrida, Jacques, *Spectres of Marx: The State of the Debt, the Work of Mourning, and the New International*, trans. Peggy Kamuf, introd. Bernd Magnus and Stephen Cullenberg (London: Routledge, 1994)

Derrida, Jacques, *Limited Inc*, trans. Samuel Weber (Northwestern University Press, 1988)

Derrida, Jacques, *The Truth in Painting*, trans. G. Bennington and

I. McLeod (Chicago and London: The University of Chicago Press, 1987)

Derrida, Jacques, *Writing and Difference*, trans. Alan Bass (London and New York: Routledge, 1997)

Derrida, Jacques, 'The Principle of Reason: the University in the Eyes of its Pupils', trans. Catherine Porter & Edward P Morris, in *diacritics*, Vol. 13 (3), 1983.

Derrida, Jacques, 'Interpretations at war: Kant, the Jew, the German', in *New Literary History*, Vol. 22 (1), 1991.

Derrida, Jacques, 'Heidegger's Ear: Philopolemology (Geschlecht IV)', in J. Sallis, ed., *Reading Heidegger: Commemorations* (Bloomington and Indianapolis: Indiana University Press, 1993), trans. J. P. Leavey, Jr.

Eliot, T. S., *Tradition and the Individual Talent, Selected Essays*, 3rd edn. (London: Faber and Faber, 1951)

Fenves, Peter, ed., *Raising the Tone of Philosophy: Late Essays by Immanuel Kant, Transformative Critique by Jacques Derrida* (Baltimore: The Johns Hopkins University Press, 1993)

von le Fort, Gertrud, ed., *The Christian Faith*, foreword Marta Troeltsch, trans. Garrett, E. Paul (Minneapolis: Fortress Press, 1991)

Gadamer, Hans-Georg, *Truth and Method*, second rev. edn., trans. revised by Joel Weinsheimer and Donald G. Marshall (New York: Continuum, 1998)

Gillespie, Michael Allen, *Nihilism before Nietzsche* (Chicago: University of Chicago Press, 1995)

Habermas, Jürgen, *The Philosophical Discourse of Modernity: Twelve Lectures*, trans. Frederick, G. Lawrence (Cambridge, Mass.: The MIT Press, 1987)

Haapala, Levinson & Rantala, eds., *The End of Art & Beyond* (Humanities Press, 1996)

von Harnack, Adolf, *What Is Christianity?*, trans. Thomas Bailey Saunders, introd. Rudolf Bultmann (Philadelphia: Fortress Press, 1986).

Heidegger, Martin, *Early Greek Thinking,* trans. David Farrell Krell and David Capuzzi, (San Francisco and London: Harper & Row, 1975)

Heidegger, Martin, *On Time and Being*, trans. Joan Stambaugh, (New York and London: Harper Torchbooks, 1972)

Heidegger, Martin, *Being and Time*, trans. John Macquarrie and Edward Robinson (New York: Harper and Row, 1962)

Heidegger, Martin, *Kant and the Problem of Metaphysics,* trans. Richard Taft (Bloomington and Indianapolis: Indiana University Press,1990).

Heidegger, Martin, *The Metaphysical Foundations of Logic*, trans. Michael Heim (Bloomington: Indiana University Press, 1984)

Heidegger, Martin, *The Principle of Reason*, trans. Reginald Lilly

(Bloomington: Indiana University Press, 1991)

Heidegger, Martin, *Ontology - The Hermeneutics of Facticity*, trans. John van Buren (Indianapolis: Indiana University Press, 1999)

Henrich, Dieter, *Kant's Transcendental Deductions,* ed. Eckhart Förster (Stanford: Stanford University Press, 1989)

Silverman, Hugh J., ed., *Derrida and Deconstruction* (London: Routledge, 1989)

Kant, Immanuel, *Grounding for the Metaphysics of Morals* (Indianapolis and Cambridge: Hackett Publishing Company, 1981)

Kant, Immanuel, *Political Writings* 2nd edn. (Cambridge: Cambridge University Press, 1991)

Kant, Immanuel, *Perpetual Peace and Other Essays on Politics, History, and Morals*, trans. Ted Humphrey (Indianapolis: Hackett Pub. Co., 1983)

Kant, Immanuel, *A Critical History of the Christian Doctrine of Justification and Reconciliation*, trans. John S. Black (Edinburgh: Edmonston and Douglas, 1872)

Kant, Immanuel, *Critique of Judgement*, trans. Werner S. Pluhar (Indianapolis and Cambridge: Hackett, 1987)

Kant, Immanuel, *Critique of Practical Reason*, trans. and ed. M. Gregor (Cambridge University Press, 1997)

Kant, Immanuel, *Critique of Practical Reason*, trans. and introd. Lewis White Beck (Indianapolis: Bobbs-Merill Educational Publishing, 1956)

Kant, Immanuel, *Critique of Pure Reason*, trans. Mieiklejohn (London: Everyman, 1991)

Kant, Immanuel, *Critique of Pure Reason*, ed. and trans. Paul Guyer and Allen W. Wood (Cambridge: Cambridge University Press, 1998)

Kant, Immanuel, *Critique of Pure Reason*, trans. Werner S. Pluhar (Indianapolis and Cambridge: Hackett Publishing, 1996)

Kant, Immanuel, *Critique of Pure Reason*, trans. Norman Kemp Smith (London: Macmillan, 1933)

Kant, Immanuel, *Critique of the Power of Judgment*, ed. Paul Guyer, trans. Paul Guyer and Eric Matthews (Cambridge: Cambridge University Press, 2000)

Kant, Immanuel, *Groundwork of the Metaphysic of Morals*, trans. and analysed by H. J. Paton (New York: Harper and Row, 1964)

Kant, Immanuel, *Philosophical Correspondence: 1759-179,*. trans. Arnulf Zweig (Chicago: The University of Chicago Press, 1967)

Kant, Immanuel, *Prolgomena to Any Future Metaphysics*, trans. Paul Carus, rev. James W. Ellington (Indianapolis: Hackett, 1977).

Kant, Immanuel, *Religion Within the Limits of Reason Alone*, trans., introd. and notes Theodore M. Greene and Hoyt H. Hudson (New York: Harper and Row, 1960)

Kant, Immanuel, *The Critique of Judgement*, trans. James Creed Meredith (Oxford: Clarendon Press, 1952)

Kant, Immanuel, *The Metaphyics of Morals*, trans. M. Gregor (Cambridge: Cambridge University Press, 1991)

Kant, Immanuel, *Anthropology from a Pragmatic Point of View*, trans. Mary J. Gregor, (The Hague: Martinus Nijhoff, 1974)

Kant, Immanuel, 'Religion Within the Boundaries of Mere Reason', in *Religion & Rational Theology*, trans. Allen W. Wood and George Di Giovanni (Cambridge: Cambridge University Press, 1996)

Kearney, Richard and Dooley, Mark, eds., *Questioning Ethics: Contemporary Debates in Philosophy* (London: Routledge, 1999)

Kearney, Richard and O'Leary, Joseph Stephen, eds., *Heidegger et la question de Dieu* (Paris: Bernard Grasset, 1980)

Kern, Andrea, *Schöne Lust: Eine Theorie der ästhetischen Erfahrung nach Kant* (Frankfurt am Main: Suhrkamp Verlag, 2000)

Kern, Andrea and Sonderegger Ruth, eds., *Falsche Gegensätze: Zeitgenössische Positionen zur philosophischen Ästhetik* (Frankfurt am Main: Suhrkamp Verlag, 2002)

Klossowski, Pierre, *Roberte ce Soir and the Revocation of the Edict of Nantes*, trans. Austin Wainhouse (London: Boyars, 1989)

Kojève, Alexandre, *Kant* (Paris: Gallimard, 1973)

Leibniz, Gottfried, *Discourse on Metaphysics, Correspondence with Arnauld, Monadology*, trans. Montgomery, rev. Albert R. Chandler, introd. Paul Janet (La Salle: Open Court Publishing, 1973)

Levinas, Emmanuel, *Nine Talmudic Readings*, trans. and introd. Annette Aronowicz (Bloomington: Indiana University Press, 1990)

Levinas, Emmanuel, *Otherwise than Being, or Beyond Essence*, trans. Alphonso Lingis (The Hague: Martinus Nijhoff, 1981)

Lisse, Michel, ed., *Passions de la littérature: pour Jacques Derrida* (Paris: Galilee, 1996)

Longuenesse, Beatrice, *Kant and the Capacity to Judge: Sensibility and Discursivity in the Transcendental Analytic of The Critique of Pure Reason*, trans. C.T. Wolfe (Princeton and Oxford: Princeton University Press, 1998)

de Lubac, Henri, *Catholicism: Christ and the Common Destiny of Man*, trans. L. C. Sheppard and Elizabeth Englund (San Francisco: Ignatius Press, 1988)

de Lubac, Henri, *Surnatural* (Paris: Aubier, 1946)

de Lubac, Henri, *The Mystery of the Supernatural*, trans. Rosemary

Sheed (London: Geoffrey Chapman, 1967)

de Man, Paul, *Aesthetic Ideology*, ed. and introd. Andrzej Warminski (Minneapolis: University of Minnesota Press, 1996)

de Man, Paul, *Allegories of Reading: Figural Language in Rousseau, Nietzsche, Rilke, and Proust* (New Haven and London: Yale University Press, 1979)

Menke, Christoph, *Die Souveränität der Kunst. Ästhetische Erfahrung nach Adorno und Derrida* (Frankfurt am Main: Suhrkamp Verlag, 1991)

Metz, Johann, *Theology of the World*, trans. William Glen-Doepel (New York: Herder and Herder, 1969)

Michalson, Gordon E., *Kant and the Problem of God* (Oxford: Basil Blackwell, 1999)

Milbank, John, Pickstock, Catherine and Ward, Graham, eds., *Radical Orthodoxy: A New Theology* (London: Routledge, 1999).

Moltmann, Jürgen, *The Coming of God: Christian Eschatology*, trans. Margaret Kohl (Minneapolis: Fortress Press, 1996)

Morgan, Diane, *Kant Trouble: The Obscurities of the Enlightened* (London: Routledge, 2000)

Mortley, Raoul, *French Philosophers in Conversation* (London: Routledge, 1991)

Nancy, J.-L., *The Birth to Presence*, trans. B. Holmes (Stanford, California: Stanford University Press, 1993)

Pannenberg, Wolfhart, *Systematic Theology*, trans. Geoffrey W. Bromiley (Edinburgh: T. and T. Clark, 1998)

Rand Richard, ed., *Logomachia: The Conflict of the Faculties* (Lincoln: University of Nebraska Press, 1992)

Rehberg, Andrea and Jones, Rachel, eds., *The Matter of Critique: Readings in Kant's Philosophy*, (Manchester: Clinamen Press, 2000)

Ritschl, *The Christian Doctrine of Justification and Reconciliation: The Positive Development of the Doctrine*, trans. H. R. Mackintosch and A. B. Macaulay (Edinburgh: T. and T. Clark, 1900)

Rollins, Mark, ed., *Danto and his Critics*, (Oxford: Blackwell, 1993)

Rotenstreich, Nathan, *On Faith*, ed. and foreword Paul Mendes-Flohr (Chicago: University of Chicago Press, 1998)

Sallis, John, ed., *Deconstruction and Philosophy: The Texts of Jacques Derrida*, (Chicago: University of Chicago Press, 1987)

Sallis, John, *Spacings - of Reason and Imagination in Texts of Kant, Fichte, Hegel* (Chicago: University of Chicago Press, 1987)

Schopenhauer, Arthur, *The Fourfold Root of the Principle of Sufficient Reason*, trans. E. F. J. Payne, intro. Richard Taylor (La Salle, IL: Open Court, 1974)

Schweitzer, Albert, *The Quest of the Historical Jesus: A Critical Study of its Progress from Reimarus to Wrede*, trans. W. Montgomery, 3rd edn. (London: Adam and Charles Black, 1954)

Waxman, Wayne, *Kant's Model of the Mind* (New York: Oxford University Press, 1991)

Weil, Eric, *Logique de la philosophie* (Paris: Vrin, 1950)

Weiss, Johannes, *Jesus' Proclamation of the Kingdom of God*, trans., ed. and introd. Richard Hyde Hiers and David Larrimore Holland (London: SCM Press, 1971)

Zavadil, Simon, *Situation et modes de présentation du 'cas' dans la philosophie kantienne* (Strasbourg, Université Marc-Bloch, 1998)

Index

a priori, 5, 9, 10, 12, 13, 19-22, 24, 29, 33, 39, 42, 43, 47n, 102n, 128-135 *passim*, 145, 173
Adieu, 172, 173
Adorno, T., 85, 110
aesthetic experience, 24, 46n, ch.6 *passim*, 124n
aesthetic judgment, 29, 41, 64n, 65n, 87, 88, 90, 91, 96, 98, 136, 191, 192, 195, 198n, 200n
aesthetic play, 109, 110, 112, 113, 118, 119, 120, 122
aesthetic pleasure, 136
aesthetic undecidability, 110-114, 116, 117, 120
alterity, 19, 28, 42, 47n, 159
'Announcement of the Near Conclusion', 70
antinomy, 10, 11, 25, 28, 33, 41, ch.5 *passim*, 64n, 187, 190, 197n, 199n
apocalypse/apocalyptic, 1, 71-73, 75, 76, 155
aporia/aporetic, 8, 20, 25, 30, 31, 33, 39, 41, 42, 48n, 161, 185, 197n
Aquinas, T., 145
Aristotle, 33, 68, 74, 77n, 144
art, 8, 25, 53, 58, 83-86, 90, 95-97, 99, 101n, 103n, ch.6 *passim*, 124n, 139, 141n
as if, ch.2 *passim*, 45n, 53, 134, 148
Augustine, 146, 147, 149-153
Barth, K., 145
beautiful, 23-26, 30, 42, 76, 88, 90, 91, 93, 98, 99, 102n, 106, 108, 109, 112, 113, 120, 122, 124n, 200n
beauty, 32, 89, 91, 101n, 198n, 200n
Being and Time, 67, 69, 74, 125n
Benjamin, W., 2, 3, 32
Bennington, G., 14n, 101n, 176

Blanchot, M., 45n, 114, 115, 116, 120, 143, 156
Bloch, E., 157
Calvin, J., 150
Capital, 74, 79n
Carrier, D., 81, 85, 100n
categorical imperative, 3, 9, 130, 132, 148
category/categories, 8, 19-23, 30, 42, 50, 64n, 66, 133, 135
chance, 7, 55, 56, 64n, 111, 188, 200n
charm, 89, 90, 91
chora, 161
Church Dogmatics, 145
city of God, 147, 150-152, 158
cognition, 5, 52, 53, 60, 70, 90-93, 102n, 107-110, 127-131, 134, 135
concept, 3, 5, 9, 10, 11, 13, ch.2 *passim*, 45n, 47n, 48n, 53-59, 62, 64n, 66, 67, 72, 78n, 83, 95, 100n, 107-112, 120, 122, 123, 128, 131, 133-137, 140n, 154, 157, ch.9 *passim*
conceptual analysis, 110, 122-123
conditional future, 30
contingency, 29, 31, 56, 57, 58, 60, 144
countersignature, 33, 144, 145, 150
critical judgment, 57
critique, 6, 8, 9, 11, 12, 13, 27, 50, 57, 63, 64n, 67, 70, 71, 82, 84, 87, 135, 197n, 198n
'Critique of Aesthetic Judgment', 4, 8, 76, 78n
Critique of Judgment, The, 13n, 15n, 23, 24, 64n, 78n, 85, 127, 132-136, 140n, 141n, 148, 166n, 187, 190, 193, 197n, 200-202n
Critique of Practical Reason, The, 4, 9, 13n, 21, 23, 131, 137
Critique of Pure Reason, The, 9, 13n,

INDEX

14n, 18, 21, 27, 30, 44n, 47n, 66, 67, 69, 70, 76, 107, 127, 135, 144, 147, 148, 200n
Danto, A., 81, 85, 97, 100n
death of God, 154, 159
deconstruction, 10, 13, 18, 20, 21, 32, 48n, 65n, 84, 85, 97, 99, 104n, 122, 143, 163, 165n, 197n, 202n
democracy, 21, 35-38, 43, 153-163 *passim*
Democritus, 54
Descartes, R., 67, 68, 81, 145
determinate concept, 109
determinative judgment, 50, 51, 56-58, 62, 134
différance, 4, 30, 31, 37, 42, 43, 139
Difference and Repetition, 31
Doctrine of Right, 177, 181
'Doctrine of the Elements of Ethics', 86, 93
duty, 8, 21, 22, 39, 40, 41, 42, 150, 154, 163, ch.9 *passim*
Eighteenth Brumaire of Louis Bonaparte, The, 75
'Elucidation by Examples', 4, 89
Encyclopaedia, 68, 74
envoi, 21, 72, 73
Epicurus, 54-57, 64n
epoché, 153, 160
ethical commonwealth, 145, 148-150, 152, 157
ethics, ch.2 *passim*, 74, 75, 78n, 145, 149, 150, 152, 155-156, 159, 165n, ch.9 *passim*, 197n, 202n, 203n
experience, 1, 3, 8, 9, 13, ch.2 *passim*, 44n, 45n, 46n, 56, 58, 72, 74, 75, 91, 92, 97, ch.6 *passim*, 124n, 127-130, 134, 135, 140n, 148, 150-152, 155, 156, 159, 161, 163, 171, 183, 185, 187, 192, 196n
external, 12, 61, 82, 85, 88, 93, 94, 100n, 120, 144
'Faith and Knowledge: the Two Sources', 2, 153, 155, 158
final causality, 50, 53

finitude, 11, 62, 72, 75, 76, 79n, 87, 102n
for itself, 19, 25, 129, 132, 137
'Force of Law', 104n, 185
forgiveness, 21, 32, 42, 43
fraternity, 32, 34, 35
freedom, 3, 10, 27, 30, 32, 88, 128-130, 133-135, 142, 145, 147, 150, 166n, 171, 179, 189, 191, 200n, 201n
friendship/friend, 21, 33-42 *passim*, 78n, 93, 95, 158, 203n
future anterior, 30
Gadamer, H-G., 111, 119
genius, 8, 71, 103n, 187-192 passim, 199n, 200n, 201n, 202n
gift, 21, 32, 72, 155, 161-162
God, 2, 9, 19, 25, 27, 36, 44n, 60, 63, 92, 95, 99, 103n, 145-164 *passim*
golden frame, 91
Grenze, 61
Groundwork of the Metaphysics of Morals, 144
Hegel, G.W., 2, 6, 10, 12, 14n, 18, 28, 29, 33, 35, 42, 67, 69, 73-75, 81, 83, 101n, 110, 111, 142, 145, 153, 158, 160
Heidegger, M., ch.1 *passim*, 43, ch.4 *passim*, 82-84, 100n, 110, 142, 158, 160-162
Herrmann, W., 145
history, 1, 6, 12, 28, 31, 32, 42, 45n, 72, 80, 81, 83-85, 100n, 102n, 148, 152, 157, 159
hospitality, 1, 6, 21, 32, 39-41, 158, 186, 197n, 203n
Husserl, E., ch.1 *passim*, 20, 43, 67, 144
Idea, 1, 4, 8, 9, 18, 20, 23, 27, 33, 34, 41, 47n, 54, 61, 62, 87, 88, 92, 93, 94, 150, 157, 183, 201n
idealist/final, 54, 55
in itself, 11, 97, 139
infinite/infinity, 12, 18, 20, 26-39 *passim*, 45n, 52, 61, 72, 75, 76, 79n, 100, 139, 140n, 171, 180
Institutes, 150

internal, 12, 85-100 *passim*, 102n
intuition, 4, 5, 9, 12, 19, 21-23, 24, 42, 47n, 68, 71, 78n, 107-110, 131, 136, 173, 201n
invention, 8, 157, 176, 185, 187, 188, 190-192, 201n
Irenaeus, 146, 148
Islam, 37, 38
Jesus Christ, 146, 147, 152, 154
Joyce, James, 36
judgment, 2, 13, 19, 24, 25, 29, 35, 41, ch.3 *passim*, 64n, 65n, 73, 76, ch.5 *passim*, 106-111, 112, 124n, 128, 134-137, 161, 191-193, 195, 201n, 203n
Juvenal, 35
Kant and the Problem of Metaphysics, 3, 14n, ch.4 *passim*, 77n
kingdom of God, 103n, 146-150, 152, 155, 165n, 168n
Klossowski, P., 40
Kojève, A., 22, 23, 28, 41, 44n, 45n
Lacan, J., 2, 69, 139
Leibniz, G.W., 31, 144, 147
Levinas, E., 156, 159, 169n
Lonergan, B., 145
Lubac, H. de, 162
Lust, 129, 138, 139
lying, 40, 70
Marechal, J., 145
margin, 29, 67, 82
Margins of Philosophy, 16n, 74
Margolis, J., 85, 102n
Marx, K., 6, 67, 73-76, 154, 158, 163
maxim, 22, 43, ch.3 *passim*, 92, 148, 178, 183, 184, 198n
mechanical causality, 24, 25, 50-59 *passim*, 64n
Memoires: For Paul de Man, 73, 75
messianism, 155, 156, 161, 162
'Methodology of Teleological Judgment', 63
Michelet, J., 35, 36
Monadology, 147
mourning, 21, 25, 27, 32, 73
Muslim, 38
Nancy, J.-L., 5, 7, 10, 15n, 16n, 36, 143

narrative, 43, 93, 97, 115-117
nature, 8, 22, 24-26, ch.3 *passim*, 128-130, 133-135, 147, 152, 158, 162, 179, 189, 192
necessity, 7, 8, 13n, 29, 34, 43, 57-60, 64n, 128, 131, 133, 140n, 174, 180, 186, 195, 197n
negative theology, 2, 156, 159
Nietzsche, F., 2, 10, 12, 13n, 30, 33, 35
noumena, 22, 23, 32, 145
'On a Newly Arisen Apocalyptic Tone in Philosophy', 67, 69
'On a Supposed Philanthropical Justification for Lying', 40
Opus Postumum, 18
organism, 50, 52, 53, 59, 76
Origen, 146, 147, 150, 152
Other, 21, 27-43 *passim*, 46n, 47n, 48n, 93, 155, 156, 159, 163
'Ousia and Grammé', 67, 69, 74, 77n
parergon/parerga, 4, 13, 24, 26, ch.5 *passim*, 142, 154
'Parergon', 14n, 46n, 83, 86, 98, 100n, 103n
'Passe-Partout', 101n
Passions, 172
Perpetual Peace, 40, 41, 43, 78n, 193, 197n
Physics, 68
Plato, 45n, 69, 144
pleasure, 24, 25, 29, 88, 90, 91, 94, 98, ch7 *passim*, 141n
Politics of Friendship, The, 8, 16n, 32, 36
politics, 25, 31-38 *passim*, 42, 43, 14-163 *passim*, 172-175, 177, 180, 181, 193, 194, 203n
Post Card, The, 8, 69
power of judgment, 1, 6, 24, 109, 128
powers, 66, 87, 90, 109, 127-137 *passim*, 152, 187, 189
practical philosophy, 69, 127, 175, 182
practical pleasure, 136
practical reason, 3, 9, 13, 19, 21, 22, 24, 29, 35, 40, 41, 45n, 66, 69, 82, 87, 197n
presence, 4, 29, 31, 68, 69, 72, 74-76,

163
progress, 12, 34, 59, 155, 181-184, 192, 199n, 202n
pure reason, 19, 22, 23, 26, 30, 41, 128, 133, 135, 147
purposiveness, 24, 53-56, 59, 62, 64n, 127, 128, 132, 133, 137
Rahner, K., 145, 162
Rauschenbusch, W., 153
reason, 2, 3, 5, 9, 10, 11, 13, 19, 22-24, 27-32, 33, 40, 47n, 51, 53, 55, 59, 61-63, 70, 71, 76, ch5. *passim*, ch.7 *passim*, 143, 144, 151-155, 160, 161, 172, 178, 179, 184, 197n
Reflexionen, 102n
Reimarus, H., 146
Religion Within the Limits of Reason Alone, 2, 78n, 86, 92, 146, 148, 153
respect, 35, 40, 88, 93, 131, 133, 158, 184-185, 189, 192
revealability, 160, 161, 162
revelation, 72, 73, 151, 156, 161, 162
rule, 22, 24, 25, 53, 91, 93, 95, 97, 101n, ch.9 *passim*
sacrifice, 158
schema/schemata, 1, 3, 5, 18, 19, 21, 32, 35, 38, 45n, 66, 69, 74, 75, 135, 139, 150, 176
Schleiermacher, F.D.E., 145
Schlösser, J.G., 71
Schmitt, K., 33, 34, 37, 38
sending, 71-73
singularity, 6, 10, 18, 21, 27, 30, 43, 163
Specters of Marx, 67, 73-76
Spinoza, B., 54, 64n, 137
St. Paul, 70, 147
subjectivity, 4, 9, 12, 20-22, 24-26, 29, 30, 32, 34, 36, 37, 40, 41, 43, 45n, 62, 67, 68, ch.5 *passim*, 108, 110, 125n, 129, 132, 145, 148, 151, 187, 201n
sublime, the, 24, 32, 76, 90, 92, 103n, 159, 177

supersensible, 22, 24, 54, 57-59, 71, 74, 148
synthetic *a priori*, 33, 34
taste, 24, 25, 83-96 *passim*, 101n, 132-134, 191
teleological judgment, 55, 58, 62, 64n, 65n
teleology/telos, 8, 12, 33, 51, 60, 63, 75, 76, 78n
'The Madness of the Day', 115, 116
'The Pit and the Pyramid', 74
theology, 2, 3, 60, 65n, 145, 146, 152, 156, 158, 161, 162, 165n, 168n
theoretical philosophy, 127
theoretical pleasure, 136
Tillich, P., 145
Time and Being, 72, 75
trace, 5, 31, 74, 133, 135
transcendent, 32, 41, 42, 60, 62, 68, 71, 79n
transcendental imagination, ch.4 *passim*, 77n
transcendental, 4, 8, 12, 15n, 20, 26, 28, 29, 32, 33, 41, 43, 44n, 51, 56, 58-61, 64n, 65n, 68, 70, 72, 76, 78n, 102n, 110, 112, 128, 135, 136, 140n, 145, 199n, 202n
Truth in Painting, The, 3, 8, 14n, 26, 46n, 79n, 101n, 164n
understanding, 3, 5, 7, 13, 18, 19, 21, 23, 24, 27, 28, 32, ch.3 *passim*, 64n, 66, 78n, 87, 89, 103n, ch.6 *passim*, 128, 130, 133-136, 140n
universalisable culture of singularities, 154, 156
Vienna Logic, 91
virtue, 28, 88, 92, 93, 94, 148, 149, 165n, 175, 182-184, 189, 190, 191, 198n
Wahl, 178, 179, 191
Weiss, J., 155
What Is Christianity?, 155
Wolff, C., 142, 144, 145

216

Also Available from Clinamen Press

The Matter of Critique: Readings in Kant's Philosophy
edited by Andrea Rehberg and Rachel Jones
1-903083-11-7 £14.99 $29.95

Nietzsche and the Divine
edited by Jim Urpeth and John Lippitt
1-903083-12-5 £14.99 $29.95

Philosophy's Literature
Andrew Benjamin
1-903083-09-5 £14.99 $29.95

Disclosing Spaces
Andrew Benjamin
1-903083-28-1 £16.00 $35.00

Walter Benjamin's Philosophy: Destruction and Experience
edited by Andrew Benjamin and Peter Osborne
1-903083-08-7 £14.99 $29.95

On Beckett
Alain Badiou, edited by Alberto Toscano and Nina Power
1-903083-30-3 £12.50 $tbc

The Formation of the Scientific Mind
Gaston Bachelard
1-903083-20-6 £17.00 $35.00

The Dialectic of Duration
Gaston Bachelard
1-903083-07-9 £14.99 $29.95

Duration and Simultaneity
Henri Bergson
1-903083-01-X £16.99 $35.00

for a full stock listing please visit www.clinamen.co.uk